AMERICAN AMBITIONS

American Ambitions

SELECTED ESSAYS ON
LITERARY AND
CULTURAL THEMES

Monroe K. Spears

THE JOHNS HOPKINS
UNIVERSITY PRESS
BALTIMORE AND LONDON

8/1987
Cent Lel

∞

*The paper used in this publication meets the
minimum requirements of American National
Standard for Information Sciences — Permanence
of Paper for Printed Library Materials,
ANSI Z39.48-1984.*

The Johns Hopkins University Press
701 West 40th Street
Baltimore, Maryland 21211
The Johns Hopkins Press Ltd., London

LIBRARY OF CONGRESS CATALOGING-IN-PUBLICATION DATA
Spears, Monroe Kirklyndorf.
  American ambitions.

  Bibliography: p.
  Includes index.
    1. American literature — History and criticism.
  2. United States — Intellectual life.   I. Title.
PS121.S547   1987   810'.9   86-21403
ISBN 0-8018-3414-7 (alk. paper)

See p. 261 for permission notices.

for Betty, Laura, and John
companions of the road

Contents

Preface

The theme that seems in retrospect to emerge from most of these essays is indicated in my title: the nature of American ambition, its great promises and liabilities, and its effects in literature as in life. One fundamental ambition is to break with the past and with the Europe that embodies it, with its decadence and corruption as well as its past glories; in literary terms this tends to mean breaking with the conventions of literary form and celebrating the self free, untrammeled, and innocent. The ultimate literary ambition is to write an American epic, or its equivalent in the novel, which will both celebrate the theme of revolution and enact its principles in the writing. Other themes—all highly ambitious—that recur in these essays are regionalism, especially in its Southern aspects, and in broad terms the relation of poetry and criticism to American history, society, and religion.

This is not, however, a book written to prove a thesis, but a selection from my writings of the last decade or so on American subjects, with a few earlier ones. (Dates and places of first publication are given on pp. 261–62.)

"Never apologize. Never explain. Say, 'No excuse, Sir.' Accept responsibility." This military maxim, learned in Officer Candidate School in World War II, is one of the few that I remember still as making good sense. So I will not apologize further for the fragmentary nature of this collection of commissioned pieces, or attempt to disarm criticism by explaining that they do not always fully represent my present views.

I am not an American literature specialist. As teacher, historical scholar, and editor (of an eighteenth-century poet, Matthew Prior), I began with academic specialties that were exclusively British. But then, for nine years, I edited the literary quarterly the *Sewanee Review,* and my writing as critic has been about evenly divided between the two countries. (Auden, about whom I have written most, might also be said to be evenly divided.) In teaching, I have ranged widely, sometimes undertaking courses as speculative as psychoanalytic criticism, science fiction, and poetry writing. If this background has any advantage (its disadvantages are all too clear), it is that I have always been amphibious and ambidextrous, not between two worlds but among several. These essays were written mostly for the literary quarterlies, with their small but highly sophisticated audiences; but some were written for periodicals of much larger circulation, and some for the book sections of Sunday newspapers with audiences in the millions. I hope the only difference apparent is in the length, for I have always believed in and written for the general reader—being one myself.

I would like to thank George Core, Daniel Hoffman, Frederick Morgan, and John Irwin for their valuable suggestions.

PART · I *Ancestors*

Cotton Mather

An embarrassing ancestor, about whom one is not eager to learn more. I suspect that many Americans feel as I did about Cotton Mather before I read Kenneth Silverman's biography:[1] that the only interesting question about him is whether he is more repulsive than he is boring. In Silverman's full-length portrait against a fully painted background, he emerges as no less repulsive, but far from boring: a complex figure, full of contradictions and paradoxes, of great interest psychologically and historically. He was a child prodigy: though entering Harvard at eleven was in those days not nearly as impressive as it would be now— the total student body numbered only twenty, and at one point was reduced to three—it was remarkable. (Katherine Anne Porter says "his mind at fourteen had reached the limit of its growth. . . . He was a typical wonder-child.")[2] He was a stammerer (parental pressures have rarely been more obvious) who became a great preacher. A Puritan of the Puritans, he went from witch-hunting to campaigning for inoculation against smallpox (leagued with Lady Mary Wortley Montagu, though unbeknownst to that most unlikely bedfellow). Always eager to be first, he went all the way from being a theocratic Puritan to becoming a more or less ecumenical and tolerant benevolist and proto-scientist, interested in common-sense practical measures to alleviate human misery and in formulating a minimum basis on which most Christians might agree.

He was America's first intellectual to gain international recognition—and terribly insecure and provincial about it, professing humility with insistent self-assertion, rushing into print at the slightest provocation (388 titles to his credit), parading his D.D. and F.R.S. on all his later title pages, hoping, like any anxious modern academic, to avoid perishing by extensive publishing. (His motives were the same, too: to establish status and convince himself of his own worth—also his father, Increase, who was not convinced and thought that he should not publish so much).

Silverman's central theme is that Cotton Mather was the first conspicuously American writer, the first person

> to write at length about the New World having never seen the old. Much of his career illustrates, for the first time, the costs and gains to America's intellectual and artistic life of its divorce from Europe. These costs and gains have been one and the same—a lack of standards or a freedom to create (depending on how it is viewed) which has often inspired works tainted by provincial crabbedness, eccentricity, and overreaching, but also often distinguished by their close kin, pungency, innovation, and grandeur. . . . In his curiousness, epic reach, and quirkily ingenious individualism he was nevertheless the first unmistakably American figure in the nation's history. (426)

It is true that even now, in Imperial America, we can see in ourselves the pushy insecurity of Cotton Mather, at once self-assertive and self-deprecatory. In Mather, this uncertain sense of identity is manifested also in an uncertain and fluctuating acceptance of the general historical shift from the self-conception of the Puritans as Saving Remnant or New Israel to that of New England as a loyal part of the British Empire. In religion, this historical shift is from the early arrogant and exclusive theocracy that tortured and executed even Quakers ("for the first intrusion, loss of an ear; for the second, loss of the second ear; for the third, a hot iron through the tongue; for repeated intrusions, death: in the early 1660s three incorrigible Quakers were hanged" [56]) to a more tolerant and ecumenical religion, professing Congregationalism as merely one among many valid religions (though not all; Mather always excluded Catholics and, of course, all non-Christians) and rejecting force in religious matters. (Mather, always clamoring to be first, claimed to be the first to testify "against the Supression of Heresy, by Persecution"; "Despite his cries about the devil reclaiming a uniquely sanctified New England for his own, in the decade following the trials he continually proclaimed that New Englanders were not a special purified remnant but were, above all, loyal colonial Englishmen" [139].)

As David Levin well says, in the introduction to his edition of Mather's *Bonifacius,* we modern Americans "continue to say, with the author of *Bonifacius,* that the ways of honest men are simple and the ways of the wicked are subtle, but we seek to devise a similar ingenuity for doing good around the world. We may also find it especially interesting that Mather the American, unlike his English predecessor

Richard Baxter, says not a word about the danger that our efforts to do good may lead to disaster."[3] The great change discussed above, according to many intellectual historians, coincides with the beginning of the "modern" world, which Paul Hazard dated specifically 1715. So we may think of Mather as not crucified (though he would have loved this figure) but caught between, or awkwardly bent over, the intersection of two great epochs, the Great Divide of modern history.

Why is Cotton Mather so repulsive? His father, Increase, with all his faults—his sour, depressive disposition, his open preference for England—is much more attractive. In the Salem trials, Increase was more concerned to prevent innocent persons from disgrace or hanging than to put down a diabolic conspiracy, whereas Cotton, publicly dissenting from his father for the first time, took the opposite view. Perhaps the fundamental trait is Cotton's incessant driving ambition, dominating, overweening, unlimited. As a child he rebuked his playmates "for their wicked *Words* and *Ways*." He dislikes and is contemptuous of blacks, Indians, common people. He intends in his *Biblia Americana* to "interpret all of Scripture in the light of 'all the Learning in the World'"; he spends "three successive days fasting and praying in his study, something he believed had never been done before by anyone"; his whole religious attitude is deeply infected with what we would now call elitism of a peculiarly obnoxious sort. "*Apocalyptical Studies* are fittest for those Raised Souls," he notes with obvious complacency, "whose *Heart-Strings* are made of a Little *Finer Clay* than other mens."[4]

In religious terms, Mather's ambition, competitiveness, and insecurity make him an extreme elitist: He is not satisifed to be saved, but wants to be more saved than others. (He seems to forget temporarily the dangers of such Catholic doctrines as the Treasury of Merits and Works of Supererogation, which so infuriated Luther and other reformers—as if man could deserve or earn salvation.) He "believed deeply in a hierarchy of the pious, and aspired to join the elite." But in contrast, on the next page he is quoted as "renouncing all Apprehension of *Merit*, in my own Duties, and relying upon the Lord Jesus Christ alone, for Acceptance and Salvation" (31). Making these "simultaneous calls for openness and exclusiveness" leads him into further exercises in ambidexterity. Openness was hard to reconcile with "the distinctive Congregational understanding of the church as an elite group of Saints." The first ceremony he participated in as a minister was the excommunication of a woman for drunkenness. His triple conception of heaven in *Tri-Paradisus* was strictly hierarchical; and he thought the literal Second Coming and the end of time were imminent.

He was not ambidexter then: When he preached on the earthquake six months before his death, "his startlingly oral depiction of a vindictive God speaking in fire and convulsion put before his listeners a lifetime of undernourishment and ill reward, its straining vatic energy a personal cry for last-minute retribution" (411). At the end he was no longer benevolist or tolerant.

His awful addiction to superlatives and to exaggeration is partly responsible for our repugnance: Everything is "amazing" or "astonishing." Of course, this style was characteristic of other Dissenters as well as Puritans, and of Grub Streeters and the lower classes generally; no doubt it helps to explain why the British middle and upper classes became so devoted to understatement. The Puritan assumption that God is concerned with every detail of personal life and every petty emotion is equally distasteful; a little of this makes the stiff upper lip understandable and attractive. But these characteristics are superficial and not peculiar to Mather in any case.

In likeability, as in most respects, Mather forms a strong contrast to, for example, his almost exact contemporary, Matthew Prior (1664–1721; Mather's dates are 1663–1728). Prior was an accomplished diplomat and poet, a polished man of the world and perhaps the greatest writer of light verse in English. Mather was apparently one of the worst poets who ever lived; as Silverman says, he had no ear for verse at all. But Prior, in spite of his Montaigneian skepticism, was also tormented by religious doubts and problems; his last (unfinished) poem was a long and agonized debate called *Predestination*. It is a curious fact, too, that the religious poetess Elizabeth Singer, whom Prior briefly courted and wrote verses to, was also briefly courted by Mather's rival Benjamin Colman. Mather's connections, however, were not with the polite world, but rather with such Dissenters as Watts, Defoe (with both of whom he corresponded), and Oldmixon, whose attack on him he bitterly resented. The City Poet, Sir Richard Blackmore, liked his writings, as one might expect. He read Dryden, Waller, Cowley; but oddly enough, there is no mention in Silverman of Bunyan or of the greatest Puritan of all, John Milton. Naturally, there is no mention of Swift, whose *Tale of a Tub* is the greatest satirical portrayal of Mather's kind of religion.

Indians were suspected instruments of the Devil, their "old landlord Satan." Like many others, Mather believed that "the Indians were a satanic parody of the Puritans, the Chosen People of the devil as the Israelites, and then the Puritans, were the Chosen People of God" (239). In missionary efforts as late as 1712, Mather hoped "not to christianize the Indians of New England but, more accurately, to

Puritanize them," abhorring the Jesuit and distrusting the Anglican missionaries. It is this adversarial, sectarian attitude that is so offensive in Mather (in spite of ambidexterity): He assumes that the Indians, the French, and the witches are all agents of the Devil in a great conspiracy to subvert the New Israel, and the Catholics and Anglicans are possibly on the Devil's side. This War in Heaven is exciting, like a theological thriller by C. S. Lewis or any good evangelical sermon; but Mather sees enemies everywhere. The contrast with, for example, William Penn, who both assumes and discovers that the Indians are good, uncorrupted, and peaceable, is extreme. (*Brotherly Love,* discussed below in "Daniel Hoffman and the American Epic," presents an unforgettable picture of Penn's relations with the Indians.) While Mather, as we have seen, moved some distance toward tolerance and quiet in his later years, and emphasized doing good, especially in his *Bonifacius,* which Benjamin Franklin admired (and gently parodied, with Mather as Silence Dogood), the contrast with Penn is striking. Mather did finally conclude that New England was not going to be a New Jerusalem and went so far as to embrace Quakers; but the tone of his late sermons is one of immpassioned exclusionism (to use the mildest possible term).

Silverman relies heavily on psychological explanations, which he presents in a sensible and nondoctrinaire fashion. His interpretation of the Salem witches is that demonic possessions prevent psychotic breaks with reality "by affording underlying conflicts expression in a culturally shared idom"; they allow "inaccessible experiences to be made public and intelligible." The bewitched children "acted out with impunity the worst fears of those ministers who denounced the rising generation for wanting to explore sex, taunt their parents and deride the ministry" (90). He is especially good on Mather's speech problems, from stuttering (he "fits a widely accepted model of stutterers as 'sensitive' children of overanxious and perfectionist parents") to his "continuing need to allay feelings of smallness and show extraordinary fecundity in producing language"— and, even more psychoanalytically, that the angel who predicted that his lengthening branches would reach Europe "in effect promised him a transatlantic penis" (129)—to his ambidexterity ("he often produced with great labor works at once his own and not his own, the extreme case being of course his 'Biblia Americana,' a gigantic collection of the works and words of others, at once toweringly self-aggrandizing and utterly self-effacing, distinctively by Cotton Mather and not by him at all" [201]) and to his final conversion to silence. At the age of sixty, when his eleventh child died, he preached a sermon later published as *Silentiarius:* "Having given

much energetic discipline to mastering his unruly speech, or much ingenuity to denying its quirks by gorgeous fluency, he now took for his
doctrine the concept that "Our GOD is never more *Praised* than by our
silence" (348).

Silverman's book is exceptionally good, partly because of its magisterial competence as history and biography, partly because of its readability without sacrifice of dignity, but most of all because of Silverman's attitude: He sees Mather sympathetically but does not attempt
to defend everything about him—does not leap automatically into a
defensive posture—or condemn him, but tries to understand. He does
not, however, assume that to understand all is to forgive all; he explains
his faults, but does not try to explain them away. He says what can be
said in defense of Mather's writings about the Salem witch trials, but
agrees with Mather's opponent Calef that Mather's attitude was at best
"perfectly ambidexter" (100). "The defining moods and gestures of
Matherese—to give this ambivalence a name—are belligerent courtesy,
self-flattering modesty, fretful calm, denigrating compliments, unacceptable offers" (255). He describes his communications to the Royal
Society as a "Matherean mixture of snobbery, altruism, resentment,
and inquisitiveness." Mather's moral deterioration in his later years
("lying, talebearing, and duplicity") is described without palliation.
His final summation of Mather's faults is sympathetic but just: "These
his inner fears and historical circumstances make comprehensible but
not less disfiguring. His submissiveness that would not grasp that at
Salem people were being legally murdered; his meddlesome ambitiousness that stopped or strutted for petty advancement; his guile that
wrote self-promoting letters under others' names; his vanity that
scented out lurking slurs yet sensed no provocations in himself; his
rashness that tendered spite as amity; his envy that sneered at what it
could not get" (425).

Silverman does not, then, attempt to "rehabilitate" Mather, but
rather to make him more understandable. To maintain a sympathetic
but detached attitude toward Mather, an easy man to dislike but also
one who begged to be championed, an obsessive self-justifier who
cried out constantly for a defender, is Silverman's most remarkable
achievement.

Reluctant though we may be to recognize ourselves in Mather, and
impossible though it may be to like him, it is, I think, difficult to resist
Silverman's modest thesis that we may see in him many of the qualities
that have been characteristic of most American intellectuals since.
Mather was a genuine prodigy, capable of astonishing intellectual
feats, endowed with a powerful mind and enormous energy. His ambi-

tion was unlimited and was certainly related to his Puritan religion; it was exacerbated by the feelings of insecurity and inferiority that always accompany provincial or colonial status. Although few of us now would oscillate as Mather did from pious humility to preposterous self-assertion, or express our attitudes in ambidexter Matherese, we have our own defenses and our own oscillations that may prove equally revealing to future readers.

William James as Culture Hero

To call William James a culture hero in anything like the anthropological sense is obviously preposterous: The great American public is aware of him, if at all, only as the author of a few trickle-down phrases such as "the stream of consciousness," "the bitch-goddess Success," "the moral equivalent of war." To say, on the other hand, that he is the hero of cultured Americans would have snobbish overtones that James would have detested. At any rate, it seems to be true that the hearts of most Americans who know his work do leap up at the very thought of his name. Because we consider him to be the greatest thinker the United States has produced? No, rather because his character is so much what we feel ours might be at our best, and his character is so fully embodied in the nature of his thought and the style of his writing.

As Elizabeth Hardwick puts it, James was "truly a hero: courteous, reasonable, liberal, witty, expressive, a first-rate writer, a profoundly original expression of the American spirit as a thinker, inconceivable in any other country, and yet at home in other countries and cultures as few of us have been."[1] He hated officialdom and refused to play the role of gentleman or professor; his sister, Alice, noted that some people "reprobate his mental pirouettes and squirm at his daring to go lightly among the solemnities."[2] Santayana complained that he was "so extremely natural that there was no knowing what his nature was, or what to expect next" (13); in Cambridge he was "a sort of Irishman among the Brahmins, and seemed hardly imposing enough for a great man." What other philosopher would call a major work *Pragmatism, a New Name for Some Old Ways of Thinking,* and try to give credit for even the name to two other philosophers, both of whom disclaimed it? In time of war he advised his students, "Don't yelp with the pack," and at the other pole of style and reference, he wrote: "The prince of darkness may be a gentleman, as we are told he is, but whatever the God of earth and heaven is, he can surely be no gentleman."[3]

Two recent books, both excellent in their very different ways, attest to the continuing interest in and admiration for James.[4] Howard M. Feinstein's *Becoming William James* is a psychoanalytical study of James's early years, his neurasthenia, depression, psychosomatic illnesses of various sorts, and other difficulties in deciding on a vocation. The psychoanalytic interpretations of James's drawings are particularly fascinating. Unlike many "psychobiographical" studies, however, it is solidly grounded in historical and biographical research and admirably nondoctrinaire. Of special interest is the emphasis on William James of Albany (William James's grandfather), the hard-fisted industrialist who made the family's money, and the whole interplay of relations within the family concerning work and vocation. Henry Senior's Swedenborgianism and indulgence of his sons was a reaction against his father's strict Calvinism, belief in hard work, and severity to him. The prodigal son syndrome and psychosomatic illness (justifying leisure and residence in Europe) play a very prominent part through three generations.

William James does not appear as hero here, but as late bloomer who suffered through neurasthenia, depression, and psychosomatic back ailments for many years and went through three apparent failures—as artist, scientist, and physician—before finding his identity and vocation at last. He "finally decided to work, not like his father, in quixotic isolation, or like his brother, as an artist abroad, but as a scientist in America—the task for which nurture and early choice had fitted him."[5] "In his beginnings at Harvard, he pursued physiology as he had pursued medicine—as a natural science that provided needed discipline. Philosophy, like painting in his youth, was labeled a self-indulgence that threatened mental stability. Psychology was a compromise between the two. . . . Having decided to work, he dared to become ambitious" (331). Feinstein's final sentence sums up the way William James resolved the various conflicts that dominated his youth: "For the rest of his life, his task would be to explain psychological science with literary grace, while defending the meaning of religious experience (such as his father's) against the tyranny of scientific materialism" (347).

The other book, Jacques Barzun's *A Stroll with William James,* is a frankly hero-worshipping one, but with all the virtues of a superlatively good academic presentation. Barzun portrays his author in the best light, making essentials clear while warning against misinterpretations and distortions, updating and giving contemporary parallels in the course of a running enthusiastic commentary. (Like many good teachers, he rides hobby-horses and pursues *bêtes noires*—especially

Freud, Eliot, and Pound, at whom he can rarely resist a shot, cheap
or expensive. But these faults do not seriously mar the book, which is
continuously informative and stimulating. The occasional irritations
merely add to its liveliness.)

Barzun begins, after a biographical chapter, with "The Masterpiece"—the *Principles of Psychology* (1890). In emphasizing this as
James's greatest work, on which all the others depend and in which
they are all to some degree implicit, Barzun follows the trend of recent
interpretation. (By long and common consent, his other masterpiece is
The Varieties of Religious Experience, 1902.) As James put his central
thesis, "the knower is not simply a mirror floating . . . and passively
reflecting an order that he comes upon and finds simply existing. The
knower is an actor and coefficient of the truth. . . . Mental interests,
hypotheses, postulates, so far as they are bases for human action—
action which to a great extent transforms the world—help to *make* the
truth which they declare. In other words, there belongs to mind . . . a
spontaneity, a vote. It is in the game, and not a mere looker on."[6] (We
note with pleasure the democratic metaphors.) James sees experience
as a field or process (or, in his persistent metaphor, a river or stream),
in which the aesthetic and the moral participate in sensation and perception. The stream of consciousness is one, prior to later distinctions.
Similarly, aesthetic and ethical factors are part of the test of truth, of
the sentiment of rationality. This radically new approach is the basis
both of his profound contributions to philosophy proper and of his
continuing relevance to everything from psychology, parapsychology,
religion, and ethics to literary criticism. Whitehead ranked him with
Aristotle, Plato, and Leibniz, calling him an "adorable genius" charac-
terized by "greatness with simplicity"; Husserl testified to his profound
influence in phenomenology; Russell accepted his radical empiricism
and said that he would, "on this ground alone, deserve a high place
among philosophers."[7] (Russell does not accept pragmatism, of
course, or James's "attempt to build a superstructure of belief upon a
foundation of scepticism.")

My concern is not, however, primarily with the importance of his
work as philosopher, but with the special affection and admiration he
evokes from his readers.

As I read Feinstein and Barzun, I began to see, superimposing itself
on the portrait of James, the large and unexpected figure of Samuel
Johnson. This conjunction seemed at first extremely implausible: the
anti-American old Tory and the open-minded American of socialist-
pacifist inclinations; the neoclassical man of letters and the romantic
scientist; the master of formal, polysyllabic, oracular prose and the

apostle of directness, informality, and simplicity. James himself, who never mentions Johnson and seems not to have read him, would certainly have been astonished at the suggestion; there can be no question of "influence." But both men were, and are, heroes of their respective cultures; and the parallels between them unfold and expand in the mind the more one thinks about them.

Perhaps the basic similarity is that both writers, in Johnson's words, "rejoice to concur with the common reader," and both assume common ground with him. Like Johnson, James was a great master of the English language, and, like Johnson, he wrote for the common reader and had small respect for those who refused to do so (though James was endlessly patient with his unfortunate friend C. S. Peirce, who could not get a teaching job because he could not communicate with students). One reason William is so much more attractive as a person than his brother, Henry, is that Henry is, as aesthete and type of the pure artist—beautifully rendered and affectionately parodied in Auden's "At the Grave of Henry James"—however admirable, also limited, fussy, and somewhat absurd. His interests and his appeal as "master of nuance and scruple" become inevitably narrower and more specialized. William, on the other hand, remains determined to write technical works in psychology, philosophy, and religion that anyone can read.

I have in mind, of course, not the elderly, sometimes pontifical Johnson portrayed by Boswell so much as the Johnson Agonistes presented in B. H. Bronson's memorable essay, W. J. Bate's fine biography, and much other recent interpretation. Bate says of Johnson, in words that apply also to James: "Few moralists have lived as he did—so close to the edge of human experience in so many different ways. We are speaking of 'experience' in the vivid Latin sense as something genuinely won the hard way—*ex periculo,* 'from danger' or 'from peril'. . . . Hence the ring of authority in so much that he says. We know that he has gone through it himself at genuine risk or peril."[8] He cites Johnson's honesty, courage, compassion, and humor—and these four characteristics describe James equally well. Johnson anticipates, he says, as no other classical moralist does, the discovery "that the mind—far from being either a serene, objective, rational instrument, or, as the radical materialists thought, a sort of recording machine . . . is something unpredictably alive in its own right."[9]

One striking biographical similarity to Johnson is James's early tendency to depression, despair, nightmarish emotional disturbances, sensations approaching a state of hallucination. The description of "The Sick Soul" in *The Varieties of Religious Experience,* which James originally attributed to a French correspondent but later acknowledged to come from his own experience, is unforgettable. James was haunted by the memory of an epileptic he had seen in an asylum: "*That shape am I,* I felt, potentially. Nothing that I possess can defend me from that fate, if the hour for it should strike for me as it struck for him."[10] (Feinstein argues plausibly that the influence of Renouvier in James's recovery from this crisis has been exaggerated; James himself said that the most important factor was "having given up the notion that all mental disorder requires to have a physical basis.") The similarity to Johnson's breakdown at the age of twenty, his despair and continuing fear of insanity and of the black dog, melancholy, and his love and dread of indolence is marked. Elizabeth Hardwick comments on James's curious procrastination, a hanging back and a reluctance to commit himself (he was thirty-six when he married, and his father chose his wife; forty-eight when his first important work, the *Principles,* was published). She says well, in words that apply equally to Johnson, "it was probably procrastination, in all its joy and sorrow, that made him such a great writer on the quirks of human nature. He was a sort of poet of 'habit' and 'will' and never able to bring himself under their pure, efficient control."[11]

Both James and Johnson, then, suffered much and had difficult early years; both worked very hard and made themselves by choice, by the conscious exercise of free will. Both were remarkably honest and candid, both gloried in their common humanity, were not without faults and limitations, but were individual, unpredictable, and distinctive. Both had remarkable and distinctive senses of humor, which contributed much of the flavor to their writings. The biographic parallel is a subject worthy of a Plutarch; but for the present we will have to restrict ourselves largely to the realm of beliefs and ideas.

Sir Joshua Reynolds said that Johnson "cleared my mind of a great deal of rubbish." Johnson himself said to Boswell, "My dear friend, clear your *mind* of cant."[12] This is one of Johnson's central achievements, and it is exactly paralleled by James. Both go back to the beginnings, to the elements and the essentials, starting afresh, taking nothing for granted; avoiding preconceptions, abstractions, illusions, self-deceptions, and the like, they confront total and concrete experience. James is, of course, being a philosopher, more profound and rigorous than Johnson. He is like the pre-Socratic philosophers, as has often been observed, in making this fresh approach prior to all distinctions and conventional categories and wisdoms. In many other ways James is obviously a more profound thinker than Johnson, and more flexible, precise, and many-dimensioned as well. On some occasions we may legitimately take satisfaction in seeing the American have the best of it against the Great Cham.

Describing his own philosophical position in a letter of 1904, James wrote: "My philosophy is what I call a radical empiricism, a pluralism, a 'tychism,' which represents order as being gradually won and always in the making. It is theistic, but not essentially so. It rejects all doctrines of the Absolute. . . . I fear that you may find my system too bottomless and romantic."[13]

Johnson was, in his way, also a radical empiricist: "Human experience, which is constantly contradicting theory, is the great test of truth."[14] True, Johnson goes on to make a point rather different from James's: He is arguing for the superior merit of collective experience through time (as embodied, presumably, in tradition and institutions), whereas James emphasizes the experience of the individual. Nevertheless, the basic principle is exactly the same: the superior validity of actual experience to any kind of theory or abstraction or doctrine, and the necessity of judging all such theories by the criterion of experience. Johnson was also, in the large sense, a kind of pragmatist: "The only end of writing is to enable the reader better to enjoy life, or better to endure it." "There is nothing, Sir, too little for so little a creature as man. It is by studying little things that we attain the great art of having as little misery and as much happiness as possible" (1:290).

Both James and Johnson are convinced that free will is a matter of immediate experience: Johnson says, "All theory is against the freedom of the will; all experience for it."[15] His refutation of Berkeley by kicking a stone and his assertions that we *know* our will is free are cruder than James's analyses of how freedom may consist in its minimum essentials of choosing what to think about, what to focus the attention on, and how the decision to believe in free will or not is itself an example of free choice. But the essential meaning is the same, and for both it is grounded in irrefutable personal experience and is intimately related to the moral life. For James as for Johnson, determinism destroys the foundation of morality and renders moral judgment or action meaningless. Wilshire, in his introduction to *The Essential Writings*, says: "James regards attention and will as the core of the self. That is, the kind of person I am is a matter of my behavior, and this is a matter of the patterned turnings of my attention; what I do is a matter of what I 'hold before me' as objects of thought."[16] Barzun says of James, in words that apply equally well to Johnson, "James, with his insistence on action as the proper end of thought and a guaranty against sentimentalism, practiced his morality of risk and faith in both private and public life."[17]

As to religion, there are great differences, but a fundamental similarity. James writes in a letter of 1900:

The problem I have set myself is a hard one: first, to defend (against all the prejudices of my "class") "experience" against "philosophy" as being the real backbone of the world's religious life — I mean prayer, guidance, and all that sort of thing immediately and privately felt, as against high and noble general views of our destiny and the world's meaning; and second, to make the hearer or reader believe, what I myself invincibly do believe, that, although all the special manifestations of religion may have been absurd (I mean its creeds and theories), yet the life of it as a whole is mankind's most important function. A task well-nigh impossible, I fear, and in which I shall fail; but to attempt it is my religious act.[18]

Johnson was in total agreement on the importance of religion, but of course was a deeply committed (though also deeply troubled) Christian and a supporter of the Church of England. James has a democratic dislike of hierarchies and intermediaries that is very American: "No American can ever attain to understanding the loyalty of a Briton towards his king, of a German towards his emperor; nor can a Briton or German ever understand the peace of heart of an American in having no king, no Kaiser, no spurious nonsense, between him and the common God of all."[19] As to the Anglican Church, he writes from England in a letter of 1903 that he has not until recently

had any sense of what a part the Church plays in the national life. So massive and all-pervasive, so authoritative, and on the whole so decent, in spite of the iniquity and farcicality of the whole thing. Never were incompatibles so happily yoked together. Talk about the genius of Romanism! It's nothing to the genius of Anglicanism, for Catholicism still contains some haggard elements, that ally it with the Palestinian desert, whereas Anglicanism remains obese and round and comfortable and decent with this world's decencies, without an *acute* note in its whole life or history, in spite of the shrill Jewish words on which its ears are fed, and the nitro-glycerine of the Gospels and epistles which has been injected into its veins. Strange feat to have achieved![20]

The position both took on ghosts and other "paranormal" phenomena is strikingly similar. Both kept open minds on the subject and, at the risk of ridicule, spent much time investigating specific instances. The story of the Cock Lane ghost is the best-known example in Boswell; in that case Johnson was "one of those by whom the imposture was detected." James was a very active member for more than twenty-five years (vice-president, 1890–1910, and president, 1894–96) of the Society for Psychical Research.[21] Neither was in the least gullible, but neither was willing to rule out any possibility or exclude any part of experience on a priori grounds. They wound up with the same baffled conclusion: that the basic question could not be answered. Whether or not "there has ever been an instance of the spirit of any person appearing after death," said Johnson, is one of the most important questions that can come before the human understanding; but after five thousand years it is still "undecided." "All argument is against it; but all belief is for it."[22]

There is, however, a basic difference. James's attitude toward religion was essentially the same as toward "psychic phenomena," though tinged with more respect, sympathy, and admiration. (He describes his own point of view in the *Varieties of Religious Experience* as "purely existential.") Johnson was, of course, a totally committed Christian and an Anglican (though ecumenical, holding that the differences among Christians were trivial, rather political than religious; was a friend of John Wesley and attracted to Catholicism; and was willing to hear all that a Confucian or a Mohammedan might say).

Barzun says that the "glaring contradiction between morality and religion makes 'scholastic theism' and 'popular Christianity' as unacceptable" to James as to him. "In practice, religion supports morality. . . . But originally and most worthily, the faith exists to forgive and unite, while morality divides and punishes."[23] But Barzun is here projecting his own view—which seems to attribute a more-than-Lutheran exaltation of Faith above Works to all Christianity—onto James. James, as we shall see, regularly argues instead that morality alone is inadequate and that religion completes it. Barzun distorts James even more seriously when he argues that James felt (as Barzun does) that Christianity is unacceptable because ungentlemanly. Barzun quotes Shaw admiringly: "Ladies and gentlemen cannot as such possibly allow anyone else to expiate their sins by suffering a cruel death" (273). (In sharp contrast, we have already noted James's remark that while the Devil may be a gentleman God certainly is not.) Barzun has limitations and prejudices that seem alien to James.

Neither Johnson nor James thinks morality or gentility self-sufficient or a substitute for religion. No gentleman would pursue James's intellectually and socially disreputable and wholly nonrespectable psychic phenomena; but James is wholly without snobbery toward these dingy, dubious, and often fraudulent characters. In fact, he obviously enjoys their vulgarity: "A plague take all white-livered, anaemic, flaccid, weak-voiced Yankee frauds! Give me a full-blooded red-lipped villain like dear old D. . . . obese, wicked, jolly, intellectual, with no end of go and animal spirits."[24] (He does complain of the "extreme triviality" of most of the spirit communications, their "curiously vague optimistic philosophy-and-water"; he and Myers joke about the "dear spirits . . . hovering around us in the Summer Land" [56].) James's utter lack of moral, as well as social or intellectual, snobbery is particularly apparent in his "Final Impressions of a Psychical Researcher" (1909). Defending mediums and other psychics for their tendency to fraud, he remarks that "man's character is too sophistically mixed for the alternative of 'honest or dishonest' to be a sharp one. Scientific men themselves will cheat—at public lectures—rather than let experiments obey their well-known tendency towards failure. . . . To compare small men with great, I have myself cheated shamelessly" (313). And he gives an account of how, in the interests of the larger truth, he once faked a demonstration of a turtle's heartbeat. "There is a hazy penumbra in us all where lying and delusion meet, where passion rules beliefs as well as conduct, and where the term 'scoundrel' does not clear up everything. . . . Our subconscious region seems, as a rule, to be dominated either by a crazy 'will to make-believe,' or by some curious external force impelling us to personation" (321–22).

That Johnson did not believe in any such contradiction or conflict between religion and morality as Barzun wrongly attributes to James hardly needs demonstration. The essential bond between the two was one of Johnson's main themes, as in his warnings against relying on natural goodness or benevolent impulses and his assertion that "to find a substitution for violated morality . . . was the leading feature in all perversions of religion."[25]

James regularly maintains that morality without religion is unsatisfactory: In an essay of 1891 he argues that "in a merely human world without God, the appeal to our moral energy falls short of its maximal stimulating power. . . . Our attitude towards concrete evils is entirely different in a world where we believe there are none but finite demanders, from what it is in one where we joyously face tragedy for an infinite demander's sake."[26] In the *Varieties* this becomes a central theme: "But the athletic attitude tends ever to break down, and it inevitably does break down even in the most stalwart when the organism begins to decay, or when morbid fears invade the mind. . . . Well, we are all such helpless failures in the last resort. The sanest and best of us are of one clay with lunatics and prison inmates, and death finally runs the robustest of us down. . . . And here religion comes to our rescue and takes our fate into her hands. . . . Fear is not held in abeyance as it is by mere morality, it is positively expunged and washed away."[27]

Balancing the claims of morbid-mindedness and healthy-mindedness, James decides that the latter does not work and "is inadequate as a philosophical doctrine, because the evil facts which it refuses positively to account for are a genuine portion of reality. . . . The lunatic's visions of horror are all drawn from the material of daily fact. Our civilization is founded on the shambles, and every individual existence goes out in a lonely spasm of helpless agony." (160).

James finds himself in agreement with "mankind's common instinct for reality," which "has always held the world to be essentially a theatre for heroism. In heroism, we feel, life's supreme mystery is hidden. . . . The folly of the cross, so inexplicable by the intellect, has yet its indestructible vital meaning. . . . Naturalistic optimism is mere syllabub and flattery and sponge-cake in comparison" (356). And in a footnote late in the *Varieties* James again concludes that "the outlook upon life of the twice-born . . . is the wider and completer. The 'heroic' or 'solemn' way in which life comes to them is a 'higher synthesis' into which healthy-mindedness and morbidity both enter and combine. Evil is not evaded, but sublated" (478n).

Johnson, too, takes an essentially tragic view of life. His generalizations in *Rasselas* and the poems are famous: Human life is "everywhere a state in which much is to be endured, and little to be enjoyed," and the vanity of human wishes allows only celestial wisdom to calm the mind, bestowing by grace the happiness it does not find. Johnson was convinced that variety, "multiplicity of agreeable consciousness," is the basis of happiness, and London therefore the most promising locus of felicity. But he maintained that man is happy in the present only when he is drunk; even driving rapidly in a post chaise, the post chaise is on its way to or from somewhere. "There is but one solid basis of happiness; and that is, the reasonable hope of a happy futurity," he wrote to Boswell.[28]

The only parallel between James and Johnson that seems to have been noted before[29] is the resemblance between the James-Lange theory of emotion and Johnson's religious attitude. The theory holds, in short, that the physical expressions of the emotion come first, the feelings later, and that the feelings are created by the action. Morally, then, the important thing is to put on the appropriate or desirable expression, and then we shall feel the proper emotion. Johnson's emphasis on religious action as prior to feeling is similar. "He that hopes to find peace by trusting God, must *obey* him": "This constant and devout *practice* is both the effect, and cause, of *confidence* in God."[30] (Johnson's attitude is, of course, by no means peculiar to him, but widely practiced and recommended, especially in Roman Catholic devotional literature: One should not wait for the proper feelings to come, but participate in the services and rituals, act properly, and let the feelings come later.) But James was against Pascal's wager, on the ground that masses and holy water are not a live option for non-Catholics,[31] though in "The Will to Believe" he reformulates it in psychological terms: "Dupery for dupery, what proof is there that dupery through hope is so much worse than dupery through fear? . . . If religion be true and the evidence for it be still insufficient, I do not wish . . . to forfeit my sole chance in life of getting upon the winning side" (324). (Hypocrisy, Johnson said, is not only the tribute vice pays to virtue but also possibly improving to the hypocrite.)

Certainly Johnson did not think either actions or outward forms enough; he believed, like all Protestants, that justification ultimately is by faith alone; and he detested most of all the complacent optimism and rationalism of deists, freethinkers, and revolutionaries. Like all Protestants, he believes that salvation cannot be earned and comes by grace, not merit. But faith is shown by works as well as feeling, and, like Luther, Johnson agonized over whether or not he had it, as judged by either testimony.

Johnson not only takes religion seriously as an intellectual problem; it is the center of his emotional life. He fears death, damnation, but even more annihilation; he prays and writes prayers, reads devotional works, goes to church, tries to amend his life, and so on. But he feels little comfort until his much-debated "conversion" in the last year of his life, after which he seems to feel assurance. James, on the other hand, was only mildly concerned about these matters as far as feelings go: he believes in their vast importance to most people, and he is concerned to prove that religion may be true, to defend the right to believe; but he leaves immortality an open question, as he does the meaning of supernatural phenomena. (Santayana said: "He did not really believe. He merely believed in the right of believing that you might be right if you believed."[32]) In *Varieties,* he says he is unable to accept either popular Christianity or scholastic theism, and supposes his "belief that in communion with the Ideal new force comes into the world . . . subjects me to being classed among the supernaturalists of the piecemeal or crasser type."[33] He accepts the Buddhist doctrine of karma, speculates on the unconscious as a link with the supernatural, and argues that the chance it all may be true is enough to give hope. But in a letter he writes, "I have no living sense of commerce with a God. I envy those who have . . . yet there is *something in me* which *makes response* when I hear utterances from that quarter made by others."[34] This is, he says, his "mystical germ." In response to a questionnaire, he says, "I can't possibly pray—I feel foolish and artificial." James says his constitution shuts him out from the "enjoyment of mystical states" almost entirely;[35] we cannot imagine Johnson speaking in this tone! These are profound differences in attitude.

James and Johnson agree in having a keen sense of the limits of human reason; the universe, they feel, is larger and richer than reason can explain. Boswell records Johnson's words: "There are innumerable questions to which the inquisitive mind can in this state receive no answer: Why do you and I exist? Why was this world created? Since it was to be created, why was it not created sooner?"[36] Johnson tends to think fearfully of the awful mystery of God. James is more hopeful, less personal; he enjoys contemplating variety, strangeness, and mystery. For example, this marvelous passage from the *Varieties:*

> Most of us can remember the strangely moving power of passages in certain poems read when we were young, irrational doorways as they were through which the mystery of fact, the wildness and the pang of life, stole into our hearts and thrilled them. The words have now perhaps become mere polished surfaces for us; but lyric poetry and music are alive and significant only in proportion as they fetch these vague vistas of a life continuous with our own, beckoning and inviting, yet ever eluding our pursuit. We are alive or dead to the eternal inner message of the arts according as we have kept or lost this mystical susceptibility.[37]

In the late essay "Humanism and Truth," James uses the familiar Romantic metaphors of the temple versus the wilderness, the man-made, fixed, and static against the organic, natural, and changing: We humanists, he says, "condemn all noble, clean-cut, fixed, eternal, rational, temple-like systems of philosophy. . . . We turn from them to the great unpent and unstayed wilderness of truth as we feel it to be constituted. . . . The fundamental fact about our experience is that it is a process of change. . . . Why should anywhere the world be absolutely fixed and finished? And if reality genuinely grows, why may it not grow in these very determinations which here and now are made?"[38] Describing the work of the great psychic researcher F. W. H. Myers, James contrasts the

> classic-academic and the romantic type of imagination. The former has a fondness for clean pure lines and noble simplicity in its constructions. . . . Until quite recently all psychology was written on classic-academic lines. The consequence was that the human mind, as it figured in this literature, was largely an abstraction. A sort of sunlit ter-

race was exhibited on which it took its exercise. And where the terrace stopped, the mind stopped. But of late years the terrace has been overrun by romantic improvers, and to pass to their work is like going from classic to gothic architecture, where few outlines are pure and where uncouth forms lurk in the shadows.[39]

But this dichotomy does not really fit Johnson, who, though a firm believer in cosmic order, was intensely aware of the shadows in which lurk melancholy, madness, and possible ghosts. And he was by temperament fiercely independent, proud, individual, eccentric, and rebellious.

What finally can we make of the parallel between James and Johnson? Does it simply show that national stereotypes are meaningless, or that these two coincide because of consanguinity—Americans and English are cousins, after all—beneath surface differences? The fact that Johnson and James are so similar in so many respects, while they are also genuinely national types, makes it obvious that the national aspect is far less significant than the universal. The common sense that distinguishes both to an uncommon degree, the firm grip on reality that constantly forces theory to the test of fact, the candor, honesty, and directness that characterize both, are not peculiar to any nation. Neither is the defense of the common reader against the pretensions of learning: "Deign on the passing world to turn thine eyes, / And pause awhile from letters, to be wise."[40]

That James is more profound than Johnson, more fully aware of the mystery of fact and the unfathomableness of ontology, the otherness of people and things, has no necessary general significance. But we may hope that it is related to the other American national trait—the reverse counterpart of ambition—of modesty, humility, awareness of limits, respect for other humans and nonhumans, and the humor that is often a consequence of this awareness and respect.

James is one of the great company of American originals and eccentrics, lovers of the unexpected and unpredictable, from Dickinson, Thoreau, and Melville, Emerson and Whitman to Marianne Moore and Charles Ives, Williams and Pound, John Cage and Robert Rauschenberg and John Ashbery. Examples may also be seen in Wallace Stevens:

> People are not going
> To dream of baboons and periwinkles.
> Only, here and there, an old sailor,
> Drunk and asleep in his boots,
> Catches tigers
> In red weather.[41]

W. H. Auden's later poety and essays ("An electron has as much right to exist as we have") or Lewis Thomas's *Lives of a Cell* are further examples. This is one reason James seems quintessentially American. Yet this quality, of course, is not exclusively American (any more than Johnson's good qualities are exclusively English): One of the great recent expressions of it is Louis MacNeice's poem "Snow":

World is suddener than we fancy it.

World is crazier and more of it than we think,
Incorrigibly plural. I peel and portion
A tangerine and spit the pips and feel
The drunkenness of things being various.[42]

"Sight of elephants and tigers at Barnum's menagerie whose existence, so individual and peculiar, yet stands there so intensely and vividly real, as much so as one's own, so that one feels again poignantly the unfathomableness of ontology . . . their foreignness confounds one's prentension to comprehend the world—while their admirableness undermines the stoic or moral frame of mind in which one says the real meaning of life is *my* action. The great world of life, in no relation with my action, is so real!"[43] Wilshire, in *Essential Writings,* uses as his first epigraph this passage written in 1873, and stresses James's sense of the mystery of fact: "Not only that *anything* should be, but that *this* very thing should be, is mysterious!"

In his essay "On a Certain Blindness in Human Beings," James tries at length to suggest what he means by the uniqueness, individuality, and incommunicability of experience. Beginning with an anecdote revealing how utterly different the same external experience may appear to two different people, he goes on to quote favorite passages (from Whitman and Tolstoy, among others) illustrating this totally nonintellectual, nondiscursive kind of awareness. He concludes, "I am sorry for the boy or girl, or man or woman, who has never been touched by the spell of this mysterious sensorial life, with its irrationality, if so you like to call it, but its vigilance and its supreme felicity." This awareness "absolutely forbids us to be forward in pronouncing on the meaninglessness of forms of existence other than our own; and it commands us to tolerate, respect, and indulge those whom we see harmlessly interested and happy in their own ways, however unintelligible these may be to us. Hands off: neither the whole of truth nor the whole of good is revealed to any single observer, although each observer gains a partial superiority of insight from the peculiar position in which he stands. Even prisons and sick-rooms have their special revelations" (342).

This is one of the great American themes. With emphasis on the concreteness, richness, and mystery of the religious attitude versus the abstraction of the scientific, it was the central thesis of Ransom's *The World's Body* and the writings of Allen Tate and others of the Fugitive-Agrarians. It is broadly a part of the whole anti-Platonic tradition, opposing otherworldliness, spiritualized idealism, and abstraction, as this tradition appears in Nietzsche, aspects of Pater and Yeats, and especially D. H. Lawrence. James does not celebrate the Pre-Socratics or spend much time abusing Socrates, but he locates the fault explicitly: "Intellectualism in the vicious sense began when Socrates and Plato taught that what a thing really is is told us by its definition. Ever since Socrates we have been taught that reality consists of essences, not of appearances, and that the essences of things are known whenever we know their definitions."[44] The supernatural as revealed by Myers, grotesque and unpredictable, queer and cactuslike, is more plausible than the "whole classic platonizing Sunday-school conception. . . . If anything is *un*likely in a world like this, it is that the next adjacent thing to the mere surface-show of our experience should be the realm of eternal essences, of platonic ideas, of crystal battlements, of absolute significance."[45]

As to immortality, James's attitude is generous, democratic, and American: He is against the exclusiveness of the "old narrow-hearted aristocratic creed" and for a

> democratic universe, in which your paltry exclusions play no regulative part. Was your taste consulted in the peopling of this globe? How, then, should it be consulted as to the peopling of the vast City of God? Let us put our hand over our mouth, like Job, and be thankful that in our personal littleness we are here at all. . . . For my own part, then, so far as logic goes, I am willing that every leaf that ever grew in this world's forests and rustled in the breeze should become immortal. . . . The heart of being can have no exclusions akin to those which our poor little hearts set up. The inner significance of other lives exceeds all our powers of sympathy and insight. If we feel a significance in our own life which would lead us spontaneously to claim its perpetuity, let us be at least tolerant of like claims made by other lives, however numerous, however unideal they may seem to us to be. (308)

If ambition is one side of the American coin (and we remember its etymology: going around [like a politician seeking votes]), the other side is modesty: awareness of limits, respect for others, human and nonhuman. It has always been a part of the national character at its best, and James is one of the grand examples. James's pervasive humor is one of its finest manifestations, based on a deep awareness of the limits of human powers and of his own limitations in particular. For the practicality of the humorless, James has nothing but contempt: "The common foe of thought is the practical, conventionally thinking man to whom nothing has true seriousness but personal interests, and whose dry earnestness in those is only exceeded by that of the brute, which takes everything for granted and never laughs."[46]

When we Americans read (usually under duress) about such ancestors as Cotton Mather, the fear arises in our breasts that we may be like that: provincially insecure, insatiably ambitious, self-righteous, humorless, ruthlessly determined to be "first," in heaven as on earth. But when we read about William James, we feel that this is the kind of person we hope that we are: modest, unpretentious, a genuine democrat, spiritually as well as politically, always warm and generous to others, candid and honest, and at the same time fearless, absolutely independent, hard-working, and productive. As admired ancestor, regarded with pride and affection, he is a true culture hero.

If the repulsive head of Cotton Mather must be imagined on one side of the American coin, let us hope that James's face—compassionate and humorous as well as profoundly intelligent—embellishes the other; and that we win the toss. Nor need the Atlantic—nor his own antipathy—sunder us from that other cultural hero, our spiritual kinsman, Samuel Johnson.

PART · 2 *Poetry*

Revolution in American Poetry

The word *revolution* is intended here to suggest not only the American military and political revolution against the British but also all those later revolutions in American poetry associated first with Whitman, then with Pound and Eliot, and later with Ginsberg, Plath, Lowell, and a never-failing succession of versifactors. The question with which I shall be chiefly concerned is that of the relation between the Revolution of 1776 and these later, specifically poetic revolutions: that is, whether the same forces of geography, character, and history that produced the political revolution may also be seen at work in the poetic ones.

First, the obligatory topic of the American Revolution as it was reflected in American poetry of the time. A little of this goes a long way. The reason is simple: There were no American poets of real talent alive at the time, and, even if there had been, this subject would almost certainly have led them into producing the kind of bad verse that patriotism, or any other propagandistic motive, almost always produces. The only American poet who is remembered at all is Philip Frenau, a poet of minimal gifts, who was an ardent Jeffersonian and wrote incessantly and interminably about the Revolution. The trouble was that, however independent his sentiments, his verse was entirely derivative from, and imitative of, his British predecessors, and even at its best trembles on the edge of absurdity. For example, "The Indian Burying Ground":

Written originally as a bicentennial lecture for a nonliterary audience, this chapter may oversimplify some complex questions, but I hope it has at least the virtues of clarity and definiteness. This revised version was presented at Vanderbilt University in April 1977.

> Thou, stranger, that shalt come this way,
>   No fraud upon the dead commit—
> Observe the swelling turf, and say
>   They do not lie, but here they sit.

Like all subsequent American poets, Frenau had a hard time making a living. In spite of diligent work as editor, hack writer, sea captain, and assorted other trades, he wound up poor. He outlived what little poetic talent he had, and one is saddened by the picture of him in old age as wandering poet declined to wandering tramp, tinker, and odd-job man, not quite a beggar but very definitely below the poverty line.

It is not surprising that there should not have been at the time a native American poet capable of celebrating the birth of the nation. What is surprising is that, when the genuine poets came, the American Revolution appealed to them so little as a theme. Aside from a few poems that seem to have been written with elementary-school audiences in mind, there is astonishingly little real poetry about the American Revolution. Perhaps the chief reason is that, by the time that poets capable of dealing with such subject arrive—and the first is, of course, Whitman—they are confronted by the Civil War, which naturally seems to them not only closer and more immediate but also inherently a more interesting and significant subject, with heroes, especially Lincoln and Lee, far more complex in their tragic predicaments. Alternatively, they have gone further back, like Whitman in "A Passage to India" or Hart Crane in *The Bridge,* to the figure of Columbus.

One of the finest poems about the significance of the Revolution (though not its specific events) is Robert Frost's "The Gift Outright." This is the poem that Frost read at President Kennedy's inauguration—or tried to read while the wind kept blowing his manuscript away. It is about the relation between the American continent and the American people, and about the development from both of an American culture:

> The land was ours before we were the land's.
> She was our land more than a hundred years
> Before we were her people . . .

We "were England's, still colonials, / Possessing what we still were unpossessed by," until we "found salvation in surrender":

> Such as we were we gave ourselves outright
> (The deed of gift was many deeds of war)
> To the land vaguely realizing westward,

But still unstoried, artless, unenhanced,
Such as she was, such as she would become.[1]

But it is exceptional for a poet to deal even this specifically with the Revolution. Pound, in some of the strangest of *The Cantos,* celebrates Jefferson as hero against Hamilton as villain (though he makes a weird conflation of Jefferson with Mussolini, Count Malatesta, and Confucius), but he has the good sense to make John Adams also a principal hero. In his early poetry, Robert Lowell presents a jaundiced view of American history from the Puritan fathers through the Revolution. The ironically titled "Children of Light" begins, "Our fathers wrung their bread from stocks and stones / And fenced their gardens with the red man's bones." And though, in "Salem," he celebrates the town that "bred the men who quartered the Leviathan's fat flanks / And fought the British lion to his knees," he says of the revolutionary shrine of Concord that "Ten thousand Fords are idle here in search / Of a tradition" and in place of the "shot heard round the world" in Emerson's "Concord Hymn" Lowell recalls "The death-dance of King Philip and his scream / Whose echo girdled this imperfect globe."

Perhaps the best long poem about revolutionary issues is Robert Penn Warren's *Brother to Dragons* (1953; rev. 1979), which is not specifically about the Revolution at all but about the murder by Jefferson's nephew of a helpless slave and Jefferson's imagined anguish in trying to reconcile this evidence of human evil with his belief in the goodness of human nature. In a later poem, Warren puts amusingly the difficulty of imagining the postrevolutionary generations. It is called "Founding Fathers, Nineteenth-Century Style, Southeast U.S.A.": "They were human, they suffered," though as they "stare from daguerreotype with severe reprehension" you'd "never guess any pain / in those merciless eyes that now remark our own time's sad declension."

> Some composed declarations, remembering Jefferson's language.
> Knew pose of the patriot, left hand in crook of the spine or
> with finger to table, while the right invokes the Lord's just rage.
> There was always a grandpa, or cousin at least, who had been a real
>   Signer.
>
> Some were given to study, read Greek in the forest, and these
> Longed for an epic to do their own deeds right honor:
> Were Nestor by pigpen, in some tavern brawl played Achilles.
> In the ring of Sam Houston they found, when he died, one word
>   engraved: *Honor.*[2]

Although the American Revolution has thus not been very important as a specific subject in American poetry, the theme of revolution in a broader sense has been central to it. For the remainder of this chapter I shall be occupied with the exploration of this larger sense of revolution in American poetry and particularly with its implications with regard to form.

The first necessary, if obvious, point to make is that *every* genuine poem is itself a little revolution in form and language. Words are coined or old words are used in new senses; syntax is often distorted or dislocated; conventions are altered and sometimes subverted. This is painfully obvious in bad poetry, for the quickest route to achieving the appearance of poetry is to make something as emphatically unlike prose as possible. But whereas the Victorian poetaster did this by writing of conventionally "poetic" themes in flowery "poetic" diction, the modern adolescent does it by abandoning the use of captial letters and punctuation, flinging the words and letters irregularly about on the page, and making sure that they make no sense whatsoever as prose.

But, however tiresome such devices may be in the hands of the untalented, they can be very effective when used by E. E. Cummings, for example, who exploited them more fully than anyone else. Consider the gradual shifting of the parts of speech in "Anyone Lived in a Pretty How Town," for a well-known but irresistible example, "(With up so floating many bells down)," and the way the spacing on the page controls the tempo and drama in many other poems.

All poetry is revolutionary in this basic sense of attempting to break through the dull film of habit and familiarity in order to wake the reader up and to make him perceive freshly. Donne liked to do it with a shocking first line: "For God's sake hold your tongue and let me love" or "Busie old fool, unruly sun," while Shakespeare is less theatrical in attacking convention: "My mistress' eyes are nothing like the sun / Coral is far more red than her lips' red." Every poet, no matter how conservative or traditional he may appear on the surface, is revolutionary in this way; and every poem makes a new and individual pattern of sounds and rhythms, whether or not this is counterpointed against a traditional one. The Frost poem that we looked at a moment ago, "The Gift Outright," for example, appears conventional, but is actually audacious and even subversive in its treatment of the language: It is based on the interplay of two meanings of *deeds* and on the paradox of salvation through surrender, taking through giving; and it changes the verb *realize* from transitive to intransitive and gives it a meaning (akin to French *réaliser*) that is quite new in English but both precise and wonderfully rich in connotation. Most American poets have always given far more prominence to this revolutionary aspect of poetic language and form. It is the total lack of it that prevents us from considering Philip Frenau a prototype. Frenau might express sentiments of poetic independence and fire-breathing defiance of the British as much as he wished, but he could not achieve *poetic* independence — or, indeed, poetic existence — as long as his language and form were hopelessly imitative and passive.

The second point to make about the revolutionary theme is that most American poets, naturally, have been moved by the moral significance of the American venture, the hope that Americans, in this new land, having shaken off the corrupt institutions of Europe, might be, or might become, a new kind of man, freer, healthier, less distorted and limited. English poets, of course, also expressed this hope, and Blake and Shelley did so very memorably. Donne calls his mistress "O my America! My newfound land!"; Miranda, in *The Tempest,* cries "How beauteous mankind is! O brave new world that has such people in't!" But with American poets, such hopes are bred in the bone. It is also a matter of timing, or, to put it in a more dignified way, of the history of Western civilization. I do not believe such hopes have commonly been associated with the settling of Australia or Africa, for example. So it is not merely that the land is new and that men will have a new start, a second chance, there; but the fact that this New World, with its possibly noble savages, was discovered by Columbus while seeking a passage to India, just before the full blossoming of the Renaissance in Europe. America, in some massive and primitive continental symbolism, thus came to represent the hopes of rebirth of post-Renaissance Western man. Even the ultrasophisticated and expatriate Henry James often names his American heroes Adam and represents them as trying to rescue their Eves from the toils of the Old Serpent of Europe.

The revolution in American poetry may be described, then, as always basically psychological, though it assumes, as an unspoken prerequisite, the military and political revolution that made democracy possible. This revolution is a full one in the etymological sense: that is, it is not merely the overthrow of old modes of thinking, feeling, and perceiving, but their replacement by new and better ones, asserting freedom and individuality and celebrating love.

All this is very clear in our first great poet. Whitman was, as everyone knows, the first great master of free verse, and he declared his independence in no uncertain terms from literary as from political authority:

Come Muse migrate from Greece and Ionia,
Cross out please those immensely overpaid accounts,

That matter of Troy and Achilles' wrath, and Aeneas',
     Odysseus' wanderings, . . .

To the States or any one of them, or any city of the States,
     Resist much, obey little,
Once unquestioning obedience, once fully enslaves,
Once fully enslaved, no nation, state, city of this earth,
     ever afterward resumes its liberty.

That the basis of his revolution is psychological is affirmed in the first
poem of *Leaves of Grass* from 1867 on; since it is Whitman's own definitive summary of his themes it must be quoted entire:

One's-Self I sing, a simple separate person,
Yet utter the word Democratic, the word En-Masse.

Of physiology from top to toe I sing,
Not physiognomy alone nor brain alone is worthy for the
     Muse, I say the Form complete is worthier far,
The Female equally with the Male I sing.

Of Life immense in passion, pulse, and power,
Cheerful, for freest action form'd under the laws divine,
The Modern Man I sing.[3]

The basis of this psychological revolution is a psychological democracy, as becomes clear later in *Song of Myself:*

In all people I see myself, none more and not one a
     barley-corn less,
And the good or bad I say of myself I say of them

                       (82)

This affirmation is easy to make, but hard to put in practice. But Whitman really does it: Accepting himself, he is able to accept others. This
is the basis of the wonderful empathy, the fellow feeling with others,
that distinguishes his poetry. He refuses to make the customary distinctions between soul and body, man and woman; he rejects all hierarchies:

I am the poet of the Body and I am the poet of the Soul,
The pleasures of heaven are with me and the pains of hell are with me,
The first I graft and increase upon myself, the latter I translate into a
    new tongue.
I am the poet of the woman the same as the man,
and I say it is as great to be a woman as to be a man . . .

Anthropomorphizing animals, he makes them ideal types of the democratic independence, self-sufficiency, and serenity that should characterize human beings, in contrast to the guilt, competitiveness, and subservience he sees everywhere:

> I think I could turn and live with animals, they are so placid and
>   self-contained,
> I stand and look at them long and long.
> They do not sweat and whine about their condition,
> They do not lie awake in the dark and weep for their sins,
> They do not make me sick discussing their duty to God,
> Not one is dissatisfied, not one is demented with the mania of owning
>   things,
> Not one kneels to another, nor to his kind that lived thousands of years
>   ago,
> Not one is respectable or unhappy over the whole earth.

Finally, he carries his rejection of hierarchy to its logical conclusion and refuses to bow to God:

> I have said that the soul is not more than the body,
> And I have said that the body is not more than the soul,
> And nothing, not God, is greater to one than one's self is,
> And whoever walks a furlong without sympathy walks to his own
>   funeral drest in his shroud,
> And I or you pocketless of a dime may purchase the pick of the
>   earth, . . .
> And I say to mankind, Be not curious about God,
> For I who am curious about each am not curious about God,
> (No array of terms can say how much I am at peace about God and
>   about death)
> I hear and behold God in every object, yet understand God not in the
>   least,
> Nor do I understand who there can be more wonderful than myself.
>   (83–121 *passim*)

In "I Sing the Body Electric" he scandalized many, celebrating the body in graphic detail and asserting its identity with the soul. The affirmation of cosmic democracy could go no farther.

Emily Dickinson, our second great poet, is far more conventional on the surface, since she writes usually in traditional forms, based most

often on the hymn stanza. Nor does she violate the strictest propriety
and decorum in language; she once remarked that she had not read
Whitman because she had heard that he was "disgraceful." But, beneath this surface primness, she is perhaps more subversive than Whitman. Not only does she refuse to bow to God, but she also seems not
to believe in him in any serious sense: He is represented as a half-comic
father figure who is to be teased out of his pretended sternness. She
sees the psychological revolution in terms very similar to Whitman's:

What Soft – Cherubic Creatures –
These Gentlewomen are –
One would as soon assault a Plush –
Or violate a Star –

Such Dimity Convictions –
A Horror so refined
Of freckled Human Nature –
Of Deity – ashamed –

It's such a common – Glory –
A Fisherman's – Degree –
Redemption – Brittle Lady –
Be so – ashamed of Thee –[4]

Her Self is hidden, while Whitman's is proclaimed to the universe,
but there is the same impulse to break through the crust of respectability and custom to the living psychological truth:

I'm Nobody! Who are you?
Are you – Nobody – too?
Then there's a pair of us!
Don't tell! they'd banish us – you know!

How dreary – to be – Somebody!
How public – like a Frog –
To tell your name – the livelong June –
To an admiring Bog!

(206)

More explicitly even than Whitman, she endorses revolution as a
cosmic principle:

Revolution is the Pod
Systems rattle from
When the Winds of Will are stirred
Excellent is Bloom

But expect its Russet Base
Every summer be
The Entomber of itself,
So of Liberty –

Left inactive on the Stalk
All its Purple fled
Revolution shakes it for
Test if it be dead.[5]

(765)

Later poets, too, perceive the needed revolution as essentially psychological, even as they denounce the present sad state of the Republic most stingingly. For example, Robinson Jeffers' "Shine, Perishing Republic" presents a wonderfully repulsive image of America in 1925 as shining with the phosphorescence of decay: "While this America settles in the mould of its vulgarity, heavily thickening to empire, / And protest, only a bubble in the molten mass, pops and sighs out, and the mass hardens." But the vulgarity comes from corrupted love of man, "the trap that catches noblest spirits, that caught—they say—God, when he walked on earth." Allen Ginsberg, in the wave of poetic revolt in the 1950s, wound up a similar but more frivolous denunciation by affirming, "America, I'm putting my queer shoulder to the wheel."

Let us move on to the closely related question: To what extent was the Modernist revolution in poetry in the English language instigated and dominated by Americans? (Chronologically, this revolution is usually described as first a groundswell beginning in the mid-nineteenth century, then Modernism proper beginning before World War I—the specific date of 1909 is sometimes given for the beginning, with 1925, 1930, or 1940 for the end. Then there was a second wave, beginning in the 1950s, called in poetry at first Beat and then Naked and finally Open, which began receding in the early 1970s but is probably still going on.)

In all three phases, it seems clear retrospectively that the leading figures were Americans. Whitman creates almost alone the groundswell of Pre- or Proto- or Ur-Modernism in English-language poetry. Hopkins, the nearest British equivalent as pioneer (though Hopkins remained largely unpublished until thirty years after his death in 1889 and without much influence until 1930), acknowledged the resemblance between himself and Whitman, as well as Whitman's priority. He wrote in a letter, "I may as well say . . . that I always knew in my heart Walt Whitman's mind to be more like my own than any other man's living. As he is a very great scoundrel, this is not a very pleasant confession."[6] And D. H. Lawrence, the most vigorous and completely committed Modernist among the British in the pre–World War I wave, gave full credit to Whitman. In his *Studies in Classic American Literature,* he said: "Whitman, the one man breaking a way ahead. Whitman, the one pioneer. And only Whitman. No English pioneers, no French. No European pioneer poets. In Europe the would-be pioneers are mere innovators . . . Whitman, like a strange, modern, American Moses. Fearfully mistaken. Accept the great leader."[7] Lawrence, of course, spent much of his time in America, and in some sense transferred his spiritual allegiance; his ashes remain in New Mexico. In "New Heaven and Earth," he uses the image of the discovery of the New World to embody his basic psychological discoveries; it is distinctively Laurentian, yet clearly stems from Whitman:

> My God, but I can only say
> I touch, I feel the unknown!
> I am the first comer!
> Cortes, Pisarro, Columbus, Cabot, they are nothing, nothing!
> I am the first comer!
> I am the discoverer!
> I have found the other world! . . .
> It was the flank of my wife
> I touched with my hand, I clutched with my hand,
> Rising, new-awakened from the tomb!
> It was the flank of my wife
> whom I married years ago.[8]

In describing the Modernist revolution proper, as it began in English verse immediately before World War I, some qualifications must be made in calling it American. Pound and Eliot, the leading revolutionaries, did their work chiefly in London, and they are sometimes said to have lost their American authenticity through expatriation or cosmopolitan sophistication or un-American political views. But Pound is a very American figure, not least when he is denouncing this country or shaking its dust from his sandals. The quickness and audacity and innovative power, the personal generosity, the eccentricity, especially about money, the tendency to be a do-it-yourselfer or cracker-barrel village philosopher, the flamboyance and cockiness—these are traits many of us recognize in ourselves. Although a professional student of the Romance languages, and obviously much influenced by French and Italian poetry, as well as by the other arts of painting and music, Pound acknowledged his roots in Whitman and in Browning and other English poets; his chief reason for coming to London was to sit at the feet of Yeats. Eliot, on the other hand, at the beginning of his career had little relation to his immediate predecessors in American or English verse: He starts by imitating Laforgue and the Jacobean dramatists, with Baudelaire and Dante in the background. But his notion of tradition, as something self-conscious, based on deliberate choice, and ranging freely throughout the centuries and languages, was, as Europeans have often pointed out, a peculiarly American and modern one. As a New Englander born and raised in the South, then sent back to New England to school, Eliot was never at home in either Missouri or Massachusetts; and this circumstance made more intense the longing for roots and for a spiritual home that is a part of the experience of most Americans. His point of view, he wrote in a letter of 1928, was that of "an American who wasn't an American, because he was born in the South . . . but who wasn't a southerner in the South because his people were northerners in a border state . . . and who so was never anything anywhere and who therefore felt himself to be more a Frenchman than an American and more an Englishman than a Frenchman and yet felt that the U.S.A. up to a hundred years ago was a family extension. It is almost too difficult even for H. J. [Henry James] who for that matter wasn't an American at all, in that sense."[9] In Pound's vivid metaphor, he was the burglar who threw the brick through the window while Eliot was the partner who made off with the swag. As revolutionist, Pound was impresario and propagandist while Eliot produced the poetry and eventually won the reputation.

At the time, however, the most prominent American poets of the Modernist golden age of the 1920s felt betrayed by the expatriation of Pound and Eliot and considered their poetry insufficiently American. All of them affirmed their own determination to write a distinctively American epic. William Carlos Williams, for example, perpetually outraged by Eliot's apostasy and arguing fiercely but good-humoredly with Pound, insisted that there must be such a thing as a distinctively American prosody, based on the variable foot (mysteriously relativistic), and produced his epic celebrating the city of Paterson, New Jersey. Wallace Stevens, whose Pennsylvania Dutch ancestry and Connecticut habitat show through clearly beneath his dandified and sometimes Frenchified surface, wrote philosophical epics in which American seasons and locales are essential, such as *The Auroras of Autumn* and the great *Notes toward a Supreme Fiction*. Hart Crane, with absolute conviction, dedicated himself to writing an epic that would prove Eliot was wrong to despair and that would demonstrate that America, symbolized by the Brooklyn Bridge, is the hope of the future.

Most of the British have never accepted, or even recognized, what Robert Graves called "Franco-American Modernism." It is hard to imagine a poet more thoroughly, consciously, and explicitly anti-modern than Philip Larkin, for example. But many of the younger poets have migrated to the United States, temporarily or permanently—Thom Gunn, Donald Davie, Jon Stallworthy, Geoffrey Hill, Charles Tomlinson, Seamus Heaney—and after Auden took up residence again in England shortly before his death, and Robert Lowell married an English wife and spent the last few years of his life in England (though he was returning to this country when he died), the situation became transatlantically very confusing. The appointment of Ted Hughes as poet laureate has at last officially domesticated the American revolution in England, however, for Hughes was married to Sylvia Plath, spent much time in the United States, and unquestionably owes much to the great Modernists as well as to his native Yorkshire roots.

In the United States, there have long been signs of backlash or undertow or riptides against the last revolutionary waves; the extremes of the 1960s in poetry as in "lifestyles" are now out of fashion. *Fuck You! A Magazine of the Arts* has died unlamented, and there have been no more books of poetry consisting of a ream of blank typing paper; this is a hard act to follow, even if you copyright the paper, as Avram Saroyan did. At least one counterrevolutionary magazine appeared, devoted to the restoration of traditional forms: this was *Counter/Measures,* edited by X. J. Kennedy, and would seem to bear out the prediction, made some years ago, that if the trend toward open poetry went far enough the sonnet would soon be rediscovered. Actually, of course, the sonnet has never been forgotten, but has been mass-produced, opened up and overworked—some would say, worked to death—by Robert Lowell, of whom more in a moment.

It should be remembered, in speaking of revolutionary excesses, that there have always been many fine American poets who are emphatically not revolutionary in form and technique, however subversive their themes may be. Emily Dickinson will serve as type or progenitress, and one thinks immediately of Robert Frost and John Crowe Ransom, both of whom were first recognized in England and had their first books published there. Other clear-cut examples are Allen Tate, J. V. Cunningham, Richard Wilbur, Howard Nemerov, Daniel Hoffman, Anthony Hecht, John Bricuth. All the strict and demanding forms are very much alive, even the most exotic: villanelle, sestina, haiku, tanka, triolet. Even the Sapphic stanza, notoriously almost impossible to reproduce in English, has been used by William Meredith to render the experience of being mugged in New York, and John Ashbery has a fine sestina based on the "Popeye" comic strip. So the tradition is quietly maintained, while the public gets the impression that all poets disintegrate, posture, and come to flamboyantly bad ends.

I will conclude with a few reflections and speculations suggested by Pound's poem about Whitman, called *A Pact:*

> I make a pact with you, Walt Whitman—
> I have detested you long enough.
> I come to you as a grown child
> Who has had a pig-headed father;
> I am old enough now to make friends.
> It was you that broke the new wood,
> Now is a time for carving.
> We have one sap and one root—
> Let there be commerce between us.[10]

It appears that ontogeny recapitulates phylogeny in psychological as well as biological terms, and hence the parallel recurs perpetually in literary history. As surely as the fetus must outgrow its vestigial gills, the child must rebel against its father and the literary present must rebel against the past. Both rebellions are necessary and proper as part of the necessary process of maturing, but neither should be terminal. After the revolt and the slaying of the Jungian dragons—or the wicked stepmother and the giant or ogre—the adolescent must come to terms and finally reestablish relations with the parents, as the literature of the present must first break with, but finally also accept, that of the past. In the history of literature as in the life of the adolescent, such rebellions are always ambivalent: They are felt first as emancipation and then as disinheritance, liberation and then impoverishment. The exhilarations of freedom end in the deprivations and confusions of self-reliance. This psychic drama tends to be far more explicit and intense in modern American poetry than in British. (It may be seen also in such American critics as Harold Bloom, whose *Anxiety of Influence* generalizes and, in my view, exaggerates it.)

Sylvia Plath's "Daddy" is the most obvious example, but the theme is as central and almost as traumatic in Robert Lowell. It appears in innumerable forms throughout his life and poetry, from the literal incident in 1936 when he knocked his father down to the identification with the criminal Caligula/Caliban and Lucifer/Satan, the ultimate rebel against the heavenly Father. He was a participant in the political and cultural revolutions of the 1960s, but also fully committed to, and ineradicably aware of, the past. The tension is often fruitful poetically (however catastrophic personally) as in such fine sonnets as "In the Back Stacks," which shows Lowell's full and ironic awareness of both sides: the transient quality of fame, but the insufficiency of mere tradition; the irrelevance of his popularity as participant in student riots, but the premature senility of art apart from life. The same self-irony is directed at the concept of openness in form and in directly autobiographical subjects—a concept established by Lowell's own *Life Studies* and worked out at enormous length in *History* and its two companion volumes of sonnets, *For Lizzie and Harriet* and *The Dolphin*—in "Reading Myself." His last volume, *Day by Day,* saw him free at last of his sonnet obsession and, to some extent, of the obsessive conflict with his long-dead parents. Adrienne Rich seems a contrasting example of a greatly gifted poet whose work has steadily diminished in power, because since *Diving into the Wreck* she has followed the monolithic feminist revolutionary line of rejection of the male-dominated culture of the past. Her position may be radically logical, but her poetry is greatly impoverished.

No doubt American poetry, in comparison with British, will continue to be revolutionary in the broad and mainly psychological sense I have tried to define. American poets will try at the same time to write the great American epic and to go beyond art to revelation; ours will continue to be a poetry of great extremes and great ambitions. But we may hope for an increasing awareness that, if every genuine poem is a little revolution, it is also a pledge of allegiance to the past; that except for the shared heritage of meaning in words and syntax, it would mean nothing; and without the rich tissue of allusion to earlier poetry in form, genre, and convention, its meaning would be vastly impoverished. In the famous phrase of E. H. Gombrich, as true of poetry as of painting, "The innocent eye sees nothing." A steady diet of revolution ends in idiocy, in the etymological if not the clinical sense.

If the political and military revolution that began in 1776 was never very important as a poetic subject, it was a necessary prerequisite for the psychological revolution that became the essential subject of American poetry from Whitman on. This predisposed American poets to the Modernist revolution, and they have dominated it to the present day. But the time has come, not for counterrevolution or for denying the revolutionary values, but for putting them in perspective and recognizing what else is needed. Demolition perhaps comes too easily to Americans; we are perhaps too likely to be impatient with the traditions and institutions of the past. (Bland formulas perhaps come too easily to academics like me.) Nevertheless, as Pound suggested in his poem of 1916, it does seem to be a time now for emphasizing continuity, for carving rather than breaking new wood, for making friends again with the past.

Life and Art in Robert Lowell

For the last three decades of his life, Robert Lowell was widely regarded as the leading American poet of the postwar era. *Lord Weary's Castle* in 1946 established him as master of a formal, elaborately allusive "metaphysical" style. But by 1959 he responded to the trend toward openness in form and personal directness in content with *Life Studies,* which rode this new wave farther up the beach than anyone else. A third stage began with *Notebook 1967–68,* recording with a new closeness the public and private involvements of a year. The first version was rapidly succeeded by two others, each larger and more incoherent. Finally, in 1973, Lowell published another revised and expanded version as *History,* with the poems about his former wife and daughter in a separate volume, *For Lizzie and Harriet,* and a new volume, *The Dolphin,* about his new wife and son. All these books from 1967 to 1973 were in the same form, the "sonnet" of fourteen unrhymed lines; Lowell's obsession with this form, and his incessant revision of his earlier work (which he appeared willing to destroy through forcing it into this later mold), left his readers confronted with an impossibly overgrown and confused body of work.

The appearance of an eminently sane and responsible *Selected Poems* in 1976 was therefore especially welcome. There was no longer any effort to make the later work swallow up the earlier; past work and past selves were treated with proper respect. To leave no doubt on the point, Lowell announced that he had made no changes in poems of the first twenty years except to cut parts of some of the longer ones. In recovering from the excesses of the 1960s, Lowell once more followed an intensely private path that mysteriously coincided with the broad highway of public attitudes; like Dryden, he changed with the nation. (He also recovered from his "sonnet" obsession; none of the poems published after 1973 is in this form.)

Lowell in this selection admirably restrained the partiality that any poet must feel for his most recent work, giving roughly 90 pages to the last decade, 150 to the first two. Especially in view of the enormous bulk of the later work, this is a reasonable proportion. In dealing with the later work, he followed the sensible procedure of choosing "possible sequences, rather than atomizing favorite poems out of context," and confined himself to "a few slight changes," which often simply go back to discarded versions.

From *History* he selected (or composed) two sequences. The first examines the whole panorama of history, from Cain and Abel to the assassinations and upheavals of 1968, in search of ultimate significance and of relation to the self. God appears in history as cruel and senseless; the self is seen as flawed, guilty, corrupting public motives by private. There are brilliant and witty perceptions, such as the portrait of Cicero as Ezra Pound ("old sheep sent out to bite the frosty stubble") and the parallel of Henry VIII and Mohammed, who "got religion / in the dangerous years, and smashed the celibates"), and wonderfully condensed portraits, such as those of Rembrandt or Charles V. But probably the best of all are those explicitly personal ones treating the ideals of revolutionary politics and open or naked poetry with the same candor and irony. For example, "The Nihilist as Hero," where the demand for immediate experience is balanced by awareness of art as illusion ("I want words meat-hooked from the living steer, / but a cold flame of tinfoil licks the metal log"): "A nihilist wants to live in the world as it is, / and yet gaze the everlasting hills to rubble." "Reading Myself" describes the book as honeycomb containing its maker, which will at most live long enough "for the sweet-tooth bear to desecrate— / this open book . . . my open coffin."

The second sequence uses the opposite method, beginning with an explicit autobiographical narrative and generalizing its significance. The subject is Lowell's relation to his parents, and specifically the incident in which he knocked his father down in 1936; this becomes the archetype of rebellion in both the psychological and the political realm. Both parents are accepted at last (now long after their deaths), and "To Daddy" makes amends for many previous revealing portraits: "I think, though I don't believe it, you were my airhole, / and resigned perhaps from the Navy to be an airhole— / that Mother not warn me to put my socks on before my shoes." (The ice image here neatly echoes that at the end of the first sequence; Lowell's selection makes the patterns of imagery plainer and more effective.)

"Mexico," the third sequence, is printed as from *History,* though in fact it comes from *For Lizzie and Harriet.* Dealing with the themes of love and cruelty in marriage, it forms an introduction to that sequence, which describes the long and agonizing process of Lowell's leaving his wife and daughter for another woman. The final sonnet, lamenting the passage of time, is particularly effective:

"Obit"

Our love will not come back on fortune's wheel—

in the end it gets us, though a man know what he'd have:
old cars, old money, old undebased pre-Lyndon
silver, no copper rubbing through . . . old wives; . . .

After loving you so much, can I forget
You for eternity, and have no other choice?

(223)

Finally, "The Dolphin" relates the story of his relation to the new wife, but also dwells on his own sickness, the continuing agony of the separation from Lizzie and Harriet, and the relation of art to life:

None of us can or wants to tell the truth,
pay fees for the over-limit we caught, while floating
the lonely river to senility
to the open ending. Sometimes in sickness,

we are weak enough to enter heaven.

(242)

The final sonnet recapitulates the images of dolphin, mermaid, and other sea creatures helpful to man, and of poetry as net; it also recapitulates the allusions to Ezra Pound, another aging poet who recognized his errors. Poetically, at least, it is a triumphant ending:

When I was troubled in mind, you made for my body
Caught in its hangman's-knot of sinking lines,
the glassy bowing and scraping of my will. . . .
I have sat and listened to too many
words of the collaborating muse,
and plotted perhaps too freely with my life,
not avoiding injury to others,
not avoiding injury to myself—
to ask compassion . . . this book, half fiction,
an eelnet made by man for the eel fighting—

my eyes have seen what my hand did.[1]

From Caligula to Philoctetes

How important is knowledge of a poet's biography to the interpretation and evaluation of his poetry? The innocent reader and the historical critic have always assumed that it is indispensable. In reaction against excessive biographical emphasis, many critics of varied persuasions—New Critics, neo-Aristotelians, deconstructionists, for example—have maintained that other kinds of knowledge and other skills (especially the ability to read well) are more important. An occasional critic—W. H. Auden is an example—has taken the extreme position that biography is totally irrelevant; but Auden went on to argue that though knowledge of the life would not help you understand the poetry, knowledge of the poetry would help you understand the life. (Auden was himself an avid reader of biography and a fine historical critic.)

Whatever one's theoretical position on these matters, it would be a doctrinaire theorist indeed who would deny that some knowledge of Lowell's life is essential to the full understanding of his poetry. The interplay between life and art became, increasingly, his central theme, with himself as prime exhibit; and the reader cannot possibly understand this counterpointing without knowing about Lowell's life from sources outside the poems. That a biography was needed to enhance and facilitate the reading of the poetry is thus hardly open to question. But quite aside from this purpose, Lowell's biography is interesting and important in its own right. Lowell was a remarkable and fascinating person; whatever his faults, nobody ever found him boring. His life obviously had a kind of representative quality: at worst, he was a scapegoat figure representing our defects in their extremity; at best, he was our culture hero, never forgetting in the heights or depths of his madness his responsibilities both to the republic of letters and to the political republic. In both, he was a loyal but critical citizen, maintaining with stubborn integrity his right to dissent. That the sixties, at least, will go down in literary history as the Age of Lowell seems a safe prophecy.

Since a biography was so clearly desirable for both these reasons, and since a large amount of primary source material was known to exist which had scarcely been touched by other scholars, Hamilton was presented with a remarkable opportunity.[2] I am happy to concur with what seems to be the general opinion that he has been fully equal to the demands of the occasion and realized most of its possibilities. He has managed to appeal to a relatively large audience—the first printing was thirty thousand, with adoptions by two book clubs—

without damaging compromises. He does not explain too much, but assumes that the reader is familiar with Lowell's poetry and with the American cultural scene. It would have been easy to go wrong by adopting too defensive or censorious or proprietary a tone, thus intruding himself between the subject and the reader as scholarly recording angel or solemn builder of a pious monument. Instead, he allows his sources to speak for themselves, through letters, written accounts published or unpublished, and especially through interviews. These interviews bring the book alive and are perhaps the most important single key to its success. Hamilton weaves them into the narrative without intruding himself as interviewer, but quoting them verbatim and at length. He has managed to interview virtually everyone still living who was significantly related to Lowell and to persuade them to talk explicitly and in great detail about him. The reader thus sees Lowell from many points of view, but close up and dramatically; and he has the sense of contact with the living man through his friends' eyes as well as the context of the biographical narrative. The people interviewed often quote Lowell's own words, since he was a memorable talker; and Hamilton quotes enough from Lowell's letters and his marvelous autobiographical writings (a long unpublished manuscript as well as the published ones) to convey his own sense of himself.

No doubt one reason Hamilton was able to get all these people to talk so fully and explicitly was simply that he is English, and therefore outside American social and literary networks, hierarchies, tensions, and suspicions. Another is that, unlike most recent authors of biographies of poets, he is not a journalist or academic, but a poet and critic himself and, as an experienced editor, thoroughly at home with both the public and private lives of writers. (As editor of the *Review,* he published much of Lowell's late poetry, and also interviewed him and reviewed him; he was therefore acquainted with him in several capacities.) Hamilton must have appeared to these people, therefore, as an informed, sympathetic, and familiar alien. At any rate, his success in arranging these interviews and the intelligence and tact with which he must have conducted them, together with the effectiveness with which he uses them—never citing them unnecessarily as window dressing, but mining them for vivid detail—should be recognized as an extraordinary achievement. Documentary or composite biographies (e.g., the Edward Nehls *Composite Biography* of D. H. Lawrence) have some of the same kinds of interest but cannot rival the immediacy of these interviews.

In interviewing, as in his other research (locating and using unpublished manuscripts and letters in numerous libraries and individual hands, for example), Hamilton is as thorough and methodical as the best American academics. He obtains from Blair Clark and Frank Parker, Lowell's closest friends from boyhood on, and from Lowell's own unpublished autobiographical manuscript, great floods of information about his early life. Jean Stafford must have died just too soon for Hamilton to interview her, but his second and third wives, Elizabeth Hardwick and Lady Caroline Blackwood, expressed themselves freely to him. So did many of his extramarital lovers: Ann Dick, Gertrude Buckman, Carley Dawson, Martha Ritter, several who remain anonymous, and, perhaps most exotic, the Latvian dancer Vija Vetra. Hamilton quotes all these people exactly, obviously transcribing from tape (though he does not say so); this procedure gives the biography a documentary value it would not otherwise have, and it is handled with such intelligence that it is never diffuse or boring; instead, the different voices are much more vivid and interesting than if they were boiled down into a single fluent style. Peter Taylor supplied much interesting material, as did Jonathan Raban and Frank Bidart, now his literary executor, on Lowell's latter days. Jonathan Miller, who directed *The Old Glory,* has some perceptive observations, and so does Eugene McCarthy.

Hamilton's decision to present these interviews and such other primary sources as letters and manuscripts at length and often verbatim gives his biography a kind of liveliness and immediacy, as well as a documentary value, that could be obtained in no other way. Its chief disadvantage is that, even in such a long book, it leaves him little space to consider backgrounds and ramifications or to interpret the poetry. What there is of critical interpretation is very good; but in most cases Hamilton takes it as his first obligation to describe the reception of Lowell's volumes, reviewing the reviewers rather than commenting directly on the poems. Some reviewers of the biography have suggested that Hamilton does not seem to recognize fully the magnitude of Lowell's accomplishment in its American context, the special significance he had for Americans in the sixties, his relation both to the culture and to the counterculture, as well as to earlier American literature. There may be something in this criticism, though it is hard to see how Hamilton, an Englishman concerned primarily with the life rather than the poetry, insofar as the two are separable, and adopting the procedures we have described, could have done all this without writing another book. His attitude toward both the man and the poetry seems to me admirably balanced, neither hero-worshipping nor censorious; since he nothing extenuates nor sets down aught in malice, he satisfies Othello's desiderata. He seems even to understand American humor, such as Elizabeth Hardwick's comment when the psychiatrist told her that Lowell, confined in a military hospital at Munich, "has left the Church and wants to join the Army:" "Dear old Cal, a born joiner" (193). Or the title she gave her manuscript memoir: "Smiling Through" (503).

Hamilton's English background enables him to interpret with assurance the episodes of Lowell's unsuccessful candidacy for the Oxford Professorship of Poetry and his marriage to Lady Caroline Blackwood. On the other hand, it may be partly responsible for his somewhat uncertain grasp of the Fugitive group. For example, he says that Ransom went to Cambridge—an astonishing mistake, since Ransom was a Rhodes Scholar—and he oversimplifies the circumstances of Ransom's leaving Vanderbilt for Kenyon (though he refers to Young's biography,[3] in which these matters are spelled out fully). His description of Merrill Moore as a "fringe" member of the group is hardly justifiable. He misunderstands the tone of Lowell's account of his 1937 visit to the Tates, which is not "sneakily whimsical but condescending."[4] It is hard to imagine Tate being "lordly and dogmatic"; Lowell's epithets, in that account, seem much more accurate: "jaunty and magisterial," and of the Tates as a couple "stately yet bohemian, leisurely yet dedicated."[5] Hamilton seems not to realize how much Tate, cast willy-nilly by Lowell in the role of substitute father, did for him and suffered at his hands. Tate not only took him in that first summer but also advised, encouraged, and helped him for the rest of his life. The Tates invited the Lowells to share their house in Monteagle in 1942–43; Tate wrote an introduction for Lowell's first book and helped him find a publisher, and thereafter was frequently involved in helping to get him jobs or extricate him from difficulties. Lowell called him a "wonderfully generous friend."[6] But the filial relationship was no joke or metaphor: When Lowell adopted a father figure, it was with a vengeance. Tate endured truly outrageous behavior during Lowell's breakdown in the spring of 1949: one of Lowell's jokes was "to provide Caroline Tate with a list of Allen's lovers, and then to implore Tate to 'repent'"; another was to hold Tate at arm's length out of his second-floor apartment window and force him to listen to a "bear's-voice recitation" of "Ode to the Confederate Dead." (As Hamilton rightly comments, the latter story is perhaps too good to be true; but that is the sort of thing that went on.) Writing to Merrill Moore a few weeks later, Tate summed up the relationship: "In the very nature of things, we cannot function as his parents. Cal, in his emotional dependence, has caused us more anxiety in the past twelve years than our own child has caused us in all her twenty-four. This has been particularly trying because he feels toward us something of the ambivalence of a child towards his real parents: love and hate, docility and disloyalty, etc. In view of this we had not sought his company since 1943; he had sought us" (160). Tate's letters are remarkably shrewd and perceptive, psychologically and otherwise; his diagnoses and prognoses usually turn out to be correct. He was not sympathetic to the "confessional" aspect of *Life Studies,* on moral as well as aesthetic grounds; he predicted, to Elizabeth Hardwick's great indignation, that those poems were symptomatic of an approaching breakdown; but when he was proved right, he was generous enough to write to Lowell, in the hospital by then, that the volume was "magnificent" (273).

Nor is it by any means a foregone conclusion that Tate was wholly wrong about *Life Studies.* His moral objection was that the poems "are composed of unassimilated details, terribly intimate, and coldly noted" (237); this tendency reached its height finally in *The Dolphin,* where Lowell not only quoted Elizabeth Hardwick's most intimate letters but also changed them to heighten the effect. The first version of *The Dolphin* provoked even Stanley Kunitz to say "some passages I can scarcely bear to read: they are too ugly, for being too cruel, too intimately cruel" (422). And Elizabeth Bishop, in a brilliant letter, complains that changing the letters is "infinite mischief": "One can use one's life as material . . . but these letters—aren't you violating a trust? IF you were given permission—IF you hadn't changed them . . . etc. *But art just isn't worth that much. . . .* It is not being gentle to use personal, tragic, anguished letters that way—it's cruel" (423). Adrienne Rich said, "The inclusion of the letter poems stands as one of the most vindictive and mean-spirited acts in the history of poetry" (433). W. H. Auden said that he would never speak to Lowell again; and even Elizabeth Hardwick lost patience (temporarily), telling Lowell, "I never want to hear from you again" (434). With his usual perceptiveness, Tate was simply recognizing these tendencies at their beginning. It is preposterous of Hamilton to suggest that the only reason Tate liked "Skunk Hour" was "perhaps because it is in neat sestets and has an almost regular rhyme scheme" (237)—as if Tate, champion of the most subtle and radical moderns, conceived of form in some simple-minded external sense! Tate's basic aesthetic objection was to a fundamental confusion between life and art; this objection is certainly tenable with regard to *Life Studies,* and is prophetic of what is carried to extremes in the later poetry. As to the personal relationship, Tate went so far as to offer himself as godfather when Lowell and Caroline had a son in 1971, though Lowell had used (and changed) in *Notebook* a quotation from Tate's letter about the death of his own infant son.

These considerations bring up the larger question of the relation between Lowell's madness and his poetic gift, as well as his behavior as private person and public figure. Hamilton, to his credit, tries not to overemphasize the pathological aspect; but there is no way to avoid making the biography sound like a case history for considerable stretches. Lowell was certainly insane for a considerable part of the time from 1949 on, requiring regular hospitalization about once a year when the mania was at its height, and for much of the intervening time suffering depression or the gradual onset of "menacing hilarity" (216). He was also drugged with chlorpromazine or, from 1967 on, lithium carbonate, in the effort to control his psychosis. The touching thing about Lowell is that he never invokes the plea of temporary insanity: He accepts full responsiblity for his actions, never suggesting that they are not his fault. At the same time he confesses that he cannot control his behavior, and he feels extreme guilt for what he has done.

Victims of manic-depressive psychosis typically find it very hard to believe that other people exist independently and are as real as they are, and they have great difficulty in establishing relations with others. For this reason, neither psychoanalysis nor other forms of psycho-therapy offers much hope to the manic-depressive: They all depend on the formation of a powerful bond between therapist and patient. Lowell's pronounced streak of cruelty to creatures ranging from turtles to fathers to women was certainly related to this psychotic aspect of his personality. Only his mother was allowed to call him Bobby; he preferred his schoolboy nickname, "Cal," derived from Caliban and Caligula, both savage, cruel, and deformed; and in later life he chose to derive it exclusively from Caligula, who was also mad. (He signed himself "Uncle Lig" during his 1949 breakdown.) As we have seen, he did not hesitate to use others ruthlessly for his own purposes, most outrageously by quoting—or misquoting—their private letters to him in his poems. This pathological egocentrism was obviously related to the confusion of life and art, or rather the blurring of the distinction between them, that is a central theme of Lowell's later poetry. Yet the inhuman and monstrous quality of his madness, which enabled him to pity and sympathize with other monsters (criminals, madmen, tyrants, heroes) throughout history from Cain to Hitler, as well as in the realms of myth, made him, in the sane intervals, more humane; for, realizing fully what he was, he tried to be kind, affectionate, responsible, and "normal." After each manic episode (always including falling in love with and wanting to marry some other girl), those with most cause to resent his behavior would welcome him back with undiminished love and admiration. As Elizabeth Hardwick said, "He 'came to' sad, worried, always ashamed and fearful; and yet there he was, this unique soul for whom one felt great pity. His fate was like a strange, almost mythical two-engined machine, one running to doom and the other to salvation." And he would return to hard labor: "The discipline, the dedication, the endless adding to his store, by reading and studying — all this had, in my view, much that was heroic about it" (258). Even after the Vija Vetra episode, most absurd and painful of them all, Elizabeth Hardwick is finally most concerned to reassure the repentant Lowell that she still admires him and still feels gratitude as well as love: "Cal my heart bleeds for you, but remember what greatness you have made of your life, what joy you have given to all of us. . . . I hate for you to get sick. I would kill myself if it would cure you. There must be something more we can lean on — medical, psychiatric, personal, the dearest love goes out to you" (332–33).

This is not the place to discuss the large question of the relationship between poetry and madness from Plato on, except to say that Lowell raises the question once more in an urgent and unignorable form and at the same time complicates it immensely. The trouble is that there is in Lowell not a clear-cut division between madness and sanity, so that one can say here he is responsible because sane and there he is not responsible because mad; instead, there are infinite degrees and shadings between the two. The madness is an integral part of his personality and intertwined inextricably with his poetic gift. It cannot be regarded as external, either as affliction or as mystical revelation; nor is it a form of perception, "reason in madness," transcending prudential wisdom. Blair Clark said that "an absolutely infallible indication of an impending manic episode was an interest in Hitler" (204); identification with Hitler, Napoleon, and other tyrants and tyrannicides throughout history was a kind of safety valve. But it remained a part of Lowell's own personality: "I think it was only when he was in hospital that he ever stood up to his full height. He sort of grew. And there was also a sort of ferocity. If one disagreed with him, he would begin to blaze. He could be very frightening" (Jonathan Raban, 449).

Lowell may well have destroyed forever the notion of Poet as Sage. Sometimes he appears to play the role of Arnold's suffering Victorian Sage — "And then we suffer! and amongst us one, / Who most has suffered, takes dejectedly / His seat upon the intellectual throne" — but he is no mere passive sufferer. He is not only sick but part criminal — not only thief and con man, like Mann's artists, but evil, violent, potentially tyrant and destroyer, torturer and murderer. If this makes possible an expansion of imaginative sympathy beyond the bounds of classical humanism to include the monstrous within as well as outside—compare, for example, the somewhat complacent note of the classical "nihil humanum mihi alienum est" with the chilling tone of "To Mother": "it has taken me the time since you died / to discover you are as human as I am . . . if I am"[7]—it puts paid rather decisively to the notion of the poet as Arnoldian interpreter of life. (It is only fair to note that the role of Sage had probably become impossible anyway. Perhaps the last poets to play it successfully were Frost, who overacted dreadfully, and Eliot and Auden, who refused it in their early careers but were driven to somewhat gingerly final acceptance. It is hard to imagine future candidates for the role: John Ashbery and James Merrill, for example, seem hopelessly miscast.)

Yet Lowell is unquestionably an example of the Poet as Hero. He is so honest that he will not claim that he is honest or tells the whole truth, nor will he ask the reader's compassion or complicity. The poet with whom he seems to identify most closely toward the end of his career is Ezra Pound—another mad, flawed, uneven, guilty figure who was accused of betraying his country and who took all history for his province. Lowell was well aware of Pound's faults: He thought the *Cantos* the "most self-indulgent long poem in English" and called Pound, whom he visited frequently at St. Elizabeth's, "absolutely the most naïve and simple man I ever met, sure that the world would be all right if people only read the right books. Pathetic and touching."[8] One of the best poems in *History* describes visiting him in the ward of the "criminal mad" and then seeing him after Eliot's death, when Pound spoke with generous affection of Eliot and with realism of his own errors:

> "Who's left alive to understand my jokes?
> My old Brother in the arts . . . besides, he was a smash of a poet."
> You showed me your blotched, bent hands, saying, "worms.
> When I talked that nonsense about Jews on the Rome
> wireless, Olga knew it was shit, and still loved me."
> and I, "Who else has been in Purgatory?"
> You, "I began with a swelled head and end with swelled feet."[9]

The last sonnet in *The Dolphin* expresses contrition and accepts responsibility in lines sounding unmistakably like the Pound of the *Pisan Cantos:* "I have sat and listened to too many / words of the collaborating muse."

Lowell's long sonnet-obsession—six years in which he wrote nothing else, in the successive *Notebooks* finally pruned, segregated, and collected in *History, For Lizzie and Harriet,* and *The Dolphin*—was, among other things a sustained working through of the possibilities in the relation of life and art, the conversion of life into art and vice versa, the enterprise being to bring the two into the closest conjunction and even to obliterate the distinction between them. Although some fine things came out of it, it was a dead end; no solution was found, either philosophically or technically. One of the best sonnets describes the impossible attempt: "I want words meat-hooked from the living steer, / but a cold flame of tinfoil licks the metal log"; and another describes its failure, in the image of the poet as bee building his works as beehive, "adding circle to circle, cell to cell, / the wax and honey of a mausoleum," and praying only that "its perishable work live long / enough for the sweet-tooth bear to desecrate— / this open book . . . my open coffin."[10] It is a paradox that the poet as activist, pursuing the present and trying to abolish time and the notion of art as separate from life, ends up imprisoned in his own book, in precisely the position of the aesthete Mallarmé: "Toute, au monde, existe pour aboutir à un livre." The quest for truth, too, ends in failure:

> None of us can or wants to tell the truth,
> pay fees for the over-limit we caught, while floating
> the lonely river to senility
> to the open ending . . .
>
> (242)

So much for the ideal of "openness."

Yet Lowell, honestly confronting his failures, arrives in his last book, *Day by Day*, at a kind of provisional resolution, decisively repudiating the sonnet form and other extremes, but not refusing responsibility. In the largest sense, his real achievement was genuinely, in the name of openness, to expand the scope of poetry. Against the historical tendency of poetry to center in the aesthetic mode of the nineties, with lyric intensity as its goal, Lowell strove to recover for it some of the territory occupied by the prose genres of autobiography, novel, and history. He tried consciously to incorporate in his poems some of the qualities of Flaubert's and Chekhov's prose and thus to reinvigorate them, increasing their range, variety, and subtlety. As "imitator" he made poets in many languages available to the American reader, and as playwright he made Greek, French, and especially American classics viable on the contemporary stage. His career will eventually be seen, I believe, as in its effect liberating and invigorating.

Whatever its minor flaws and major limitations, Hamilton's is certainly the liveliest and most readable, and probably the most satisfactory, biography of any contemporary poet. Lowell is thus lucky posthumously, as he was so often—though it seems strange to say it of one so obviously doomed—in life. Lowell knew this, and said himself that his life had been happier than his poetry, that he had "felt mostly the joys of living; in remembering, in recording, thanks to the gift of the Muse, it is the pain."

What else remains to be done? As we have noted, Hamilton has little space for specific discussion of the poetry. There has been no lack of good criticism of Lowell's poetry—the examples that come immediately to mind are Alan Williamson's *Pity the Monsters*, Vereen Bell's *Nihilist as Hero*, and the essays of Helen Vendler[11]—but the full job of interpretation of his whole career and its significance has hardly yet been attempted. Perhaps it is still too early for this. For one thing, more information is needed about Lowell's manuscripts—he was a compulsive and incessant reviser—and related matters. Presumably his literary executor, Frank Bidart, will eventually publish some of this material; one gathers that there is so much that the thought of a variorum makes the mind reel. For another, more information may become available about some of the biographical enigmas that remain; for example, about Merrill Moore's relationship to Lowell's mother and about his role in these events and his interpretation of them. Lowell speculates about this in "Unwanted":

Dead he is still a mystery,
once a crutch to writers in crisis.
I am two-tongued, I will not admit
his Tennessee rattling saved my life.
Did he become mother's lover
and prey
by rescuing her from me?[12]

A third and final example: Lowell's curious "bear" joke that he continued all his life and that expanded in his manic periods cries out for interpretation. It seems to have been a strange blend of regression to childhood (is Milne's Pooh in the background?) and disguised aggression, for Lowell would seize people in a bear hug that was also a policeman's restraint, his persona being a bear who was also a Boston policeman called "Arms-of-the-Law." He invented extended narratives, with bear-personae (called "berts") for his friends; many of these seemed funny only to Lowell, though he was delighted to find common ground with Roethke (also a manic-depressive, but of a different sort), who sometimes thought of himself as a dancing bear.

"The victim of a malodorous disease which renders him abhorrent to society and periodically degrades him and makes him helpless is also the master of a superhuman art which everybody has to respect and which the normal man finds he needs. . . . How then is the gulf to be got over between the ineffective plight of the bowman and the proper use of his bow, between his ignominy and his destined glory? Only by the intervention of one who is guileless enough and human enough to treat him, not as a monster, nor yet as a mere magical property which is wanted for accomplishing some end, but simply as another man, whose sufferings elicit his sympathy and whose courage and pride he admires." So Edmund Wilson, summing up the meaning of the Philoctetes myth in his *The Wound and the Bow*.[13] (Hamilton, it should be noted, wisely leaves untouched all such theoretical questions as the relation of artistic gifts to incurable wounds; the Philoctetes myth is my importation.) However much we may hesitate to generalize about the relation of art to sickness, mental or physical, we can hardly doubt that this myth, as here interpreted by Wilson, applies with remarkable aptness to Lowell. And if Lowell is Philoctetes, Hamilton must be Neoptolemus, who treats him as man rather than monster and brings him back into human society. It is a very important role, and Hamilton performs it with real distinction.

Daniel Hoffman and the American Epic

What is a major poet? The two criteria most often invoked are range and development: a major poet is one whose work encompasses a variety of different kinds, covers broad bands of the emotional and formal spectra, and has also a shape in time, forming a pattern into which the individual poems can be seen to fit.

Daniel Hoffman's *The Center of Attention* (1975) — his sixth collection of verse, published more than twenty years after Auden introduced his first in the Yale Series of Younger Poets — seems to me to establish his claim to the title of major poet. If I attach the label to him somewhat aggressively, it is because I have long felt that he has not received the kind of recognition he deserves, and I rejoice to find in the present volume both confirming evidence for my opinion and the ideal occasion for proclaiming it. Hoffman has not been neglected — his poetry has been widely published and he has received many honors, including the consultantship in poetry at the Library of Congress — but his reception has always seemed, though respectful, somewhat muted. I would like to end this decorous hush by sounding a loud (if necessarily brief) fanfare in honor of *The Center of Attention*.

This volume is not only Hoffman's best (though of course it does not in any sense supersede the earlier ones, each of which is still to be cherished for its own distinctive achievement) but also, through the happiest of coincidences, the one of widest popular appeal. As we are too well aware, the qualities that attract a larger public are not necessarily those that mark a genuine advance in poetic art. But on occasion they can be, and such occasions should be celebrated by dancing in the streets.

Hoffman is an academic poet in the sense that he is a dedicated teacher and a member of academia. But, like such other academic poets as Nemerov, Wilbur, and Meredith, he is untouched by the academic vices of timidity, ineffectuality, unawareness of present reality. By their intense involvement with the true realities of the present, these poets have greatly helped to diminish such vices in the academy. At the same time they have kept alive in poetry the academic virtues of intelligence, a sense of the past, and a respect for civilization and its institutions. Two of Hoffman's most explicitly academic poems are also among his most topical. "The Princess Casamassima" present a teacher reading of a former student now turned dynamiter:

> But I can't remember now
> One word she wrote for me.
> —Good God,
> Was it something *I* said
> About Thoreau
> Shorted her fuse? Oh,
> Such unbalanced, mad
> Action is surely extra-curricular—
>
> If the discourse of our liberal arts
> Which entertains all rival truths as friends
> And rival visions reconciles
> Could but bring the pleasures of its wholeness
> To a mind
> Rent by frenzy—
> But how conceive what hatred
> Of the self, turned inside-out, reviles
>
> The whole great beckoning world, or what desire
> Sentenced the soul
> To that dark cellar where all life became
> So foul
> With the pitch of rage,
> Rage, rage, rage to set aflame
> Father's house—what can assuage
> That fire or that misfire?[1]

The analysis is deeply compassionate but uncompromising, beyond all fashionable jargon, and the images and rhythms have a tragic power. "The Sonnet," honoring Louise Bogan, is in its much lighter way equally effective:

> The Sonnet, she told the crowd of bearded
>   youths, their hands exploring
>   rumpled girls,
>   is a sacred

vessel: it takes a civilization
>to conceive its shape or know
>>its uses. The kids
>>stared. . . .

All the poems in the first section of this book are concerned with
the realities of present-day society. "Power" employs the same kind of
psychological imagery as "The Princess Casamassima," and as that
poem is the definitive treatment of student revolutionaries, so this one
is the best ever written about political assassins:

. . . When he thinks of his folks he smiles oddly.
"It was broken but was it a home?"

At night, the wet dream. Arising,
He is afraid of women. . . .

One day he will fondle a snub-nosed
Pistol deep in his pants. . . .

His trigger will make him bigger.
He will become his victim.

When he steps from his rented room
History is in his hand.

Power, violence, history, the fusing images of pistol and penis, continue
to resonate in the mind.

Even more haunting, however, is the natural symbolism of the title
poem. The Center of Attention is a man who has climbed a bridge pylon
and is threatening to jump. The crowd gives him contradictory advice:
"This is a tough decision. The man beside me / Reaches into his lunch-
box and lets him have it, / *Jump!* before he bites his sandwich. . . . "

Up there he hasn't made his mind up either.
He has climbed and climbed on spikes imbedded in the pylon

To get where he has arrived at.
Is he sure now that this is where he was going?
He looks down one way into the river.
He looks down the other way into the people.

He seems to be looking for something
Or for somebody in particular.
Is there anyone here who is that person
Or can give him what it is that he needs?

(8)

He lights a cigarette, "looks down on the people gathered, and sprinkles / Some of his ashes upon them." A soon as he starts down, the crowd disperses:

> It was his aloneness that clutched them together.
> They were spellbound by his despair
>
> And now each rung brings him nearer,
> Nearer to their condition
> Which is not sufficiently interesting
> To detain them from business or idleness either,
>
> Or is too close to a despair
> They do not dare
> Exhibit before a crowd
> Or admit to themselves they share.

At the end the man "looks round as though searching for what he came down for. / Traffic flows over the bridge." Among the many levels of meaning in this poem is one in which the man has Made It to the Top and his ritual ash-sprinkling is a blank substitute for religious ceremonies, since this crowd is united only by an image of desolation and despair. The Quest figure or archetype, perhaps the central one throughout Hoffman's work, here reaches a dead end. ("The City of Satisfactions," the title poem of an earlier volume, is one of his most powerful renderings: an obsessional nightmare of the Great American Dream, the trip westward in search of treasure, in endlessly receding images evoked by the perpetual recession of land, treasure, and satisfactions. Other Quest poems in the present volume are "The Wanderer," "Runner," "The Way," "West," "Path," and "Shell"—the last a particularly beautiful poem in subtly changing rhythms about a psychic journey and a metamorphosis.)

The poems in the first section are ambitious, dealing with the great issues, but in most cases indirectly and with reticence. "After God," however, directly treats the religious significance of space exploration (or rather, of the experience of watching it on television). Taking his basic image from Cotton Mather, Hoffman ranges from Caedmon to Marlowe for poignant allusions as he prays to this "After-God" of Space to "send us a sign."

Hoffman is, however, basically a poet of hard-won affirmations, not of the disintegrations and decreations so fashionable now. Addressing British readers, he has said:

A poet's obligation should be to restore to the center of life the numinous objects, relationships, and feelings menaced by the mechanism of mass society. . . . If the culture seems in the throes of a nervous breakdown, some poets will exacerbate the symptoms of its affliction. Others will be driven back upon their own resources. In the celebration of love, in the revelation of the instinctual rhythms of feeling, in the discovery of the movements the mind makes in reassembling the dry bones of the broken world into a living unity, such poets may help us to define our humanity.[2]

Although he does not claim to have written such poetry, but only to want to, the description applies very well to most of his work. "Striking the stones to make them sing" was his image for the poet's task in an earlier volume. In this collection the second group contains poems dealing with nature and the truths of the self as manifested in it. Some of them render violence and ruthlessness as powerfully as Ted Hughes ("Dogfish," "Shrew," "Boar"— and "Raven," which seems closely akin to Hughes's Crow). But Hoffman's vision is ultimately quite different from Hughes's: where Hughes sees savagery at the heart of things, Hoffman in "Comanches" assumes the Redskin persona and says the poet is "half a savage"— but only half. "Rats" and "Egg" indict not violence but calculating selfishness and unimaginativeness. The contrast is clearest if one compares with Hughes's hawk Hoffman's wonderful poem "Eagles," which celebrates fidelity and nobility:

When things are creatures and the creatures speak
We can lose, for a moment, the desolation
Of our being

Imperfect images of an indifferent god.
If we listen to our fellows then,
If we heed them,

The brotherhood that links the stars in one
Communion with the feathery dust of earth
And with the dead

Is ours. I have seen bald eagles flying,
Heard their cries. Defiant emblems of
An immature

Republic, when they spread their noble wings
They possess the earth that drifts beneath them.
I've learned how

Those savage hunters when they mate are wed
For life. In woods a barbarous man shot one
In the wing.

He fluttered to an island in the river.
After nearly half a year, someone,
Exploring, found

Him crippled in a circle of the bones
Of hen and hare his partner brought to him.
Close above,

She shrieked and plunged to defend her helpless mate.
Eagles, when they mate, mate in the air.
He'll never fly.

His festered wing's cut off, he's in the zoo.
They've set out meat to tranquillize his queen
And catch her too.

Who'll see them caged yet regal still, but thinks
Of eagles swooping, paired in the crystal air
On hurtling wings?[3]

In these times, a poem like this is very daring. Hoffman even writes a fine poem about married love, obviously a tribute to his wife, ending, "Your love is the weather of my being. / What is an island without the sea?" and others about his troubled concern for his children ("A Dread," "A Woe"). I do not mean to make Hoffman sound offensively wholesome; as we all know, what matters is not whether ideals are affirmed or denied but how they work in the poetry. But it does appear that if a poet is, like Hoffman, fully and intensely aware of all the pressures of the time, neither isolated nor insulated, a greater range of feeling gets into the poetry if responses are not limited to the negative. Hoffman has a Virgilian or Wordsworthian sense of the natural pieties, affections, and joys; but his keen sense of form preserves him from Wordsworthian slackness. Furthermore, Hoffman always remains aware of the ultimate mysteries as well as the ultimate simplicities. There is a kind of Dark Night apparent in some of these poems, but the formal restraint and the mythical pattern keep them from seeming overly personal. For example, "Sickness" is developed from a single metaphor, and "Thought I Was Dying" is kept close to folk song.

The poems mentioned in the preceding paragraph are all in the third section, which seems to group together poems dealing with archetypal things or experience (e.g., "Path," "Door," "Window," "My Hand," the Quest poems previously cited, and those dealing with the Dark Night). Writing poetry is clearly a joyful experience for Hoffman, and there are some marvelous light verse pieces about it in the first section ("The Outwit Song," "Delusions," "O Personages"). But the last poem in the book, seeming to create its own simple but very effective incremental form, best sums up his poetic, which is both archetypal and personal:

"The Poem"

Arriving at last,

It has stumbled across the harsh
Stones, the black marshes.

True to itself, by what craft
And strength it has, it has come
As a sole survivor returns

From the steep pass.
Carved on memory's staff
The legend is nearly decipherable.
It has lived up to its vows

If it endures
The journey through the dark places
To bear witness,
Casting its message
In a sort of singing.

(77)

Brotherly Love *(1981)*

"Come Muse migrate from Greece and Ionia," sang Whitman; and many an American poet since has repeated his hopeful invitation to the epic muse. So far, she has played hard to get. We have had great novels that have interpreted distinctively American experience and history, but not long poems. *Hiawatha* and *John Brown's Body,* though appealing, cannot be taken seriously by adults; *Song of Myself* has no action; *The Waste Land* and *The Cantos* are international. *The Bridge,* though American, is more esoteric than Eliot or Pound; *Paterson,* though not esoteric, is often flat or incoherent. In short, no long poem has yet established itself as at once American, a sustained poetic success, and attractive to a wide audience.

Brotherly Love seems to qualify on all three grounds. Hoffman invokes Clio, Muse of History, rather than Calliope; I suppose his reason, aside from modesty, is that he wants to emphasize that his poem is more seriously and scrupulously historical than any preceding epic. His Clio presides over Indian history as well as white, and she inspires the poet to interpret both histories through faithful presentation of the documents as well as imaginative reconstruction. His hero, William Penn, is epic in that he is an exceptional and admirable man whose deeds are important in his country's history. Because 1981 was the three-hundredth anniversary of the legendary occasion celebrated in Benjamin West's famous painting *William Penn's Treaty with the Indians 1681* and later in Edward Hicks's *A Peaceable Kingdom,* this was a singularly appropriate time for such a poem to appear. Its subject has both wide appeal and obvious relevance to contemporary problems: It poses the central question of American national identity in terms that are at once faithful to history and perennially recurrent.

Like most modern long poems, Hoffman's is broken up into short segments composed in a variety of different meters or in prose. (This is not "imitative form," or making form chaotic to represent chaos, but a device to gain intensity and to reflect multiple perspectives.) Specifically, its sixty-one numbered sections are divided into three larger groupings (we may follow epic tradition and call them "books") entitled "Treating with Indians," "An Opening of Joy," and "The Structure of Reality." The first is about the 1681 treaty and its historical context, especially the Indian, the second about Penn's inner life and the religion that came to dominate it, and the third about the subsequent history of the persons and places involved. (Since book two chronologically precedes book one, Hoffman is following epic tradition in beginning *in medias res.*) Notes at the end of the poem give the historical sources for each section; these are not pedantry or padding, but part of the poem's authentic historicity.

By selecting and shaping on the page passages from letters and other primary documents, Hoffman makes their significance appear, without comment, as the sculptor reveals the form that was already there in the wood or stone. At least half the poem consists of quotations from contemporary documents. Yet the selections are so artfully made, shaped, and arranged that they become, in context, genuine poetry.

To perceive the poetry in historical documents and reveal it without losing the historical immediacy that only such documents can give is a technique not invented but carried to new heights by Hoffman. His use of it is much more extensive, complex, and subtle than that of such pioneers as Pound. The best example is the Indians' account of their own history followed by Penn's description of them and then by a later traveler's encounter with their last doomed remnants (nos. 6–7, 12–20, 26, and 57). A more complex type is no. 51, where Voltaire's praise of Penn is rearranged into tercets, which alternate with couplets expressing the Indians' feelings.

The techniques of allusion, in which an older poem is evoked as a parallel and a contrast to a new one, and of pastiche, in which a new poem is written in a consistently "period" style, are similar in effect to the one just described. It is not too much to say that Hoffman's use of these techniques is the most brilliant since Eliot's.

To see how these techniques work and what extraordinary and varied effects are produced by the juxtaposition of contrasting styles, tones, and attitudes, let us look briefly at the second book, which is the shortest and most intense of the three. The first poem (or section) describes the statue of Penn on modern Philadelphia's City Hall. This is the same image that dominates the first poem of the whole volume—"over Wanamaker's lights / Billy Penn extends indulgent arms"—and the last—"his head in the clouds, his mood / benign, though slum-blocks sprawl." It is an obvious but effective device for bringing together the present city and its founder, as the poet meditates on what Penn was like and how he could "Dream into being this wrangling 'City / Of Brotherly Love.'"

This modern poem is followed by a marvelous pastiche in seventeenth-century couplets celebrating Admiral Penn's victory and loyally hoping that his rebellious son will soon come to his senses. Next comes a poem modern in form but seventeenth-century in spirit, imagining what it must have been like for Penn but not presuming to speak for him in first person, as a bad historical novelist or poet would do: "It is not easy, being son / To the hero of the English nation. / One thing is sure: You'll never go to sea." Not only the conflict with his father but the underlying conflict in his own mind between his attraction to the "Glory / Of the World" and his yearning for purity in withdrawal from the world are vividly evoked: "you are torn / Between your father and the Son."

All these poems lead up to "Instructions to a Painter" for the portrait of the young Penn in armor. This poem employs allusion with remarkable effectiveness. In the first place, an earlier section (no. 21) has reminded the reader of the association of the genre of "Instructions" with the celebration of the admiral's victory. In the second and more important place, this poem dares to evoke the greatest political poem in English, Marvell's "Horatian Ode" on Cromwell, employing the same stanza, style, and tone. Its function, however, is not to rival its great predecessor but to use to the full Marvell's implications about the ambiguities of power, its ambivalence about action and history as against withdrawal and contemplation. Praising Penn's early martial exploits that made him seem likely to follow in his father's footsteps, Hoffman exploits all the overtones of his great original; for the point is that Penn, unlike Cromwell, did hang up his armor for good and renounce the use of force.

The next poem describes in a contrastingly prosaic style Penn's return to the Quakers after the portrait in armor. There follow two beautiful lyrics expressing the essence of Quakerism, the first on Silence (with which every Quaker service begins) and the second, based on the sermon by Thomas Loe which convinced Penn, on faith in God's immediate action on the believer. In sharp contrast, the next section is a realistic prose description of the persecution of the Quakers, followed by two lyrics, the first vividly describing Penn's suffering and the second his final convincement, "This vessel of my flesh / Is the chalice of my soul."

After a prosaic description of his actual joining of the Society of Friends and giving up his sword, the final and most impressive section describes in modern style Penn's misery in prison, then his vision of the Indians and Philadelphia, with his conviction of divine love and joy. He "feels the Lord open his soul with a love that embraces all" and sees what he must do:

> In the Lord's love for each person
> Is His revelation
> Perpetual and unending,
>
> And they shall come together in a city. . . .
>
> For the Lord is the home of the soul
> And the world which is far from God
> Is history, the body's prison,
>
> But the House of Stuart shall deed to the House of Penn
> A Province
> Of the New World
>
> Where history has not yet begun,
>
> A city of brotherly love.

This sketchy description has been intended only to show how artfully the poem is patterned and how much each individual section gains from the whole context. What is true of each book is true also of the structure of the whole poem. Dealing with Penn alone, book two is the most limited and intense. Book one deals with the other principal subject, the Indians, and with Penn as perceived by them; it concludes with the wonderful idyllic picture of Penn and the Indians leaping on the lawn at Pennsbury: "They leap far from a standing start / But he, Miquon, their good friend and host, / He leaps farther, to their cheers." After the close-up of Penn in book two (which, as noted, chronologically precedes book one), book three has the sad task of telling what went wrong after Penn left.

The poems (nos. 1, 28, 61) that meditate on Penn's statue in modern Philadelphia recall Robert Lowell's great poem "For the Union Dead." But Lowell's poem ends in despair at the contrast between the hero's statue and the modern city—predatory, servile, doomed. Hoffman, though equally aware of urban horrors, nevertheless feels that "there's a spirit in this place" to be grasped only in time, and "possibilities of grace":

> Like fragrance from our rich compost cling
> to leaves where our each deed
> and misdeed fall. The Seed
> stirs, even now is quickening.

Hoffman's involvement with American history is like Lowell's, but does not issue in a final nihilism; and his elegant and varied sense of form is at the opposite pole from the arbitrary "sonnet" compulsion in which Lowell was so long imprisoned. As Lowell's *History* grew longer, his life got away from him. Hoffman's concluding poem contains two lines that are so characteristically Lowellian that they are surely meant as an affectionate tribute: "Our history grows longer, longer. / It's life that's getting away from us."

A closer parallel and perhaps stronger influence is the work of Robert Penn Warren, to whom the book is dedicated. It seems likely that Hoffman's dialogues between ghosts and spirits in book three derive from Warren's dialogues of the dead, and of the dead and living, in *Brother to Dragons*. Warren is similarly immersed in American history and its questions of guilt and identity, has a realistic view of the wilderness and the people, white and Indian, who inhabited it, but is, like Hoffman, convinced of the possibility of heroism and even of grace.

The poem is an astonishing feat of historical and literary imagination, and at the same time a work that should appeal to a very wide audience. Among other attractive features, the three paintings—the *Treaty,* the Portrait in Armor, and *A Peaceable Kingdom*—each preside over one of the three books; all are reproduced in the volume and all are commented on in poems that are entertaining as well as good. *Brotherly Love* is not *Paradise Lost,* but it is perhaps the nearest equivalent now possible; and its theme is precisely paradise lost, the peaceable kingdom destroyed, though without a Satan. (Hoffman suggests, reasonably, that both weak and wicked men—"Before there was a Philadelphia / There was a Philadelphia lawyer"—and economic and political forces were responsible.) It lacks the visionary heights of *The Bridge,* but its brotherly love offers a more feasible common ground. (Suspicious of theology and talk, relying instead on inner light, leadings, openings—on these and good works, for the Great Schism, described in no. 60, was over the question of how far the good man should involve himself in the world, in history—Quakerism should be acceptable to most audiences, at least as a basis for poetry.)

Brotherly Love is not merely a "long poem containing history" defined as "tales of the tribe," as is *The Cantos;* instead, it realizes fully the perspectives of both past and present and relates them coherently. It preserves and gives meaning to the American past; its hero embodies a worthy ideal; and it raises the great issues of national identity and policy. If it is not an American epic, I do not know how one could be written now. I have not even begun, in this brief account, to describe it properly; with each rereading it grows, expands, and develops richer meanings and further resonances in the mind.

James Dickey: Southern Visionary as Celestial Navigator

Some years ago James Dickey responded to an interviewer's question about the sense in which he was a Southern writer with the ringing declaration that "the best thing that ever happened to me was to have been born a Southerner. First as a man and then as a writer." He would not want to feel that he was limited in any way by being a Southerner or was expected to "indulge in the kind of regional chauvinism that has sometimes been indulged in by Southern writers," he said, but the tragic history of the South gave him a set of values, "some of which are deplorable, obviously, but also some of which are the best things that I have ever had as a human being." Southerners, he suggested, let their ancestors help: "I have only run-of-the-mill ancestors but they knew that one was supposed to do certain things. Even the sense of evil, which is very strong with me, would not exist if I had no sense of what evil was."[1]

Dickey is convinced, then, that being Southern is central to the way he thinks and feels, but he does not want to be thought of as *merely* regional; he suggests that the most valuable Southern quality is a special awareness of the personal past in the sense of inheriting traditions and codes of values from one's ancestors, and a special awareness of the regional past in its full tragic meaning, including the sense of evil. But rather than continue to depend on Dickey's own statements, now that I have used him to run interference for me, let me try to define more specifically just what kind of Southern writer he is and how he is related to other Southern writers.

The obvious starting point is his relation to the Fugitive-Agrarian

A part of this chapter was given as a lecture at the University of South Carolina on the occasion of Dickey's sixtieth birthday in February 1983, and was published in the *Virginia Quarterly Review* (Winter 1986–87).

groups. Except for Donald Davidson, all of the Fugitives and most of the Agrarians had left Vanderbilt long before Dickey arrived; thus there was no possibility of personal influence. But Ransom, Tate, and Warren had become major figures in the literary world, and Brooks, Jarrell, and others were establishing high reputations. Vanderbilt students and faculty—most of them—were proud of the connection, and the campus was alive with legends of the days when giants had walked that very earth. In this context, creative writing seemed exciting and important to a good many students, and so did being a Southerner. It seems plain enough that Dickey's commitment to poetry and his awareness of his identity as a Southerner owed much both to his reading of the Fugitive-Agrarian writers and to the Vanderbilt tradition of respect for serious writing. R. V. Cassill is amusing but quite wrong when he portrays Dickey as a rebellious Young Turk who refused to conform to the Southern ruling circles by speaking "smartly about Miss Eudora and Mr. Ransom" and being "reverent about Traveler" while snickering down Whitman and the Midwesterners.[2] In the first place, the Southern literary estblishment, insofar as there ever was one, was not reverential about Traveler; Tate abandoned his biography of Lee because he had ceased to believe in him, and the *Fugitive* announced early that it fled nothing so much as the genteel pieties of the Old South. In the second place, Dickey was recognized early by the Southerners and usually given whatever awards they had to offer. Although he never had the rare good luck that the Fugitives did of close association with a group of like-minded peers, the fact that the tradition of serious writing was still alive at Vanderbilt kept him from the near-total isolation of a writer such as Faulkner. Tate has gone on record with the opinion that Dickey is the best poet the South has produced since the heyday of the Fugitives, and Warren has said in the *South Carolina Review* that he is "among Jim's greatest admirers"[3] and in the *New York Times Book Review* that *The Zodiac* is a major achievement, worthy of comparison to Hart Crane's *The Bridge*.

In recent years some nostalgic epigones of the Fugitive-Agrarians at Vanderbilt have written requiems for the Southern Literary Renascence, maintaining that it has suffered death by melancholy. Their thesis is that Southern literature has been dying since World War II, when Modernism triumphed over the South; and any hope is illusory. I have never quite believed in the Southern Renascence, suspecting that it was created artifically, like Frankenstein's monster, in the laboratories of academic critics; and reports of the loss of such artificial life need not disturb us. At any rate, Dickey, thank God, like Madison Jones and others of his contemporaries at Vanderbilt, and like such older Southern writers as Robert Penn Warren, Walker Percy, and Eudora Welty, does not know he is dead and refuses to lie down. As stubbornly as the astronomical phenomena that Galileo saw through his telescope in spite of the irrefutable arguments of his learned opponents that they could not possibly be there, the works of these writers continue to exist and to grow, unquestionably alive. Most of us, however we may feel about the modern world, would rather have the poems and novels than have a thesis about it demonstrated; and our own Poe has taught us to beware of premature burial. So we will be grateful that some of our writers flourish and we will refuse to abandon hope.

While Dickey seems to have no interest in Agrarianism as a political or economic program, he shares with the Agrarians a deep concern about man's relation to nature and the distortions produced in this relation by the increasing urbanism and commercialism of our society. Dickey's true subject, however, is neither rural nor urban, but *suburban*. Because Southern cities are smaller, their suburbs are not wholly distinct from nearby small towns, and both maintain more connection with the country than their Northern counterparts. Compare, in this respect, those Dickey represents with John Cheever's dormitory suburbs around New York, with swimming pools linked in one giant fantasy. But both writers describe the modern nuclear family—nuclear both in being small and without the connections families used to have and in being under the threat of nuclear war. In these respects there is little difference between North and South, though the South may be slightly less nuclear simply because it is less urban.

Dickey's remarkable achievement is that he has taken his subject seriously and redeemed the word *suburban* from its comic or pejorative overtones. Instead of describing bored wives at the country club, adulteries in commuterdom, hysteria and desperation breaking out from the pressures of enforced uniformity, or the absurdities of Little League baseball, he shows us a suburban world that is still in touch with a nature that remains wild, not tamed or prettified. Dickey's suburbs have no cute ceramic animals, no dear little Bambis or gnomes on the lawns, but the call of the real wild, and inner nature answering to outer. *Deliverance* is the most extended example, with its gradual revelation that the wilderness has always been present in the suburbs, whose security is an illusion. On the other hand, "The Firebombing" treats the homeowner's longing for security sympathetically because of his vivid awareness of its precariousness in view of what he did to his Japanese counterparts. "Dark Ones" transmutes into poetry the evening ritual of the arrival home of the commuters.

To say that Dickey is a visionary poet is a paralyzingly obvious assertion: Almost every poem he has written describes a vision of one kind or another, and in recent years he has dealt explicitly with the loss of physical vision in works such as the unfinished novel "Cahill Is Blind." Perhaps he will become the patron or mascot of ophthalmologists, as Wallace Stevens was adopted by ice-cream manufacturers after writing "The Emperor of Ice-Cream." Yet the truism is worth repeating, for it says something about his relation to Southern literature. Dickey belongs to the line of visionaries running from Blake through Rimbaud and Whitman to such modern exemplars as Hart Crane, George Barker, Dylan Thomas, and Theodore Roethke. It is noteworthy that there are no Southern names on this list, since as far as I know there are few Southern poets who could be called visionary. Tate and Warren, for example, are in their different ways primarily concerned with history, with attempting to relate the past to the present. Perhaps one reason good Southern poets have shied away from the visionary mode is that they remember how much older Southern poetry was emasculated by the necessity of avoiding politics and hence driven from reality into fake vision. The old Southern tradition of escapism and sentimentality—of "gutless swooning," to borrow a phrase from Faulkner—was certainly one thing the Fugitives were fleeing. I am afraid Henry Timrod often exemplified this tradition, and Tate surely intended a contrast with Timrod's "Ode Sung at the Decoration of the Graves of the Confederate Dead at Magnolia Cemetery" when he wrote his own ironic "Ode to the Confederate Dead." Timrod's "Ethnogenesis" is a kind of vision, it is true, but appallingly detached from any sense of reality: In it the new Confederacy, with its economy based on cotton and slavery, is seen as bringing wealth, moral improvement, and a better climate to the whole world.

Before Dickey, the only Southern poet who was a true visionary was Poe; and his visions, as every schoolchild knows, were very peculiar indeed. Although one might argue that Dickey's poetic rhythms are often incantatory, and intended to put the reader into a kind of trance state, they are far more subtle than Poe's blatantly hypnagogic music; and though both poets are most interested in states of consciousness beyond normal waking life, they are not interested in the same states. Much as I would like to, I do not see how I can make a case for any resemblance beyond the fact that they are both visionaries. Dickey has none of Poe's morbid preoccupation with death, his concern being rather with new and different modes of life; you cannot imagine him saying that the ideal poetic subject is the *death* of a beautiful woman. Poe strives obsessively to make the reader feel the horror of being a living soul in a dead body, of an irreparable crack or split in the edifice of the mind, of long-ago irremediable losses. Dickey, in contrast, produces in the reader a new awareness of nonhuman forms of life, from dogs on the feet to owls in the woods and panthers in the zoo; the poems seek new forms of union, wider possibilities of consciousness. Mind and body are not separated as they are in Poe, but totally fused. Finally, Dickey gets into his poems a solid feeling of everyday reality and normal experience before moving to transcend them. It is this feeling or rendering that distinguishes him not only from Poe but also from the kind of fantasy that is now so enormously popular in movies and cheap fiction. Dickey's visions have nothing in common with these self-indulgent daydreams unrelated to any kind of reality.

Dickey's most ambitious visionary poem is certainly *The Zodiac* (1976). It is, I may concede to begin with, impossibly ambitious and hence foredoomed to failure. Dickey has said (in unpublished interviews) that he knew it would be a failure but is glad he did it and has a special affection for it because it explores that part of creativity that depends on being drunk. Robert Penn Warren observed that no poem since Hart Crane's *The Bridge* has been "so stylistically ambitious and has aimed to stir such depths of emotion," and that *The Zodiac* "can be said to be about the over-ambitiousness of poetry—even as it celebrates its ambitiousness." But, mentioning some of its limitations and defects, he finds that "the audacity of imagery, assemblage of rhythms, the power of language redeems all."[4]

To write a long poem that will rival the epics of the ancient world is still, as it has been since the Renaissance, the ultimate challenge for modern poets. (The shores of literary history are littered with the massive and curious wreckage of their attempts, from Ronsard's *Françiade* through Cowley's *Davideis,* Davenant's *Gondibert,* Chamberlayne's *Pharonnida,* and Blackmore's *The Creation* to Pound's *Cantos* and Williams's *Paterson.* Only *Paradise Lost* is still afloat, with the comic epics in verse from *The Rape of the Lock* to *Don Juan,* and in prose from *Tom Jones* to *Ulysses.*) Because James Dickey is a poet who has always sought out challenges, scorned the safe and prudent way, and aimed unblushingly at the sublime, accepting the roles of Icarus and Prometheus with full awareness of their risks, it is not at all surprising that he should attempt a long poem. (Long, that is, for a modern poem: more than twice the length of *The Waste Land.*) Nor is it surprising that *The Zodiac* should deal with nothing less than the meaning of the visible universe. What is surprising is that *The Zodiac* should be neither Southern nor even American in subject, but based on a Dutch poem with a Dutch protagonist whose experiences are distinctively European.

According to the dust jacket of *The Zodiac*, Dickey "finds inspiration in the experiences of a real-life Dutch sailor, Hendrik Marsman, who during a lifetime at sea was bedazzled by the constellations and possessed by the mysteries of the zodiac. On the verge of madness, he wrote bits of poetry, and it is from these fragments of Marsman's verse that Dickey has fashioned" his poem. This statement is staggeringly inaccurate and misleading, even for a jacket blurb. Marsman (1899–1940) was a well-known poet in real life, not a mad sailor. The publication of his *Verzen* in 1923 was a major event in Dutch literary history and established the Vitalist movement. After this he wrote mainly critical and narrative prose, editing an influential magazine, *Vrije Bladen,* beginning in 1925. After traveling for some years, he returned home to fight totalitarianism. His last great poem, *Tempel en Kruis (Temple and Cross),* a kind of poetic autobiography, appeared in 1939. *The Zodiac* is a part of this work. It is not a collection of bits or fragments, but a carefully wrought long poem in twelve sections.

Dickey's own statement in his headnote that his poem is "based on" Marsman's poem but is "in no sense a translation" is accurate and generous, with its concluding "homage to Hendrik Marsman, lost at sea, 1940–"; but it does not convey a full sense of the relationship. While Dickey's poem is not a translation, it is an "imitation" in the sense popularized by Robert Lowell. Because Dickey reproduces Marsman's situation, protagonist, narrative, and principal images, each of his twelve sections corresponding in detail to its original, his poem is rather closer to its source than are many of Lowell's "imitations." Though naturally enough, Dickey, like Lowell, wants the reader to see his work primarily as a contemporary poem, its relation to its original constitutes a significant dimension of its meaning.

Where did Dickey discover Marsman's poem—which is, to say the least, not well known in America? Probably in the *Sewanee Review,* where it appeared in 1947.[5] A. J. Barnouw, the translator, reprinted it in an anthology, *Coming After,* the following year; but because Dickey was certainly reading the magazine in those years at Vanderbilt (his first published poem appeared in it), it seems likely that he encountered it there. Whether it lay fallow in his imagination for nearly thirty years, or was discovered—or rediscovered—by him at some later date is a question of some interest that Dickey does not seem to have answered in any of his subsequent interviews or essays.

The most interesting question, however, is why Dickey chose this poem—certainly unfamiliar to most of his readers—to imitate. My guess is that the Marsman persona was attractive because it provided him with an alternative to his own established role. Writing as

Marsman, Dickey has a different mask of the self and different memories. Instead of writing about the South or the wartime Pacific, he writes as a man of an earlier European generation about Amsterdam; instead of writing as a survivor, he is now one who died early in the same war. Even the name *Marsman* may have reinforced this appeal: an author with a message from outer space. But on a deeper level, Marsman's poem expresses interests and beliefs that Dickey shares. He has been fascinated by astronomy since he studied it at Vanderbilt and has kept up his interest; a few years ago he completed a correspondence course in celestial navigation and is now a certified marine navigator. His primary religious sense is of "how wild, inexplicable, marvelous, and endless creation is," and religion, he says, "to me involves myself and the universe, and it does not admit of any kind of intermediary, such as Jesus or the Bible."[6] He would like to be reincarnated as a migratory sea bird like a tern or a wandering albatross, he says, and "Reincarnations II" is a vivid imagining of just this possibility. The themes of the aging wanderer returning home and so finding his own identity, and of the poet's reexamination and reaffirmation of his poetic faith and vocation, must also have appealed to Dickey with peculiar force in this poem. "Imitating," then, frees Dickey from his public self and gives him a fresh start at the same time that it provides him with a way of expressing some of his most deeply felt convictions from a different perspective.

Marsman's poem, as translated by Barnouw, is relatively conventional in language and versification. The first section, for example, is in regular blank verse. It begins:

The man of whom I tell this narrative
Returned, some time ago, to his native land.
He has since lived, for nearly a full year,
Over the peaceful broker's offices. . . .
The square lies, like an empty crater bowl,
Amid the agonized obscurity
Of the dead city's hellish neon light.

(238)

Dickey shatters and transforms this:

      The man I'm telling you about brought himself back alive
A couple of years ago. He's here,
      Making no trouble
             over the broker's peaceful. . . .
The town square below, deserted as a Siberian crater, lies in the middle

> Of his white-writing darkness   stroboscoped   red-stopped by the
>   stammering mess
>   Of the City's unbombed neon, sent through river and many cities
>   By fourth-class mail from Hell.
>
> (9–10)

It is by this transformation of language that Dickey makes the poem his own. He makes it emphatically contemporary and personal, with a tone quite different from Marsman's and with far more dramatic power and variety. In the process of expanding and loosening the language, and through adding new material, Dickey makes his poem about twice the length of Marsman's.

The protagonist (who is never named) is neither Marsman nor Dickey, but a dramatic character, given distance and universality by his anonymous condition. As the passage quoted indicates, he is technically not the speaker of the poem, but when he does speak directly the language does not change. The situation and narrative remain exactly what they were in Marsman's poem: The scene is Amsterdam in 1938–39, and, insofar as the protagonist's self-doubt and near-despair have historical referents, they relate to the coming of World War II: "The gods are in pieces / All over Europe"; "What does his soul matter, saved like a Caesar-headed goldpiece, / When the world's dying?"[7]

The central fact about the protagonist is that he is a poet dedicated to the belief that poetry reveals ultimate truth and that it comes from sources above or beyond the rational intellect. Under the pressures of impending catastrophe, both personal and collective, this "drunken and perhaps dying Dutch poet" (to quote Dickey's headnote) re-examines his visionary faith. He feels that he has misused and wasted his life, and he sees his world moving swiftly to destruction. Returning to his home in Amsterdam, he "tries desperately to relate himself, by means of stars, to the universe." He seeks the answer in the stars partly because his father was an amateur astronomer, partly because he has spent much time at sea, and partly because of the ancient and widespread beliefs embodied in the symbolism of the zodiac.

A final word about the relation of Dickey's poem to Marsman's. Perhaps the most important change Dickey makes is to have the protagonist drunk throughout the poem. (Belief in intoxication as a cognitive mode, drunkenness as a way of knowing, has of course always been central to the Dionysiac tradition, in poetry as elsewhere; Dickey is merely making the case an extreme one.) The protagonist becomes more dramatic: His moods change abruptly and are exaggerated by the drink; his rhetoric is unshackled and his inhibitions and pretenses are gone; we feel that he speaks truth, or tries to. Dickey provides him with a richly symbolic drink, *aquavit:* In Marsman he drinks only on one occasion, and plain gin at that. Dickey also gives him, as the single ornament in his bedroom, a crude mobile made from coat hangers and a shattered whiskey bottle. This is developed from a hint in Marsman, but becomes far more important in Dickey: It comes to represent a little man-made universe and hence the world of Art, a microcosmic counterpart to the zodiac. (Other central features of the poem's symbolism, such as Orion and Pythagoras, have no basis at all in Marsman.)

The essential theme is, in the largest terms, the same as Crane's: the nature of the poetic imagination and its relation to reality. The drama, as by implication in *The Bridge* and more explicitly in such other poems of Crane's as "The Broken Tower," consists in the protagonist's struggle to clarify and reaffirm his faith that poetry is vision and that what it reveals is the deepest truth. Except for walks around Amsterdam, Dickey's protagonist travels only in memory, but his quest is the same as that of countless poet-voyagers from the Ancient Mariner to Crane's Columbus. Like almost all poets who conceive of their art as lamp rather than mirror, he worries that the light will die with the guttering lamp and he vacillates about the reality of what it reveals; but he has the additional problems of distinguishing the hallucinations produced by delirium tremens from reality and of reconciling an awareness of modern astronomy with belief in the significance of the zodiac. There is some dramatic suspense: Will he be able to retain and affirm his faith that poetry can decipher the meaning of the universe through the stars? The zodiac may seem at first a curiously archaic and arbitrary locus of poetic faith, but it is this archaism and richness of mythological association that make it the supreme test case of the relation between man's imagination and God's. To believe in its significance is to bear witness that the universe is not meaningless, that there is a connection between the little world of man and the great world of the stars, between the world inside and that outside.

Waking with a hangover, the protagonist surveys the desolate city from his empty room and reflects on his futile, drunken life:

> He moves among stars.
>   Sure. We all do, but he is star-*crazed,* mad
> With *Einfühling,* with connecting and joining things that lay their
>   meanings

> Over billions of light years
> eons of time—Ah,
> Years of light: billions of them: they are pictures
> Of some sort of meaning. He thinks the secret
> Can be read. But human faces swim through[8]

and a "young face comes on" like the "faint, structural light / Of Alnilam, without which Orion / would have no center the Hunter / Could not hunt, in the winter clouds." She "is eternal / As long as *he* lives—the stars and his balls meet." The zodiac is his only way beyond the room: "He must solve it must believe it learn to read it." Seasick and airsick, he looks at the little mobile he has set spinning like a model of the universe:

> Even drunk
> Even in the white, whiskey-struck, splintered star of a bottle-room
> dancing
> He knows he's not fooling himself he knows
> Not a damn thing of stars of God of space
> Of time love night death sex fire numbers signs words,
> Not much of poetry. But by God, we've got a *universe*
> Here
> Those designs of time are saying *some*thing
>
> (17)

He tries to write, but "he can't get rid of himself enough / To write poetry." But then, in a dawn flash of inspiration, he realizes that "Everybody writes / With blackness" and that whiteness alone is death; it "is dying / For human words to raise it from purity from the grave / Of too much light." "The secret is that on whiteness you can release / The blackness, / The night sky." Getting drunker, he imagines himself creating a new beast for the zodiac: a healing Lobster to replace Cancer. But he cannot sustain the illusion: "I've failed again. My lobster can't make it / To Heaven." In a brilliant passage, he reproaches his "old lyre-picking buddy" Pythagoras, but reaffirms allegiance to him:

> By GOD the poem is *in* there out there
> Somewhere the lines that will change
> Everything, like your squares and square roots
> Creating the heavenly music.
> It's somewhere,
> Old great crazy thinker
> ah
> farther down

In the abyss.   It takes triangular eyes
        To see Heaven.   I got 'em from you.

(25)

He decides to put his favorite constellation, Orion, in the zodiac. The stars, he says, are gasping for understanding; they have had Ptolemy and Babylon, and now they want Hubbell, Fred Hoyle, and the steady state. "But what they really want   need / Is a poet and / I'm going to have to be it." The sight of birds brings him back to earth, and he says

                    . . . . I can always come back to earth.
But I want to come back with the secret
                                with the poem
That links up my balls and the strange, silent words
        Of God   his scrambled zoo   and my own words
                                and includes the earth
        Among the symbols.

(29)

The rest of the poem can be quickly summarized. The poet goes out into the neon hell of the city, meditates on a black church, and comes back to nightmares of the one-eyed animals of light:

. . . Is all this nothing but the clock-stunned light
Of my mind, or a kind of river-reflection of my basic sleep
Breaking down   sleeping down into reprisal-fear of God:
        The Zodiac standing over, pouring into
            The dreams that are killing me?

(45)

He vacillates between spirit and flesh, his star-obsession and ordinary life. He adjures himself to give up this poetry "that's draining your bones / Of marrow"; leave it, and get out. "Go back to the life of a man. / Leave the stars. They're not saying what you think." Daylight comes, and he walks around the city, free for twelve hours from his obsession; he returns to the house in which he spent his childhood and remembers his parents and early sweetheart, but imagines his mother telling him not to come back, not to be a memory-animal like the lizard on the wall (Scorpio?). He spends the night with a young girl, but "knows that nothing, / Even love, can kill off his lonesomeness." A party with friends thaws him out; he "shakes free of two years of wandering / Like melting-off European snows," and he is "back home." But that night he is once more in the grip of his obsession:

A day like that. But afterwards the fire
Comes straight down through the roof, white-lightning nightfall,
A face-up flash. Poetry. Triangular eyesight. It draws his
fingers together at the edge
Around a pencil.   He crouches bestially,
    The darkness stretched out on the waters
    Pulls back, humming Genesis. From wave-stars lifts
      A single island wild with sunlight,
    The white sheet of paper in the room.

(60)

The whole last section, of which this passage is the beginning, is a triumph in which Dickey recapitulates the main themes of the poem and brings it to a magnificent close. Perhaps in part because of the translation, Marsman's conclusion is rather awkward and anticlimactic. For the sake of one last comparison with Dickey, I will quote it:

I pray thee, spirit, grant to this small hand
The quiet and the still tenacity
To steer the ship onto the morning land
That slumbering in each horizon waits.
And grant the man who listens to the note
That hums along the dancing of the planets
And through the seething of the emerald sea
To tune the instrument upon the fork
Which, at the touch, reveals the structural form
Of the immemorial European song
That sounded at the dawn of culture when
It started on its course in the azure sea,
And will resound throughout the western world
As long as exaltation spans around space
A firmament of intellect and dream.

(251)

Here is Dickey's version:

    Oh my own soul, put me in a solar boat.
      Come into one of these hands
      Bringing quietness and the rare belief
    That I can steer this strange craft to the morning
Land that sleeps   in the universe on all horizons
    And give his home-come man who listens in his room

    To the rush and flare of his father

Drawn at the speed of light to Heaven
Through the wrong end of his telescope, expanding the universe,
    The instrument   the tuning-fork—
He'll flick it with his bandless wedding-finger—
    Which at a touch reveals the form
    Of the time-loaded European music
    That poetry has never really found
Undecipherable as God's bad, Heavenly sketches,
Involving fortress and flower, vine and wine and bone,

    And shall vibrate through the western world
So long as the hand can hold its island
    Of blazing paper, and bleed for its images:
    Make what it can of what is:

    So long as the spirit hurls on space
The star-beasts of intellect and madness.

(61–62)

Dickey's essential affirmation is the same one made by his predecessors in the visionary line, from Blake through Hart Crane and the Dylan Thomas of *Altarwise by Owllight:* the analogy, or identity, of the poetic imagination and the divine power that created the stars. (For this symbolic affirmation, the little mobile in the protagonist's room, which is counterpart to the universe outside, seems more plausible than Brooklyn Bridge—though of course I am not suggesting that Dickey's poem is therefore better than Crane's). The subject of *The Zodiac,* then, is not astrology but the nature of reality and its relation to the poet's creative imagination, treated not in post-Kantian philosophical terms but dramatically and mythologically.

Dickey's poet, as we have seen, tries to change the zodiac through his own creative powers. He makes Cancer into a Lobster, and he adds his favorite constellation, Orion. Of course, he fails in both attempts. (If we recall the story of Orion, it is easy to see why the myth, as well as the constellation itself, would be Dickey's own favorite: The great hunter was blinded while drunk—Merope's vengeful father did this to him—and regained his eyesight by walking on water until he reached the east; he was killed at last by Scorpio. Dickey's preoccupation with vision and blindness, both literal and symbolic, is well known, from his time as a night-fighter pilot to his novel-in-progress with its temporarily blinded hero.)

The question, then, is not whether or not *the Zodiac* fails, since all such poems inevitably fail, but how and how badly. As Warren remarked, there are some flaws in the "dramatic pivots": the dramatic logic of the protagonist's movements and shifts of moods is not always clear. Although the language is always dramatically appropriate, the protagonist's drunken ranting sometimes becomes a little insistent and hectoring, so that the reader feels trapped as if by a real drunk; and his assertions of the connection between the stars and his balls seem crude by comparison to, say, Eliot's subtle intimation of the link between the dance along the artery, the circulation of the lymph, and the drift of stars, or his tapestried boarhound and boar reconciled among the stars. But the power is there when needed at dramatic high points of the poem, and abundantly in the whole last section.

The Zodiac belongs in some respects with that galaxy of poems produced during World War II, of which the most notable are Four Quartets, Notes Toward a Supreme Fiction, Seasons of the Soul, For the Time Being, and The Sea and the Mirror. In all these poems, an action that is essentially subjective has been successfully embodied in a traditional objective form: most obviously, the string quartet in Eliot, the oratorio and closet-drama in Auden. For Dickey, the same function is performed through Marsman's poem, with its traditional symbolism and structure. The poem is at once fixed in time and space (in these respects another poem of World War II) and made universal, since the voice is so clearly that of Dickey, a survivor of that war and a contemporary, speaking through the mask of Marsman, who died early in it.

Poets of other persuasions do not seek meaning in the stars. Auden could say cheerfully, "Looking up at the stars, I know quite well / That for all they care, I can go to hell," and Warren that the stars "are only a backdrop for / The human condition" and the sky "has murder in the eye, and I / Have murder in the heart, for I / Am only human. We look at each other, the sky and I. / We understand each other."[9] Visionary poets, however, affirm that there is a relation, that the stars are saying something to man. Just what they say is, naturally, impossible to state in cool discursive prose. But Dickey, like his visionary predecessors, affirms the ultimate analogy, or identity, of the poetic imagination and the divine power that created the stars. For this symbolic affirmation, the zodiac works better than the Brooklyn Bridge.

To say that visionary poets do not age well is an academic understatement, or litotes. Rimbaud gave up poetry for gunrunning at the age of nineteen, and Hart Crane leaped into the sea at thirty; Dylan Thomas drank himself to death at thirty-nine, and Roethke, after increasingly harrowing bouts of mania and depression, in his fifties. Blake and Smart, under cover of madness, made it into their fifties. But except for Whitman, who was only in one sense a visionary poet, it is hard to think of any who attained the age of sixty. Dickey's achievement in surviving not only two wars but the special hazards that beset his kind of poet is, then, a notable one: Like Faulkner's Dilsey, he has endured.

Dickey has not only remained very much alive, but he has continued to grow and develop. *Puella* (1982) marks his entrance into a distinctive new stage. In *Puella* there is a shift from the cosmic vision of *The Zodiac* to a very different kind of vision that might be called domestic. The poet is not tamed but gentled as he lovingly describes what Hopkins called the *mundus muliebris,* the woman's world inhabited by the daughter-wife figure whose girlhood he relives. At the risk of embarrassing Dickey, I might suggest a large and vague parallel with the change in Shakespeare's career from tragedies such as *Lear* to romances such as *Cymbeline, The Winter's Tale,* and *the Tempest,* with their themes of reconciliation, fulfillment, the joy of recovering what was thought to be lost forever. Deborah in these poems has something in common with Marina, Perdita, Miranda, and other such young girls in these plays; with Yeats's Dancers and the daughter for whom he wrote the great prayer; and with the young girls in Hopkins—in "Margaret, are you grieving" and the "Echo" poems, for example. (I am beginning to sound like those nineteenth-century studies of the girlhood of Shakespeare's heroines; but that is the mood of the book, with its charming epitaph from T. Sturge Moore: "I lived in thee, and dreamed, and waked / Twice what I had been." If the word mellow had not been preempted by the Californians of "Doonesbury," it would be hard to avoid using it here. This is also the first time the word *charming* has been conceivable as a description of Dickey's poetry.)

The girl in the poems is intensely herself, yet she is also representative of all young girls, as the title *Puella* suggests. She is pictured in scenes that are archetypal, sometimes *rites de passage,* sometimes with mythical or historical contexts; sometimes heraldic as if in medieval tapestry, sometimes heraldic as if in medieval tapestry, sometimes playfully absurd as if in a modern folk-naive painting. While the poems are obviously very personal, they exhibit a new kind of formality, both in the speaker's attitude toward his subject—affection tinged with gentle humor, folk ceremoniousness, a degree of detachment making possible fresh appreciation of physical beauty—and in the verse itself. Dickey has always treasured the "wildness" aspect of Hopkins, as did Roethke—"long live the weeds and the wildness yet!"—but these poems show a new sense of the beauty of formal sound patterns that is often reminiscent of Hopkins. There is a tenderness, a delicacy, a fresh appreciation of the beauty of the visible universe that seem to owe something to Hopkins while being also strongly individual.

The beginning of "Heraldic: Deborah and Horse in Morning Forest" has an epigraph from Hopkins and is a kind of homage to that poet:

> It could be that nothing you could do
> Could keep you from stepping out and blooding-in
> An all-out blinding heraldry for this:
> A blurred momentum-flag
> That must be seen sleep-weathered and six-legged,
> Brindling and throwing off limbo-light
>
> Of barns. . . . [10]

In another, Hopkins' verse techniques are used to describe Deborah's piano-playing:

> With a fresh, gangling resonance
> Truing handsomely, I draw on left-handed space
> For a brave ballast shelving and bracing, and from it,
>   then, the light
> Prowling lift-off, the treble's strewn search and
>   wide-angle glitter.
>   (39)

As for playful folk-ceremony poems—a world apart from what one critic calls the "country surrealism" of "May Day Sermon"—there are "Deborah and Deirdre as Drunk Bridesmaids Foot-Racing at Daybreak" and "Veer-Voices: Two Sisters under Crows," in both of which the titles are enough for present purposes. But I cannot resist quoting the end of my favorite poem in the book, "Deborah in Ancient Lingerie, in Thin Oak over Creek." This is both a vision, at once tender and absurd, of Deborah in her "album bloomers" diving into the creek, and a ritual acted out in the poem itself:

>   . . . snake-screaming,
>   Withering, foster-parenting for animals
>   I can do
>   very gently from just about
>   Right over you, I can do
>   at no great height I can do
>   and bear
>   And counter-balance and do

and half-sway and do

and sway

and outsway and

do.

(22)

The poems move from the realism of "Deborah and Scion," where she is seen "In Lace and Whalebone" thinking of the kind of looks she has inherited—"Bull-headed, big-busted . . . I am totally them in the / eyebrows, / Breasts, breath and butt" (32)—to the visionary heights of "The Lyric Beasts," where she speaks as "Dancer to Audience" and becomes a kind of goddess challenging the audience to "Rise and on faith / Follow" (35). In a sense, I suppose the book is Dickey's reply to the radical feminists, for Deborah in it is both herself and Dickey's ideal modern woman, enacting her archetypal feminine role in full mythic resonance, but not enslaved or swallowed up by it. If so, Kate Millett and Adrienne Rich may eat their hearts out!

I have not mentioned many qualities in Dickey that might be called distinctively Southern, on the ground that they are large, vague, and obvious—more obvious in the novel *Deliverance* and the two books about the South, *Jericho* and *God's Images,* than in the poetry—but perhaps they should be summed up briefly. A strong sense of place is the first, as in the poems about Cherrylog Road, kudzu, chenille, the Buckhead boys, the woman preacher, and the lawyer's daughter whose dive from the Eugene Talmadge Bridge brought revelation from the burning bush. Love of storytelling, and hence of communal myth, is important, and from this it is a short step to love of ceremony and ritual both within the family and with other life-forms, from the Owl King to *Puella.* Dickey's humor is more frequently present than most people seem to realize, but its most characteristic form is the preposterous lie or grotesquely implausible vision that outrages the reader, but then turns out to be, in a deeper sense, true. Like most Southerners, he has a strong religious sense: His poems are often sermons or prayers or invocations. But his creed might be called natural supernaturalism, or fundamentalism so fundamental that it concerns man's relation to all other life forms.

As we have seen, Dickey has little significant relation to earlier Southern writing; it would take a truly ingenious academic to show how he was influenced by Sidney Lanier! Poe seems to be his only Southern predecessor in being a genuine visionary; but he was a very different kind: Whereas Poe's visions are of horror and death-in-life,

Dickey's are of larger modes of life. Dickey is so far from being a regionalist in any exclusive sense that the spiritual ancestors most prominent in his recent poetry are that New Englander of the New Englanders, Joseph Trumbull Stickney, who lies behind the wonderful poem "Exchanges"; the Dutch poet and sailor Hendrik Marsman, who lies behind *The Zodiac;* and the English Jesuit Gerard Manley Hopkins, who lies behind *Puella.*

In contrast to more recent Southern poets such as Tate and Warren, Dickey has not been interested in communion with other humans through acceptance of the human condition but in getting beyond ordinary humanity to participate in the life of nonhuman creatures and in more-than-human forces. His essential subject has been exchange or metamorphosis or *participation mystique* between man and wild animals, fish, or birds; or, in *Zodiac,* stars and the mysterious universe in general. Since the rational mind is a hindrance, or at best irrelevant, to this quest, his poems represent extreme states of consciousness: intoxication, terror, rage, lust, hallucination, somnambulism, or mystical exaltation. His concern is not the limitations but the possibilities of human and nonhuman nature, not history but vision.

As I have tried to suggest, *Puella* constitutes a new kind of vision, back from the cosmic extremities of *The Zodiac* to the human and domestic world. The figure of the daughter-wife is suffused with a new tenderness, gentleness, and humor, and the verse takes on a new formal musicality. A Jungian would say that the girl in these poems is an anima figure; but whether the sense of fulfillment and joy in these poems comes from integration of the personality or from some deeper cause, I will not attempt to decide. Nor will I comment on the fact that Deborah is not only Southern but South Carolinian; Southern chivalry toward ladies who have the misfortune to be born elsewhere forbids it. But I will risk the charge of Southern chauvinism by saying that the book is a most notable contribution to Southern letters.

Robert Penn Warren as Hardy American

Selected Poems, 1923–1975

It is hard to think of Warren as old. He was the youngest and most precocious of the Fugitive group, and the qualities one associates with him are youthful: prodigality of talent, versatility, copiousness, idealism coupled with a determination to know the world, willingness to learn from history and to change. But the dates on this volume remind us that his poetic career now spans more than fifty years, and in the portrait on the dust jacket he has something of the aquiline look of the elder Yeats. "Myself must I remake," Yeats resolved once more in a poem written when he was past seventy, taking as his models Blake and Michelangelo, Timon and Lear: "An old man's eagle mind." Although Warren is in many ways a very different kind of poet from Yeats, he has the same dedication to remaking his poetic self and the same tenacity in continuing the process into old age.

Far from marking the end of Warren's career as poet, this volume does not appear to signal even the end of a phase. The occasion of this third version of *Selected Poems* seems to have been mainly that ten richly productive years had passed since the second, in 1967. (Warren does not, by the way, use *Selected Poems* to mean a small anthology or sampling taken from a larger *Collected Poems;* he includes in these selections all the poems he wants to preserve, carefully revising, pruning, and rearranging them into what seems, for the time being at least, a definitive state.)

In all of his *Selected Poems,* Warren has arranged the poems in reverse chronological order, beginning with the most recent. Thus the present volume begins with ten poems written in 1975 and not previously published in book form, then moves back through the three volumes published since the last *Selected Poems* in 1967: *Or Else— Poem/Poems, 1968–1974, Audubon: A Vision,* and *Incarnations: Poems, 1966–1968.* The *Selected Poems* of 1944 is now reduced to little more than half its original length.

Warren, in thus giving pride of place and preference in bulk to his later poetry, makes his sense of the shape of his own career very plain. More than five-sixths of this volume—268 of its 325 pages—dates from 1954 or later; it is work, then, of the poet's middle and later years, from the age of forty-nine on. In making up his volume in this unusual way—and reverse chronological order is very rare indeed—has Warren fallen victim to the natural partiality that every poet feels for his latest work (but that most poets conclude sadly to be unjustified) or to an excessive concern for contemporary relevance? I do not think so. In the first place, he does not abandon the early work, but preserves and sometimes improves the best of it; in revising he tries "not to tamper with meanings, only to sharpen old meanings—for poems are, in one perspective at least, always a life record, and live their own life by that fact."[1] In the second place, few would deny that the kind of poetry Warren began writing after the ten-year interval in which he wrote none except for the long "play for verse and voices," *Brother to Dragons* (1953), is more inclusive, richer in human and dramatic qualities, and far more accessible than the early verse.

In most of his early poetry, Warren was more open in texture and personal in tone than his fellow Fugitives; when he returned to poetry in 1954 these tendencies were much accentuated. No doubt partly in response to the same pressures that produced the "confessional" movement at about the same time, and partly as a result of private and internal developments, Warren's poems have grown steadily more open, more unabashedly personal, more overtly psychological and religious, and more interdependent. The titles of the later volumes show Warren's desire to make his themes perfectly explicit (in contrast, the titles of his two early volumes were totally uninformative: *Thirty-six Poems* and *Eleven Poems on the Same Theme*). Thus *Promises* (1957) begins with a sequence dedicated to his daughter, born in 1953, and contains as its title sequence a group dedicated to his son, born in 1955, the same year his father died. *Promises* suggests both the new hope and promise that the children bring and the commitment to the future that they represent; and through them he relives his own childhood. The title also designates a theme new to Warren's poetry: the promise of joy as a real possibility, if Time is accepted. To live fully in the present is to accept the world as real and to accept both past and future, for the present takes part of its reality from them. Hence the volume begins with the poet's vision of his dead parents repeating their promises to him, and it reaches one of its high points in the ballad about the grandmother who must submit to being eaten by the hogs (eating being a natural symbol for acceptance, communion, incorporation). It is not fanciful to see analogies between *Promises* and Yeats's *Responsibilities,* each marking at about the same age the beginning of a new phase in the poet's career.

You, Emperors, and Others: Poems 1957–1960 (1960) is about the "you" who is both the reader and the poet, as well as the "Roman citizen of no historical importance, under the empire" whose epitaph is quoted in the first poem, which begins: "Whoever you are, this poem is clearly about you," and the Roman emperors dealt with in other poems. Warren, seeking a direct and candid relation to the reader, is characteristically the poet of the second person, and this volume makes explicit that mode of address. *Incarnations* (1969) is religious but non-theological: The communion it celebrates is chiefly one of suffering, and the flesh most prominently that of an old convict dying of cancer in a Southern penitentiary and a black maid dying in a meaningless accident in New York. *Or Else* (1974) is in my opinion Warren's best single volume. Certainly it is his most fully achieved structure in the mode he has been developing since 1954, for whereas earlier volumes have been made up of several sequences, this whole book is, as Warren said in the preface, "conceived as a single long poem composed to a number of shorter poems as sections or chapters." The nature of time and of evil, the ambivalent and guilty relation to the parents ("In the rain and naked old father is dancing, he will get wet. / . . . They must learn to stay in their graves. That is what graves are for"), the un-pleasant sources of creativity in Flaubert and Dreiser, the false visions produced by drink, passion, and stargazing, but the real embodiments of the "unsleeping principle of delight" and even love and joy, implaus-ible as a floating mountain — all these and other themes are integrated into a complex unity made up of twenty-three sections and eight "In-terjections." Among them is what seems to me the best poem yet written about Vietnam: "Bad Year, Bad War: A New Year's Card, 1969." It is an ironic poem without any assumption of moral superior-ity on the part of the ironist, for Warren sees the liberal attitude toward the war as another example of that quest for a false innocence that be-trays us all. It begins, "That was the year of the bad war. The others — / Wars, that is — had been virtuous" and it ends, "Dear God, we pray / To be restored to that purity of heart / That sanctifies the shed-ding of blood."[2]

Let us look briefly at the ten new poems, dated 1975, with which the 1977 *Selected Poems* begins. The last of these, "Old Nigger on One-Mule Cart Encountered Late at Night When Driving Home from Party in the Back Country," is a vivid evocation of a long-ago incident in which the poet, drunk on booze, music, and the desires of the flesh, was driving through the Louisiana night and was almost killed when he suddenly encountered, "On the fool-nigger, ass-hole wrong side of / The road, naturally," an old black man on a mule cart piled high with junk. The encounter haunts him through the years; he remembers the couplet of a sonnet he once tried to write about it:

> One of those who gather junk and wire to use
> For purposes that we cannot peruse.

As I said, Jesus Christ. . . .

Now, looking at the whiteness of snow-filled forest on the mountain, he imagines the man arriving home and going to bed after the incident; and this becomes an image of his own death. The poem ends,

> And so I say:
> Brother, Rebuker, my Philosopher past all
> Casuistry, will you be with me when
> I arrive and leave my own cart of junk
> Unfended from the storm of starlight and
> The howl, like wind, of the world's monstrous blessedness,
> To enter, by a bare field, a shack unlit?
> Entering into that darkness to fumble
> My way to a place to lie down, but holding,
> I trust, in my hand, a name—
> Like a shell, a dry flower, a worn stone, a toy—merely
> A hard-won something that may, while Time
> Backward unblooms out of time toward peace, utter
> Its small, sober, and inestimable
> Glow, trophy of truth.
>
> Can I see Arcturus from where I stand?

This passage is a good example of the difference between Warren's and "naked" or "confessional" poetry. Warren does not expose himself to reveal exceptional wickedness or misfortune; there is in him no touch of the *poète maudit,* suffering exceptionally for us all. Instead, he offers himself rather as Auden does in his later verse, as a representative man, accepting himself as part of accepting the flesh of common humanity: "A man ain't nuthin but a man" is one of the epigraphs to *Incarnations.* The trophy he seeks is truth, the truth of the human condition primarily as found in himself. Although the poem seems open and direct, much of its power comes from the symbolic interplay between whiteness (suggesting, as usually in Warren, emptiness, desolation, meaninglessness, death) and darkness, associated with sensual pleasure. For example, the beginning:

Flesh, of a sudden, gone nameless in music, flesh
Of the dancer, under your hand, flowing to music, girl-
Flesh sliding, flesh flowing, sweeter than
Honey, slicker than Essolube, over
The music-swayed, delicate trellis of bone
That is white and secret in flesh-darkness.

Much of the poem is written in the second person, as is most of Warren's later verse. "You" is most often both the reader and the poet; and this rhetorical device, which in other hands can seem offensive, is in Warren a declaration of fraternity and common ground. The shift in meaning of the vision from confronting the old black man as death to identifying with him is the ultimate assertion of fraternity. It is also comic, in a grotesque and ironic way. I have not said enough about the element of humor in Warren, but it is very important, from the salty vulgarity of the folk ballads to the parody headlines and clichés of "Mortmain" and the wild surrealism of "Ballad of a Sweet Dream of Peace."

The last line ("Can I see Arcturus from where I stand?") of the poem just discussed forms the title for the group of new poems. The first of them, "A Way to Love God," embodies Warren's recurrent vision of the worst evil as blankness, meaninglessness, "forgetting the crime," symbolized by images of whiteness, and his view of nature as no more innocent than man. But "Answer to Prayer" states, as a fact of experience, that prayers are sometimes answered, and even for happiness, though how this can be the poet cannot explain:

Who does not know the savvy insanity and wit
Of history! and how its most savage peripeteia always
Has the shape of a joke—if you find the heart to laugh at it.
In such a world, then, one must be pretty careful how one prays.

Her prayer, yes, was answered, for in spite of my meager desert,
Of a sudden, life—it was bingo! was bells and all ringing like mad,
Lights flashing, fruit spinning, the machine spurting dollars like dirt—
Nevada dollars, that is—but all just a metaphor for the luck I now had.[3]

Some years ago I heard several of Warren's elders among the Fugitives agree that the proper phrase to describe him was "a hard-bitten saint," and, though they were speaking of him as man rather than poet, the phrase applies well to his verse. Warren's poetry exhibits tough-minded awareness of what the world is like and what history is. He is perhaps more deeply immersed in American history and literature than any other contemporary poet; all his novels are in a sense historical, and he has dealt in prose with most of the major American writers. One of the tasks he undertakes in his verse is to reconcile the doctrines of American sages with the facts of American history and of human nature. *Brother to Dragons* forces Jefferson, believing in man's natural goodness and perfectibility, to confront the hideous crime committed by his nephew; as "RPW" sums up at the end, "The recognition of complicity is the beginning of innocence. / The recognition of necessity is the beginning of freedom." "There is," he says in "The Day Dr. Knox Did It," "no water to wash the world away"; "We are the world, and it is too late / To pretend we are children at dusk watching fireflies." "Homage to Emerson, On Night Flight to New York" observes that Emerson thought "There is / No sin. Not even error," and at 38,000 feet he is dead right, but only in the "womb-gloom" of the airplane, where the heart is "as abstract as an empty / Coca-Cola bottle." In contrast, the poem cites much earth-level evidence. Instead of taking refuge in such dreams of innocence, the solution is to "eat the dead," to accept the past, including one's own past self, however unpleasant it may be: "You must eat them completely, bone, blood, flesh, gristle, even / Such hair as can be forced." This done, "Immortality is not impossible, / Even joy."[4]

Unlike visionary poets, Warren finds no revelation in drink or passion: "Drunk, drunk, drunk, amid the blaze of noon," in New Orleans, he quoted Milton for magnificence: "But let / Bells ring in all the churches. / Let likker, like philosophy, roar / In the skull. Passion / Is all. Even / The sleaziest":

> A cop,
> Of brachycephalic head and garlic breath,
> Toothpick from side of mouth and pants ass-bagged and holster low,
> From eyes the color of old coffee grounds,
> Regarded with imperfect sympathy
> *La condition humaine* —
> Which was sure-God what we were.
>
> (123)

But Warren also celebrates the capacity for idealism and sacrifice and the yearning for love and forgiveness that are equally part of the human condition. In his stubbornly skeptical way, he is a deeply religious poet. He holds hard to the facts. But, as he discovers repeatedly, prominent among the facts is the possibility of joy, even of blessedness and redemption. Once the guilty self and the past are accepted in the present—once the dead are eaten and incorporated, and communion thus affirmed—then joy becomes possible and the future real. To summarize this hard-won knowledge briefly is almost to parody it, for Warren rejects all abstract doctrines and dogmas and refuses to simplify. His view of life is essentially tragic, for he is vividly aware of how men's best qualities are betrayed by their worst and how the two intertwine and shift; and of the prevalence of suffering and meaningless accident, as well as evil and malice, in the world. No one could be further removed from the bland formulas of the pop psychologists, though the themes as I describe them abstractly may sound similar. His poem to Theodore Dreiser begins, in very American terza rima:

> Who is the ugly one slump-slopping down the street?
> Who is the chinless wonder with the potato-nose?
> Can't you hear the soft *plop* of the pancake-shaped feet?

"Born with one hand in his pants and one in the till, / He knows that the filth of self, to be loved, must be clad in glory, / . . . May I present Mr. Dreiser? He will write a great novel, someday." It concludes:

> He is no philosopher.
> His only gift is to enact
> All that his deepest self abhors,
> And learn, in his self-contemplative distress,
> The secret worth
> Of all our human worthlessness.

> (59)

Yeats wrote: "The rhetorician would deceive his neighbours, / The sentimentalist himself; while art / Is but a vision of reality." Warren would emphatically agree, though his pursuit of his goal has taken him in a different direction from Yeats's. His aim has been not to produce a Sacred Book of the Arts as Yeats did, above or outside of time, but a poetry closer to prose and to the novel, sacrificing the intensity of the individual lyric to larger dramatic effects; a poetry direct and open in its approach to the reader, candidly personal and truthful, both grounded in and remaining a part of history. But Yeats is, in conclusion, not the right poet with whom to compare Warren, though it is tempting to say that Warren strives to hold reality and justice in a single thought without the help of *A Vision*.

For Warren is the most American of poets. In contrast to James Dickey, who is a visionary poet whose aim is to transcend the human,

Warren is a poet of history, whose aim is to accept the human, including the self. (With characteristic generosity, however, Warren was one of the first to hail Dickey's *The Zodiac.*) Both poets represent traditions originating with Whitman: on the one hand, the transcendental and pantheist; on the other, the good gray poet who is one of the roughs, and who is deeply concerned for the Republic. Finally, however, all these comparisons are misleading, for Warren, though he is the poet of common humanity, is not much like any other poet. Let us hope that his late flowering will outlast those of Yeats, Frost, and Williams, and take him into the company of Picasso, Stravinsky, and Chagall.

Warren at Seventy-five

Warren has done it again: In the face of advancing years, he has produced another collection[5] that is at least as good as any of its predecessors and that manifests continued growth and change. His progress is a joy to contemplate, and an inspiration to us all.

In *Being Here,* Warren's second collection since the *Selected Poems* of 1975, he is still experimenting with different kinds of structure, playing off thematic arrangements against a "shadowy autobiography," and trying new meters and new kinds of poems. Of all Warren's volumes, this one is most open and accessible to the reader: Not only are the poems given descriptive titles and arranged in sequences so that they provide contexts for each other, both thematic and autobiographical, but even the dedication and the epigraphs are functional, and there is an "Afterthought" as a further guide. The epigraphs indicate the central theme of the volume—the nature and meaning of Time—and the dedication, to Warren's maternal grandfather, Gabriel Penn, evokes the memory and situation that lies behind many poems:

> OLD MAN: You get old and you can't do anybody any good any more.
> BOY: You do me some good, Grandpa. You tell me things.

As Warren has frequently remarked in interviews, he spent many boyhood summers on his grandfather's farm, and was tremendously impressed by the old man, who, though opposed to slavery, became a captain in Forrest's cavalry when the war came, and was all his life a great reader of history and poetry. Some of the best poems vividly recall such boyhood scenes, but now sometimes with roles reversed, as the poet identifies with the grandfather rather than the boy; in a sense, the poems are substitutes for such colloquies, for in them the poem attempts to tell somebody things that may do him good.

Although this tableau characterizes the volume accurately, since most of the poems deal with boyhood memories interpreted in age, Warren rarely speaks as a self-consciously old man. (There are, for instance, no poems like Hardy's "An Ancient to Ancients" or "Afterwards.") Instead, he stresses the essential humanity that is common to youth and age, boy and grandfather. His atittude is realistic, unsentimental, hard-bitten, without self-pity or easy consolations. He preaches no doctrine; but he affirms, on the basis of his own experience, that joy and love are possible; and he yearns for significance. Lack of meaning, blankness, whiteness—most often imaged as snow—is the ultimate horror in the poems; and it is a possibility never dismissed. Thematically, each of the five sequences expresses a tension between this vision of despair and the search for meaning: poems such as "Empty White Blotch on Map of Universe: A Possible View" and "Ballad of Your Puzzlement" are, in Warren's unpretentious metaphor, like backboards against which the other poems in their sequences are bounced.

To single out individual poems is misleading, for an important part of their meaning derives from their context. Nevertheless, a few of the most outstanding must be noticed. "Speleology" develops early memories of cave exploration into an image of death; "Recollection in Upper Ontario, from Long Before" describes an incident witnessed in boyhood when a female hobo was killed by a train, possibly pushed by her husband. These are wonderfully vivid poems.

"When Life Begins" presents the tableau of boy and grandfather, the boy wondering when life would begin, while "Time crouched, like a great cat, motionless / But for the tail's twitch. Night comes. Eyes glare." "Function of Blizzard" is an ironic effort to accept even snow, "coverings-over, forgettings."

> Bless snow! Bless God, Who must work under the hand of
> Fate, who has no name. God does the best
> He can, . . . And bless me, even
> With no glass in my hand, and far from New York, as I rise
> From bed, feet bare, heart freezing, to stare out at
> The whitening fields and forest, and wonder what
>
> Item of the past I'd most like God to let
> Snow fall on, keep falling on, and never
>
> Melt, for I, like you, am only a man, after all.

(45)

"Cocktail Party" is a powerful and funny meditation, with beautifully controlled tone, on the dangers of truth. "Auto-Da-Fé" is a meditation on the body and its destruction by flame; "The Cross," a wistful and compassionate description of burying a monkey drowned in a storm at sea. But these are only a sampling: there are others equally good.

In general, the images in this volume are sharper and more powerful than ever. There is a particularly vivid one of the future as suction: the man with a passion for Truth,

> . . . clutching his balance-pole,
> Looks down the sickening distance
> On the crowd-swarm like ants, far below,
>
> And he sways, high on the fated
> And human high-wire of lies.
> Does he feel the pitiless suction
>
> Their eyes exert on him?
> Does he know they wait the orgasmic
> Gasp of relief as he falls?
>
> (78)

Another poem images the future as tornado:

> That all-devouring, funnel-shaped, mad and high-spiraling,
> Dark suction that
> We have, as the Future, named. . . .
>
> (92),

and another speaks of the "suction of years yet to come" (101).

Perhaps the most powerful repeated image and situation, however, is that of night walking, whether "Snowshoeing Back to Camp in Gloaming" or wandering "The Asphalt of Midnight," and looking up at the stars in the inhuman vastness of space. The last poem, "Passers-By on Snowy Night," is perhaps the most beautiful version. A daringly regular poem for these times, it is a kind of envoy to the reader, making its limited affirmation of human good will in the indifferent universe of snow and "mocking moonlight":

> Black the coniferous darkness,
> White the snow track between,
> And the moon, skull-white in its starkness,
> Watches upper ledges lean,
>
> And regards with the same distant stare,
> And equal indifference,

How your breath goes white in steel air
As you trudge to *whither* from *whence.*

           . . . Alone,
I wish you well in your night
As I pass you in my own.

We each hear the distant friction,
Then crack of bough burdened with snow,
And each takes the owl's benediction,
And each goes the way he will go.

                                                          (105)

The "owl's benediction," though a lovely musical phrase, is in Warren's poems not soothing or reassuring, but ominous: The owl asks his
question "to make your conscience ask if it's you who—*who-who*— /
Did whatever it was"; it is his "mystic question that follows his glut."
The effect is somewhat like that Frost produces in poems such as
"Stopping by Woods" or "Acquainted with the Night," of a beautiful,
rather bland surface masking depths of bleakness within. But in Warren the emphasis is on the good will, the common humanity despite
all limitations and barriers.

Hardy American

An American Hardy? Not exactly. Although we have not had such a
prolonged late flowering of a poet since Thomas Hardy's (which lasted
until his eighty-eighth year), and though Warren's poetry resembles
Hardy's in many ways—perhaps most in the religious attitude of yearning unbelief coupled with grim irony and the metrical virtuosity based
on stretching traditional forms—Warren is obviously not merely an
American version of Hardy. He is unique, original, and, for me at
least, a far more profound, moving, and satisfying poet than Hardy.
At the risk of being thought a precious paronomasiac, I have therefore
shifted the word order in my title so as to stress Warren's hardiness and
hardihood. He is strong and durable, a tough-minded survivor who
never shirks a full look at the worst. And he is supremely American,
immersed as he is in American history and feeling a personal responsibility for older American literature (reviving Melville's and Whittier's
poetry, Dreiser's novels) and for the state of the Republic (a concern
shown not only in his poetry but also in his prose studies of the Civil
War, of segregation, and of Jefferson Davis). That Warren's character
embodies many of the qualities that we like to think peculiarly Ameri-

can is a statement that is nebulous but not, I think, meaningless: great energy and vigor, a willingness to take risks, a kind of omnicompetence that impels him to turn his hand to everything from biography and history to children's books, as well as criticism, plays, novels, and poems of all varieties; a deep understanding of and sympathy for the ordinary or, as he used to be called, "common" man. Generalizing even more recklessly, I might suggest that in the largest terms the essential theme of all his work is one which, while universal, is specially applicable to Americans and to our national foreign policy: the dangers of innocence, self-righteousness, moral isolation that allow us to believe that only we have escaped from history.

Rumor Verified,[6] Warren's third collection since the *Selected Poems* of 1977, is not quite up to its predecessor, *Being Here;* yet this does not mean any decline, but merely the ebb and flow inevitable in the productions of so large and prodigal a talent. (His latest volume, *Chief Joseph,*[7] is not the mixture as before but a new and quite different kind of poem.) *Rumor Verified* lacks the clarity of theme and organization that helped to make *Being Here* so effective. The title poem makes the theme explicit enough—the verified rumor is "That you are simply a man, with a man's dead reckoning, nothing more"—and the sequences are given such titles as "Paradox of Time," "If This Is the Way It Is," "But Also," and "Fear and Trembling." A more dramatic and effective principle of organization is constituted by the ghostly figure of Thomas Hardy, which seems to hover in the background of many of these poems. Warren does not imitate or reply to Hardy directly, but he does deal with Hardyan themes in his own way; and he seems deliberately to evoke Hardy so that the reader will be conscious of the parallels and differences. An obvious example is "Convergences," in which the meter as well as the title recalls Hardy's "Convergence of the Twain"; but instead of Hardy's grim but impersonal irony of the Spinner of the Years humbling man's pride, Warren has the more disquieting image of the personal future as rails converging into a dark tunnel to embody the memory of human evil in the tramp who robbed him and of his own responsive hatred. The image of "God's palsied hand shaking / The dice-cup? Ah, blessèd accident!" can hardly fail to recall "Hap" and other Hardy poems, and "Immanence" Hardy's Immanent Will, and "Afterward" Hardy's beautiful poem of the same name—though Warren offers even less consolation than Hardy for mortality. But Warren is in general much less bleak and grim than Hardy, much less defensive. He is a purer agnostic because he is unsure that God does not exist and that Fate always is hostile or indifferent. He often sounds like someone who has escaped the Hardyan trap; he does not understand how or why, but he believes in the existence of joy and love because he has experienced them; and therefore he has hope. He has far more humor than Hardy, and he is capable of fear and trembling, which is foreign to Hardy's grim stoicism. He is more compassionate, a yearner after, more than a denouncer of, the absent God. He has his own belief in a kind of secular Eucharist, in which the parents and the dead past must be eaten and digested; and we too must be ready to be eaten. (An alternative metaphor, more prominent in the prose than in the poetry, is that of "osmosis of being," a membranal interpenetration of being between self and others and man and nature.) The Dionysiac or surreal aspect of Warren—as in the mystical Eucharist just mentioned, or the visions of the dead grandmother eaten perpetually by the hogs, or the ghost of the dead father dancing, or the experiences of pure joy, of feeling that "everything that lives is blest"—suggests Yeats; but it is striking that one does not feel the presence of Yeats in Warren's later poetry.

I fear that I have been tempted into too many generalizations, and so I will conclude with a few more words about *Rumor Verified*. Although it is full of images of sleeplessness and nightmare, of the terror of meaninglessness in life and death, it is a hopeful volume. The epigraph, fittingly, is the passage from Dante about emerging from Hell to see the stars again. The first poem, "Chthonian Revelation: A Myth," describes a sexual communion in the nave of a hidden sea-cave, a hermetic revelation that is wordless; and as the lovers are swimming home, each drop of water falling from a fingertip is "a perfect universe defined / By its single, minuscule, radiant, enshrinèd star." So the transient waterdrop and the eternal star are equated in the mystery of time. The quest for meaning is often equated with the writing of poetry, as in the beginning of "Minneapolis Story":

Whatever pops into your head, and whitely
Breaks surface on the dark stream that is you,

May do to make a poem—for every accident
Yearns to be more than itself, yearns,

In the way you dumbly do, to participate
In the world's blind, groping rage toward meaning. . . .[8]

Again, "The Corner of the Eye" images the poem as alternatively a small fugitive animal or a Jamesian "Beast in the Jungle":

The poem is just beyond the corner of the eye.
You cannot see it—not yet—but sense the faint gleam,

Or stir. It may be like a poor little shivering fieldmouse,
One tiny paw lifted from snow while, far off, the owl

Utters. Or like breakers, far off, almost as soundless as dream.
Or the rhythmic rasp of your father's last breath. . . .

.   .   .   .

It has stalked you all day, or years, breath rarely heard, fangs dripping.

And now, any moment, great hindquarters may hunch, ready—
Or is it merely a poem, after all?

(64)

The final poem, "Fear and Trembling," in a section called "Coda,"
seems again to identify poetry and the discovery of meaning: only at
the death of ambition "does the deep / Energy crack crust, spurt forth,
and leap / From grottoes, dark—and from the caverned enchain-
ment?" But the volume is full of splendid and varied poems that I wish
I had space to comment on. "Redwing Blackbirds" is an American
equivalent of Yeats's "Wild Swans at Coole," and "If" ("If this is the
way it is, we must live through it")—surely consciously?—of Kipling's
dreadful inspirational poem.

Warren's long poem is a new departure in several ways. Whereas
Brother to Dragons is a "play for verse and voices" and *Audubon* "a
vision" (described by Warren in an interview as a series of snapshots
or fragments), *Chief Joseph* is simply called "a poem," and it is
Warren's closest approach to a traditional narrative poem. Most of it
is spoken by Chief Joseph himself, after a brief introduction; Warren
does not enter in his own person until the last section, when he describes his visit to the burial site. In a collage technique Warren inter-
sperses prose excerpts throughout the poem; these are extracted from
contemporary and later documents of many kinds, from records and
reports to letters, biographies, and newspapers. Since the prose constitutes a running commentary on, and counterpoint to, the old chief's
words in the poem, the technique is very effective.

Chief Joseph is an American epic. In many ways it is the third point
on a line of development that begins with *Brother to Dragons,* and in
which *Audubon* is the middle work. In *Brother to Dragons* the action
is in every sense tragic: the ghost of Jefferson and the persona R.P.W.
recognize their own complicity in evil and are changed by the reenact-
ment. *Audubon* is, in contrast, not dramatic: The Audubon of the
poem is made far more serene than the historical Audubon ever was
(as James Justus notes), a hero-saint, a mythic rather than a tragic protagonist. Chief Joseph is faultless—the only Warren protagonist who

is wholly good. (The only things he can find to reproach himself with are pride in his position and possible minor errors of judgment.) Hence there is no psychological conflict in the poem and no irony. Joseph is not passive: he fights; but since the fight is hopeless, his main function is to suffer. His only alienation is physical: Deprived of his homeland, he remains true to the eyes of the fathers who watch from darkness.

The aesthetic problem is how to avoid making this situation overly simple and sentimental: When the Indians are all good and most of the whites bad, and the good suffer wholly undeserved evil, the result is likely to be pathos. This result is avoided in two ways. The first is the characterization of Joseph. Throughout his long speeches he exhibits no trace of self-pity or vindictiveness: He is the noble Indian of legend realized in life. The second is the characterization of the whites, who range from noble spirits like Jefferson through many soldiers and statesmen of mixed character to real villains like Sherman. Who was responsible for the final betrayal? "General Sherman, it was, and the name he bore, / That of the greatest Indian chief— / Tecumseh. William Tecumseh Sherman, of course." The whites even offered bounties for Indian scalps: "One hundred dollars per buck, fifty / Per woman, only twenty-five for a child's." In the "predictably obscene" procession to dedicate Grant's tomb,

> Joseph, whose people had never taken
> A scalp, rode beside Buffalo Bill—
> Who had once sent his wife a yet-warm scalp,
> He himself had sliced from the pate
> Of a red man who'd missed him. Joseph rode
> Beside Buffalo Bill, who broke clay pigeons—
> One-two-three-four-five—just like that.
>
> Joseph rode by the clown, the magician who could transform
> For howling patriots, or royalty,
> The blood of history into red ketchup,
> A favorite American condiment. . . .

$$(55-56)$$

In the final section Warren describes his own visit to the battlefield, his vision of Joseph

> While he, eyes fixed on what strange stars, knew
> That eyes were fixed on him, eyes of
> Those fathers that incessantly, with
> The accuracy of that old Winchester, rifled

Through all, through darkness, distance, Time,
To know if he had proved a man. . . .[9]

Reflecting that "There is only / Process, which is one name for history. Often / Pitiful. But, sometimes, under / The scrutinizing prism of Time, / Triumphant," he imagines a future stranger, in a similar moment of decision while the mob rushes onward, who will "into / His own heart look while he asks / From what undefinable distance, years, and direction, / Eyes of fathers are suddenly fixed on him. To know."

Turning now to some studies of Warren, let us begin with *Then and Now*, by Floyd C. Watkins. This is a hard book to classify. The subtitle, "The Personal Past in the Poetry of Robert Penn Warren," is not much help, except that it indicates certain limits. Although Watkins disclaims any biographical intention, the book is more biographical than anything else; even the exhaustive analyses of poems are biographical in emphasis. The thesis is that Warren creates in his poetry an imaginary town, a "created village of the mind and art," like Faulkner's Jefferson, Wolfe's Altamont, Anderson's Winesburg, or Robinson's Tilbury Town; and with the poet's help Watkins proceeds to explore the relation between the poetic town and the "reality" of Guthrie and Cerulean Springs, Kentucky, as represented in historical documents and in the memories of Warren's surviving contemporaries. There are various assumptions here that one might question, from the rationale of these limits—why exclude the novels?—to the notion that Warren has been much concerned with creating an imaginary town. But rather than quibble about such matters, let us rejoice that the study did produce some valuable results. With his customary generosity, Warren cooperated very fully with Watkins, not only providing material and suggestions but also discussing each chapter in detail and making elaborate suggestions for revision. The resulting book is perhaps most like an expanded interview, though for the most part Warren's words are absorbed into Watkins's commentary rather than given verbatim. Warren has said that he does not intend to write an autobiography and does not want a biography written; but, on the other hand, he has been more generous than any other poet known to me (except James Dickey in his *Self-Interviews*) in giving interviews that supply just about everything that a reader might find helpful. Watkins has published not only one of these interviews, but also (with John T. Hiers) a collection of them, *Robert Penn Warren Talking* (1980). So this book grows naturally out of that kind of activity. Whether it adds much to the understanding of Warren's poetry is debatable; but, literary appreciation being always impure and not completely divorceable from curiosity, many of Warren's readers will be glad to have this book.

The second chapter, "The Penns, the Warrens, and the Boy," is much the best part of the book. It contains the fullest account I have seen of Warren's family background and boyhood, with new material on such matters as Warren's accidental blinding in one eye. This injury was obviously of enormous importance psychologically, aside from its practical effect in disqualifying him for Annapolis; but Warren—a man who successfully protects his privacy—has refused to talk about it until recently. He told Watkins: "I felt sort of alienated rather than emasculated, but alienated. . . . Alienation and separation from other people, and I felt a kind of shame—shame is not the word—but disqualification for life, as if I had lost a leg, say, or an arm or something. . . . It made you feel unattractive, and it made you also express your anger quite a lot."[10] He worried about losing the other eye, and no doubt this was all related to his attempt at suicide. (He discusses these matters also in the summer 1982 *Georgia Review.*)

Little of what Watkins reveals is surprising, though he gratifies curiosity and provides interesting details. The Guthrie that Warren remembers is not the town other people remember; nor does it always correspond to what facts are now discoverable. Being precocious and gifted, Warren as a boy was not popular; he was regarded with a good deal of envy and malice. Guthrie is now totally unaware of its most famous citizen.

Neil Nakadate's collection of essays, *Robert Penn Warren: Critical Perspectives,*[11] is the first general collection about Warren since John Longley's of 1965. It is a useful and engaging selection, and it illustrates the high level of most criticism of Warren. (That Warren is well treated by critics is not merely good luck. He has always avoided literary politics, and has spoken well of fellow writers or remained silent; even his commercial success has provoked remarkably little envy. Furthermore, his work offers many fruitful challenges to critics.) Unfortunately, Nakadate's book is done in photo-offset and is cheap-looking though not cheap.

The other collection of essays, James A. Grimshaw's on *Brother to Dragons,*[12] is a handsome book and a good complement to Nakadate's, since all these pieces deal with the same work. (There is little duplication; only three essays appear in both volumes.) Grimshaw's collection has two important sources of interest. First, *Brother to Dragons* occupies a unique place in Warren's career. He wrote it after a ten-year dry spell when he was unable to finish poems, and it was his writing of this work in 1953, his including his father and his own persona as

R.P.W., that heralded and made possible his entire later poetic career that began with *Promises* (1956). Second, he published a dramatic version of *Brother to Dragons* in 1976 and a drastically revised version of the original "play for verse and voices" in 1979. In the meantime a historical study had appeared—*Jefferson's Nephews: A Frontier Tragedy*, by Boynton Merrill, Jr. (1976)—that demonstrated the lack of correspondence to historical fact in many details of the first version and that questioned the whole matter of its relation to history. *Brother to Dragons* is thus Warren's most controversial work, both with regard to the comparative merits of the two versions and with regard to the matter of historicity. Most critics, whatever positions they have taken on these controversies, have also thought it (or one version of it) to be among Warren's finest works: many would rank it with *All the King's Men* as one of his two supreme achievements.

Grimshaw's volume, then, has every attraction to appeal to a very wide audience, since it deals on a high level with controversial matters of the widest range and the greatest importance. The first section consists of essays about the 1953 version, ranging from Frederick P. W. McDowell's 1955 essay "Psychology and Theme" (the only essay to be reprinted in all three collections, Longley's, Nakadate's, and Grimshaw's—and well worth it) to Dennis Dooley's study of the "Persona R.P.W." and Richard G. Law's on "The Fact of Violence vs the Possibility of Love." Space does not permit even the listing of all these, but they are uniformly good. The second section consists of reviews, the first five of the 1953 edition and the remaining two of the 1979 edition. Jarrell and Lowell (who curiously seems to be trying to imitate Jarrell's style) are marvelous on the earlier version; Harold Bloom, a late convert to Warren's poetry on the basis of *Incarnations* and *Audubon*, does not really like either version (too anti- Jefferson and -Emerson) but finds the new one improved. Irvin Ehrenpreis does not like either version and does a rousing academic hatchet job, which is, at least, a comprehensive statement of everything that can be said against them. The third section is a group of interpretations of the 1979 edition. The late Hugh Holman faults Warren for not making it clearer that he is not a practitioner of historical fiction, for *Brother* does not, as the Merrill book shows, correspond even to the "general outline" of the facts, as Warren claims it does. But Holman performs this service for the poet, and does it well. *Brother,* he points out, began with folk tales and garbled legends; and Warren's change of the victim's name from the historical George to John "is a quiet but emphatic declaration to Clio, in the guise of Boynton Merrill, of 'non serviam.'" Warren, Holman makes very clear, "embraces a purpose and a method older by far

than that of historical fiction as it was practiced by Sir Walter Scott";
whereas historical fiction is realistic, seeking to displace myth with
fact, myth exists "when what is unique about periods is dissolved
away, when time becomes meaningless and space replaces time as the
dominant ingredient in fiction" (196–97). When Warren locates
Brother in "no place" and at "no time," he is indicating that he is concerned with myth rather than history, or rather with the permanent
meaning of history. His Jefferson, with his faith in human goodness
and perfectibility shattered by the depravity of his nephews, is totally
unhistorical; Warren is obviously not trying to describe a historical
Jefferson but to criticize the view of man which Jefferson is generally
considered to embody. Holman suggests that *Brother* might be aptly
subtitled "Original Sin on the Dark and Bloody Ground"; and he remarks that this use of history is very old, going back to Shakespeare
and Homer. (I hope Warren reads this essay; the only times I have
heard him complain about critics have been when they have labeled
him a "historical" novelist in the wrong sense.) Richard N. Chrisman
makes a better case against the revision than did Ehrenpreis. He argues
that, though Warren insists that the new version is not a play, it was
strongly influenced by the dramatic version published in 1976, and that
these changes, while improving the poem as drama, disrupt its former
coherence as poem. But Warren's "fundamental poetic task in *Brother
to Dragons* of framing a 'new definition of joy' in the light of new
definitions of humanity has nevertheless survived the editing" (224).
There are several other fine essays, among which must be mentioned
Richard G. Law's analysis of the figure of R.P.W.'s father as the polar
opposite to Lilburn. Finally there is an appendix containing the historical documents in the case: Merrill's account of the murder, a genea-
logical chart of the Jefferson family, and Warren's foreword to the
dramatic version of 1976. The whole book resembles a glorified version
of the casebooks that used to be popular for use as texts; but it would
take celestial freshmen, or infernal and professional critics only, to
make proper use of this one. The controversy is fascinating and most
instructive.

Charles H. Bohner's *Robert Penn Warren*[13] is a revision of a volume
that first appeared in 1964. Bohner's is much superior to most volumes
in the Twayne series. He writes with clarity, concision, and vigor, and
he gets the facts straight and complete. For an account of Warren's
background and early life, and for a brief survey of his whole career,
this book is a good one to start with. Bohner thinks *A Place to Come
To* Warren's best novel since *All the King's Men; Or Else,* his best
volume of poetry since *Promises.* He does not like the new version of

Brother to Dragons as well as the original, but makes sensible comments on the questions of historicity and dramatic quality. This is an intelligent and useful book.

I have saved the best of all these books on Warren until last. James H. Justus's *the Achievement of Robert Penn Warren* is the best single volume covering all of Warren's work yet to appear. Justus makes full use of earlier critics—his preface begins disarmingly: "I would like to think that my views of Robert Penn Warren are fully original, but of course they are not"—but writes freshly, intelligently, and imaginatively. His book is continuously interesting; there is hardly a dull paragraph in it. It is so good that it inspires even this weary reviewer at the end of this long review with the impulse to discuss various points at length, not to disagree but to refine and develop. I will confine myself to noting a few of these points. First, I wish he had been able to think of a better word than *Achievement,* which Matthiessen preempted for Eliot. Second, to say that Warren's career "compares favorably with that of . . . Edmund Wilson and Allen Tate" seems both vague and invidious (it is repeated on the dust jacket): Warren is long past the stage when he needs to be bolstered by such comparisons. Third, I wish he had given more time to the poetry as compared to the novels. Fourth, I wish he did not insist on fitting Warren into an Emerson-Hawthorne dialectic so frequently, though he is certainly right in stressing Warren's continuity with earlier American literature.

These quibbles are nothing compared to the qualities that deserve unquestioning praise. First, readability: Justus grinds no axes, is unfailingly intelligent and perceptive. He is good on the question of historicity in the novels, on Warren's "border" quality, on Warren's scholarship and his deep respect for learning and for history. Although he avoids generalization, Justus is capable of such fine statements as this: "All of Warren's fiction, as well as much of his other work, seems intended, as it were, to counter Thomas Jefferson's extravagant vision of America as a people 'not chosen to fulfill history but a people freed from history.'"[14]

PART · 3 *Criticism*

The Function of Literary Quarterlies

You may expect me to say that the literary situation is very bad and that the critical quarterly is our only hope, the only repository of intelligence and virtue in an evil time. It is fatally easy to let one's defensiveness at the fact that nobody loves the quarterlies express itself in rhetorical exaggerations. Far from believing that the quarterlies are perfect, however, I maintain that they are necessary evils, produced by the peculiar cultural situation of our time, and that they would not have to exist in their present form if the culture were what it should be. But I hold also that the quarterlies are not only symptomatic of our malaise but embodiments, however imperfect, of an ideal of health. I object to the not uncommon diagnosis that identifies the quarterlies as the cause of whatever the diagnostician thinks is wrong with the culture, that makes them—to abandon my overdeveloped medical figure—scapegoats. My purpose is not, however, to offer a blanket defense of them or a jeremiad against our culture, but to consider, with what I hope is reasonable detachment, the nature and function of these magazines.

This chapter, written toward the end of my editorship of the *Sewanee Review* (1952–61) as a lecture to be delivered at the University of Texas, was published in *Texas Quarterly* in 1960. I have left it unchanged except for a few brief additions and deletions. To cover in detail the twenty-six years since it was written would require another essay of equal length, and it seems to me that the basic situation remains much the same. An excellent account of the quarterlies up to 1950 has appeared— G. A. M. Janssens, *The American Literary Review: A Critical History, 1920–1950* (The Hague, 1968)—and George Core, editor of the *Sewanee Review* since 1974, has described the contemporary scene in "*The Sewanee Review* and the Editorial Performance" (*Yearbook of English Studies,* 1979).

The list of "major" quarterlies has often changed over the years: After Ransom's retirement in 1958, *Kenyon* gradually lessened its critical emphasis until in 1966 the editor, Robie Macauley, was simultaneously fiction editor of *Playboy;* after its

To begin with the crudest kind of definition: The literary quarterly or critical review is a noncommercial magazine, uncompromisingly highbrow in character, which publishes criticism of literature and to some extent of the other arts in the form of essays, book reviews, and chronicles, together with fiction and poetry selected according to the kind of high standards defined and employed in the criticism. The proportion tends to be about three parts criticism to one part fiction and poetry. Some quarterlies emphasize political and social criticism; others restrict themselves to an approach primarily aesthetic. All of them give some attention to foreign literatures and ideas, recognizing the ideal of an international community of letters; and all of them make a special effort to discover and help new writers. Although they are always published at a deficit, the quarterlies pay contributors, print some dignified advertising, and are distributed (on a very small scale) to bookstores and newstands.

In its fully developed form, this kind of magazine is peculiar to modern America. It is, of course, a descendant of the *Edinburgh, Quarterly,* and other great critical reviews of nineteenth-century England, though without their political orientation; it is influenced both by the intense aestheticism of the *Yellow Book* and by the

---

rebirth in a new series in 1978, it was certainly no longer a critical quarterly, though lately it seems to be veering back toward that format. Its place was taken, however, by the *Southern Review,* which was revived in 1965 and has followed the old definition. *Partisan* became somewhat less critical and less controversial as it moved from New York to Rutgers and then to Boston University and so lost its New York ambience. Its place was taken, in some ways, by the *New York Review of Books,* which began in the newspaper strike of 1963 and is entirely devoted to criticism (except for the occasional poem); but it is, of course, neither a quarterly nor primarily literary, and it has a vastly larger audience than do the quarterlies. In the seventies, there was a spectacular metamorphosis of the *Georgia Review* under John Irwin, rousing it from somnolent respectability to exciting new critical ventures; and *Tri-Quarterly* appeared, publishing exclusively fiction and poetry, without criticism, like the older *Paris Review* (though both allow interviews and chronicles).

Government subsidy has helped small magazines and small presses, and there seem to be more of them than ever; annual anthologies such as the *Pushcart Prizes* help bring them attention. General magazines, such as *Esquire, Harper's,* and the *Atlantic,* seem to publish even less good fiction and poetry (with occasional exceptions, especially in the *Atlantic*). But neither government subsidy nor the growth of writing programs in universities seems to have had much effect on the fundamental problems. The number of writers, presses, and magazines has increased, but not the size of the audience for serious writing. The audience for the quarterlies does not keep pace with the growth of the population in general; but costs do increase, and subsidies are more necessary than ever.

examples of responsible intellectual leadership provided by such European journals as the *Nouvelle Revue Française.* The two chief immediate predecessors were T. S. Eliot's *Criterion,* published in London from 1922 to 1939, which gave most of its space to discussion of fundamental issues in literary and cultural criticism, and the *Dial,* which, in its second incarnation (1920–29), was strongly aesthetic in emphasis. The *Southern Review* (1935–42) was the first full-fledged example of the form, and a brilliantly successful one.

For more than twenty years, the four dominant literary quarterlies have been the *Sewanee* (1892), *Partisan* (1934), the new *Southern* (1965), and *Hudson* (1948) reviews. (I have given the dates of their founding, but it should be noted that the two older ones did not become primarily literary until after the establishment of the *Kenyon Review* in 1939.) Although they differ widely from one another in history, provenance, and means of support, and each has its individual character and flavor, all of them follow the same basic pattern and share the same problems. In some respects they have come uneasily to regard themselves as collaborators rather than competitors. Throughout this chapter, these four (with the original *Kenyon* and *Southern* reviews) are my primary referents for the term *literary quarterly.*

The literary quarterlies are often called *little magazines* or, more irritatingly, *little mags;* thus they are classed with—and usually by implication compared unfavorably to—the exciting, rebellious, and unpredictable little magazines of the twenties. But to want the quarterlies to be "little mags" is to ignore history: The twenties were a period of vigorous experimentation and revolt in the arts at a time when printing costs—especially abroad, where most of the magazines were published—were very low. *Broom, Blast, Transition, Little Review,* and other little magazines were founded to publish experimental poetry and fiction, and most of them paid little attention to criticism. They were intense and impudent, carefree about deadlines and business arrangements, living very much for the moment. The literary quarterlies represent a different function in a different age: They try to be mature, responsible, and dignified, and they prefer to attract rather than to shock or antagonize the reader. They are institutions, not mere temporary organs for a movement or for publishing a few new writers. To want them to be "little mags" is unrealistic and, one suspects, sentimental: a part of the nostalgia for the twenties so characteristic of our time, a kind of lament for vanished youth. There are, in fact, plenty of "little mags" still appearing and disappearing in this country and abroad, being doggedly experimental and Bohemian in the manner of the twenties; but few people seem to be aware of their existence.

Poetry, the nearest thing to a surviving "little mag," became an institution early and has changed with the times. Together with the group that might be labeled Minor Quarterlies, it has carried on the essential legitimate function of the little magazines: special hospitality to experimentation and innovation. These minor quarterlies—such as *Shenandoah, Prairie Schooner, Antaeus, Grand Street, Salmagundi,* and the late-lamented *Accent, Perspective, Furioso,* and *Hopkins* and *Western* reviews—publish more fiction and poetry than criticism, and tend to concentrate on new and younger writers. (I call them minor because they are smaller in format and circulation, and usually shorter-lived, than the major quarterlies. Two others, however, the *Paris* and *Chicago* reviews, have more professional distribution and promotion, and therefore reputedly larger circulations, than the major ones.) Some members of this group have also managed to carry on the greater tradition of the little magazines—irreverence; any tendency of the major quarterlies to take themselves too solemnly has been promptly ridiculed, and in this as well as other aspects the smaller quarterlies have served as valuable correctives to the larger.

The literary reviews are sometimes confused with two other types of quarterlies that are addressed to intellectual minorities and usually sponsored by universities. One such is the quarterly of general culture which finds its center of interest in public affairs—political, economic, and social issues. Prominent examples are the *Yale* and *Virginia Quarterly* reviews and the *American Scholar.* The audience that is interested in serious discussion of these matters being much larger than that for serious literature, these quarterlies usually have considerably larger circulations than the literary ones, though they are not self-supporting. Most of them publish some criticism, fiction, and poetry; but, presumably because of the larger audience, their literary standards are less rigorous than those of the critical reviews. The second type of intellectual quarterly is the "learned journal," addressed exclusively to specialists and often having a circulation of only a few hundred: for example, in literature, *Philological Quarterly, Studies in Philology, Modern Philology, English Literary History.* The difference between the kind of study published by these journals and the kind published by the literary quarterlies is not absolute but is real; and now that the former bitterness between scholar and critic has abated it can be described neutrally. The learned journals are primarily historical in point of view: They are the repositories of fact and interpretation which will contribute to the understanding of the literature of the past, considered as far as possible for its own sake. The literary quarterlies, on the other hand, are concerned primarily with the present; they are interested in historical studies only if they are relevant in a fairly direct way to contemporary problems, trends, or ideas.

Now that the literary quarterly has been roughly defined and distinguished from other magazines, some attempt must be made to explain what forces brought it into existence. It is impossible to deal adequately here with this large and complex question, and I shall content myself with a few generalizations.

First, the new kinds of literature that rose and flourished in the twenties required a new kind of criticism to explain and justify them. A literary revolution always brings a critical revolution in its wake; and in one obvious and simple sense, this is the origin of the "New Criticism." But the poetry of Pound and Yeats and Eliot, and the fiction of Joyce and James and Faulkner, in complexity and in alienation from their potential audience, went far beyond past literary movements; and a criticism of unprecedented intensity and scope was required to perform the necessary functions of exegesis, mediation, and judgment. In addition, the cultural climate of the age, fundamentally "positivistic" and hostile not only to literature but to the other arts and humanities, required of this criticism a larger function: the defense of the unique value of the imagination and the arts in general. Thus the literary critics were driven, somewhat unwillingly, to the task of trying to impose some order upon cultural chaos. These are the chief reasons why the quarterlies felt it necessary to devote themselves to criticism.

To explain why the literary quarterlies had to be noncommercial magazines, published at a deficit and addressed to a very small minority, we need to consider the sharp division in our time between "serious" and commercial or popular writing. This division is nothing new: It becomes apparent as soon as the literary audience starts to expand in the eighteenth century and Grub Street grows up to pander to the newly literate; but not until the twentieth century does it become the dominant fact of the literary world. As a result of numerous and complex factors—such as the spread of minimum literacy, the development of the mass media of communication (newspapers, comic books, picture magazines, movies, radio, television), with a concomitant decline in the ability to read intelligently, the growth of publishing as a really big business tied up with the book clubs and with Hollywood— a kind of commercialized literature and subliterature to fit the taste of the mass audience is manufactured on a scale and in a variety unknown before. The tremendous pressures of these commodities have tended to push honest or "serious" writing out of the commercial market and leave it without economic status.

The division between "middlebrow" and "highbrow" is much more

pronounced in the United States than in England and France, where
the tradition of the intelligent general reader still persists, as well as
that of support of high culture by those who do not expect to understand it. For example, the taxpayers in both countries support opera,
ballet, and music of the highest quality, and a number of radio programs intended exclusively for the cultivated listener—most notably
the B.B.C. Third Programme, which has provided a kind of state
patronage for serious writers. In both countries there are lively intellectual weeklies, dealing at a high level with literature, the other arts,
politics, religion, and science, combined with some entertainment and
topical journalism—for example, the *New Statesman* and *Times
Literary Supplement* in England, and *Figaro* and innumerable others
in France. The kind of "highbrow-middlebrow" audience that supports
these, together with such monthlies as *Encounter* and the now-defunct
London Magazine, seems not to exist in the United States. The high
degree of specialization among American intellectuals and the rigid
stratification of American culture, which draws a sharp line between
"highbrow" and "middlebrow," have forced the literary quarterlies to
become themselves specialized in appeal.

The fragmentation of our culture of which this division is one sign
is something that every responsible person will try to resist. Could the
quarterlies appeal to some part of the middlebrow audience, without
compromising their standards, merely by avoiding solemnity and un-
necessary austerity and trying to make themselves more attractive?
This is a hope that no man of good will can ever surrender completely.
But the recent history of the "middlebrow" monthlies is not encouraging. The *Atlantic* and *Harper's* used to be addressed to the intelligent
general reader. But because the intelligent general reader apparently no
longer exists in the United States, having perished in the division between "middlebrow" and "highbrow," the monthlies have had to
choose one side or the other, and they have not chosen the higher and
smaller. They are commercial enterprises and therefore driven to try to
increase their circulations so that they can obtain more advertising in
order to show a profit in spite of rising costs. Hence they tend to compete more and more with the mass magazines in offering topical news
and information, superficial "think pieces" on current affairs, "human
interest" pieces by or about celebrities; the poetry and fiction they publish tends to be increasingly superficial and sensational. As everyone
knows, some commercial periodicals do publish good fiction—*The
New Yorker* and *Mademoiselle* and *Harper's Bazaar* and *Vogue*—as did
the old *Life* and the *Saturday Evening Post,* though preferably after the
author had won the Nobel Prize. *Esquire* publishes some good fiction

and even poetry once more, leaving the cartoons and ribald classics to *Playboy.* But these are exceptions, small rocks appearing briefly among the great waves of trash that keep the commercial magazines afloat. The quarterlies would soon find themselves out of their depth and overwhelmed in these dangerous seas if they made any serious effort to appeal to the larger audience.

I

Although the quarterlies are thus resigned to their noncommercial status, they have never been willing to separate themselves entirely from the commercial world. They are dedicated to an ideal, rather than tailored to fit the facts of their circulation; their audience is specialized, but they stubbornly resist specialization. They behave *as if* their contributors were all professional men of letters and their readers were intelligent general readers, responsible patrons of the arts. Hence they pay contributors as well as they can; they try to achieve an attractive format; that carry some dignified advertising; they are distributed (at a loss) to newsstands and bookstores. Refusing to "adjust to reality," they act *as if* there were a profession of letters operating at the center of a unified culture. Sometimes they seem forlorn monuments to the departed "intelligent general reader"; in more hopeful moods they believe that they can accomplish something toward making the facts correspond to the fiction, or ideal, of cultural unity. Whereas other periodicals reflect the fragmentation of our culture into specialized groups, the quarterlies at least make an effort to keep the ideal of cultural unity alive and to reach any surviving, or potential, general readers.

The quarterlies are themselves obviously specialized, in one sense, because they deal chiefly with literary criticism at a professional or technical level. But it is not a trivial paradox to say that this is specializing in the unspecializable. Literature is experience incarnated in form, and all other experience is ultimately relevant to it. In the quarterlies the focus has tended to be on the literature itself, and especially its formal aspects; but the rest of the picture has not been ignored. They have often been described as organs of the New Criticism, which is popularly conceived of as a sterile and pretentious aestheticism. In the first place, the quarterlies have all published attacks on the New Criticism, and they all publish critics whom nobody would describe as New. None of them has ever been committed to any specific aesthetic doctrine: they have never attempted to maintain the kind of orthodoxy that *Scrutiny,* for example, did. Their only commitment is to the belief that criticism is possible and is important. The New Critics have tended to dominate the quarterlies because they have been the best critics available, and not because they have formed a back-slapping clique or sinister conspiracy; when other critics have exhibited a seriousness and competence of the same order, they have been published. Furthermore, the notion that New Critics are pure aesthetes is a product of ignorance or malice. Against those who would reduce literature to philosophy or sociology or history, they have always insisted upon its autonomy as formed experience, its unique ontological status, its cognitive function. But as the threat of tyranny from historicism or "social realism" or Americanism has diminished, this polemical emphasis has also diminished; in their later work most of these critics write explicitly and extensively of the relation of literature to the rest of man's experience.

The quarterlies, then, have the responsibility of maintaining literature as a unifying center for the culture. They have it both by inheritance and by default, since other periodicals do not recognize it. Only in the quarterlies can one hope to find serious and coherent evaluation, independent of the pressures of commercialism and mass opinion, and responsible to the highest intellectual standards. One may not often find it; but at least the ideal is kept alive. As more and more of the quarterlies' contributors and readers come from the universities, there is an increasing temptation for them to become academic and withdraw completely from the world of commercial publishing. But it is vitally important that they maintain their connections with the commercial world, in the hope of influencing it, and that they direct themselves at an imaginary audience of cultivated but unspecialized readers, in the hope of creating such an audience. Instead of lowering their standards to appeal to a larger public, they hope to educate some part of the public into accepting their standards.

Judged by their circulation figures, the quarterlies have had no success whatever in this effort: Most of them have only a few thousand subscribers, no more than the *Dial* in the latter twenties or the *Southern Review* in the thirties, although the population of the United States is half again as large. Circulation figures do not accurately indicate the number of readers: Most of the quarterlies send almost half their copies to libraries, and many of the other copies are read by several persons (since unfortunately many of those most interested in the quarterlies are unable to subscribe). Nevertheless, it would appear that in terms of the size of the immediate audience, the quarterlies have been losing ground by standing still. On the other hand, the immediate audience consists chiefly of writers and would-be writers, critics (including many popularizing critics and reviewers), college teachers and students, and some miscellaneous or general readers, chiefly business and professional men. These are, of course, precisely those people who are in a position to influence a wider public. There is plenty of evidence that the quarterlies achieve an influence out of all proportion to their circulation, and that, indirectly and cumulatively, they do have some effect in educating the public. The point does not need to be argued, for no one denies that they have a considerable influence; the common tendency is to exaggerate this influence and hold the quarterlies responsible for whatever is wrong in the literary world.

Let us consider now some of these criticisms of the quarterlies. They expect to be attacked, and they are resigned to having nobody really like them. Their regular contributors are not happy, both because they would like to have a larger audience and because the quarterlies usually are not able, for reasons of space, to take everything they write. And for every contributor there are hundreds of would-be contributors who quite naturally blame the quarterlies' timidity or snobbery or stupidity or corruption for their rejection. The middlebrow world, when it is aware of the existence of the quarterlies, resents them because it does not understand them and feels that they are exponents of intellectual snobbery. The academic world suspects them of dilettantism and superficiality. There is a vague feeling in many quarters that they are un-American because they are noncompetitive, noncommercial, and dedicated to the fostering of an intellectual elite: This was revealed clearly in the controversy about the Bollingen Award to Pound, when the quarterlies were pictured as agents of a sinister Fascist conspiracy—though they were simultaneously pictured as organs of a frivolous and irresponsible aestheticism. Publishers resent them because they ignore—or, worse, label accurately—most of the books that make money for the publishers. With justice, the quarterlies are sometimes called "unpopular" magazines.

II

These resentments and suspicions are probably inevitable; at any rate, they cannot be dispelled by fact or argument. It may be worthwhile, however, to discuss two plausible criticisms made fairly recently from within the fold, by critics who have themselves written for the quarterlies and who seem to be motivated by genuine concern for literature. Randall Jarrell, in *Poetry and the Age,* argues that the quarterlies are chiefly responsible for making this an age of criticism:

The common reader does not know that it is an age of criticism, and for him it is not. He reads (seldomer and seldomer now) historical novels, the memoirs of generals, whatever is successful. . . . He . . . is neither helped nor hindered by criticism—to him a critic is a best-seller list, only less so. Such a reader lives in a pleasant, anarchic, oblivious world, a world as democratic, almost, as the warm dark depths below, where nobody reads anything but newspapers and drugstore books and comic books and the *Reader's Digest* at the dentist's. This common reader knows what he likes, but is uncomfortable when other people do not read it or do not like it—for what people read and like is good; that is what *good* means.

On the slopes above (as a fabulist might put it) live many races of animals; the most numerous are the members of Book Clubs and the dwellers in the Land of Book Reviews. These find out from their leaders weekly, monthly, what they ought to read, what they ought to like; and since, thank goodness, that is almost always what they would have read and liked anyway, without the help of the reviewers, they all live in unity and amity. It is the country of King Log, the fabulist would say: thousands of logs booming on the hillside, while their subjects croak around them; if you shut your eyes it is hard to tell who reads, who writes, and who reviews. Nearby one finds readers of scholarly journals, readers of magazines of experiment, readers of magazines of verse. But highest of all, in crevices of the naked rock, cowering beneath the keen bills of the industrious storks, dwell our most conscious and, perhaps, most troubled readers; and for these—cultivated or academic folk, intellectuals, "serious readers," the leaven of our queer half-risen loaf—this is truly an age of criticism. It is about them and their Stork Kings that I am going to talk. . . . Four times a year these people read, or try to read, or wish that they had read, large magazines called literary quarterlies. Each of these contains several poems and a piece of fiction—sometimes two pieces; the rest is criticism.[1]

In brief, Jarrell's complaints are, first, that the quarterlies have fostered the belief that criticism is superior to "creative" writing; and second, that they have diverted the talent of young writers from creative writing into criticism. He hopes to make "a few people read a story instead of a crticism, write a poem instead of a review, pay no attention to what the most systematic and definitive critic says against some work of art they love." This is all very persuasive; but, on reflection, it appears to be merely a sophisticated version of an old complaint: "Wordsworth holds the critical power very low, infinitely lower than the inventive; and he said today that if the quantity of time consumed in writing critiques on the works of others were given to original composition, it would be much better employed. . . . A false or malicious criticism may do much injury to the minds of others; a stupid invention, either in prose or verse, is quite harmless." Thus Matthew Arnold, quoting Wordsworth's reported conversation at the beginning of "The Function of Criticism at the Present Time" (1865). You will remember that Arnold first makes the common-sense point that it is not certain that Johnson would have been better employed in producing more *Irenes* than in writing the *Lives of the Poets* or even "that Wordsworth himself was better employed in making his Ecclesiastical Sonnets than when he made his celebrated Preface." He then proceeds to his central argument that the purpose of criticism is to create the free play of ideas as background and material for the production of great literature, "a disinterested endeavor to learn and propagate the best that is known and thought in the world and thus to establish a current of fresh and true ideas." T. S. Eliot's essay "The Function of Criticism" (1923) is in one aspect a commentary on Arnold's. Refusing to make Arnold's large claims for criticism, Eliot defines it as "the commentation and exposition of works of art by means of written words"; its purpose "in this limited sense" is "the elucidation of works of art and the correction of taste." Though he implies that Arnold expects too much of criticism, Eliot agrees as to its importance and necessity; in fact, he says that Arnold has overlooked the capital importance of criticism in the work of creation itself and has distinguished too sharply between the two activities. "The critical activity finds its highest, its true fulfillment in a kind of union with creation in the labor of the artist."

Criticism, then, is not necessarily opposed to, completely separate from, and inferior to the "creative." If a critic succeeds in enriching our experience and awareness, not merely of one poem but of all poetry, it is not self-evident that he has made a less valuable contribution to our self-knowledge and pleasure and understanding than the poet who produces a fifth-rate poem. Some years ago Stanley Hyman, in *The Armed Vision,* argued that

> modern criticism for the most part no longer accepts its traditional status as an adjunct to "creative" or "imaginative" literature. If we define art as the creation of meaningful patterns of experience, or the manipulation of human experience into meaningful patterns, . . . it is obvious that both imaginative and critical writings are art as defined. Imaginative literature organizes its experiences out of life at first hand; criticism organizes its experiences out of imaginative literature, life at

second-hand, or once-removed. Both are, if you wish, kinds of poetry, and one is precisely as independent as the other, or as dependent.[2]

This seems to me to define neatly the false assumption underlying much bad modern criticism: In reassuring the critic that he is just as good as the artist, it also justifies the inferior artist in masquerading as critic and calling his second-hand or fake poetry criticism. Good criticism is not poetry, and it is not autotelic. On the other hand, it need not be limited to the "commentation and exposition" of particular works so that its value is ancillary and exhausted when it has illuminated the work. The larger function of the "correction of taste" requires not only the interpretation of literary experience but also the relating of it to other modes of experience. In performing this larger function, criticism may become literature in at least the same sense that philosophical, historical, or biographical writing may, and may have at least this kind of independent value and permanent interest.

Jarrell's second complaint is that the quarterlies have diverted the talent of young writers from creative writing into criticism. If this ever really happened, it was probably a good thing: Only a feeble talent could be influenced this way, and the stories or poems that might have been produced instead of criticism would almost certainly have been bad. Laborious but uninspired criticism may just possibly be of some use; but unsuccessful poems and stories are certainly worthless unless accidentally funny. But I think Jarrell's impression that promising young writers are all trying to do criticism is simply mistaken: Even now the young writer dreams of being a novelist or poet, not a critic; and, in my experience as an editor, unsolicited manuscripts of poems and stories outnumber those of criticism by at least twenty to one. I do not know of a single example of a promising young creative writer being misled into criticism; it seems more likely, as Norman Podhoretz observed, that some good critics and essayists have been diverted into writing second-rate stories and poems by the excessive piety toward the "creative" manifested by critics such as Jarrell. The leading modern critics have been also fine poets—Eliot, Tate, Ransom, Warren, Blackmur, Empson, Winters; perhaps they would have written more poetry if they had not written so much criticism, but they did not themselves complain of any opposition between the two, and to posit such a conflict seems a rather impertinent speculation.

The notion that the literary quarterlies seldom publish new writers and generally undervalue the "creative" seems to have become a part of our literary mythology. As to new writers, the facts are easy to ascertain, and a glance over the files will show that the quarterlies do publish them regularly. As to the amount of space devoted to poetry and fiction, this is not governed by any assumption of relative values—as if to say that criticism is three times as valuable as "creative" writing— but is what seems sufficient to include most of the poems and stories of real interest and distinction that are available. The amount of poetry and fiction capable of meeting the highest standards which is produced each quarter is not, after all, very large, and a good deal of it never reaches the quarterlies, in spite of their best efforts. There is, fortunately, some competition for good fiction and sometimes even for poetry; and the quarterlies regularly and gladly lose out to magazines that can pay better and reach more readers. There is, after all, no special point in their publishing stories that could be published elsewhere to the author's advantage. But there is no other market—with rare exceptions—for good criticism; and to publish this is, for reasons indicated above, the primary reason for the existence of the reviews.

The other plausible criticism is that made by Malcolm Cowley in *The Literary Situation*.[3] Cowley suggests that the quarterlies, as instruments of the New Criticism, are responsible for producing what he calls the New Fiction. This fiction, he says, is purely aesthetic in emphasis, avoiding social issues and dealing with individual problems in a limited way; it is overly preoccupied with formal qualities and with symbolism. He yearns for naturalistic novels dealing with social issues, instead of this concern with sensitive adolescents, religious questions, private worlds. There are two chief things wrong with this argument. In the first place, it is obvious that the state of the world in general, and social and economic forces in particular, have had far more influence on the writers than any aesthetic doctrine. (Cowley knows this and, after he has finished damning the quarterlies, admits it; but it cannot be dealt with as merely a qualification of the argument.)

In the second place, Cowley says that he is trying to look at these matters as a "cultivated Hindu sociologist" might look at them, and his point of view is thus deliberately naïve and superficial. Thus he lumps together very dissimilar writers, ignores any sort of indirect concern with social issues, and describes only subject matter in the crudest sense. More seriously, he also ignores exceptions to his generalizations, as, for example, Robert Penn Warren, who for many years has regularly written criticism and verse, as well as fiction, for the quarterlies and has helped to edit several of them. He is certainly a master of the New Criticism, and one would expect his novels to exhibit its influence in the most complete way. Yet the novels are very far from agreeing with Cowley's description of the New Fiction: they deal with social issues and confront political questions explicitly; they show mature men and women in a realistic fashion, and not merely as isolated individuals; there is hardly a sensitive adolescent in the lot. Or consider, for another example, Lionel Trilling. Whether he was a New Critic is debatable, but he is certainly typical of one kind of regular critic for the quarterlies. His novel *The Middle of the Journey* and his short story "The Other Margaret" deal with politics as explicitly as anyone could desire. Both Trilling and Warren treat politics in human terms: They show the self-deceptions we are guilty of in the political realm, the corruptions of power. Neither seems to believe that political terms are ultimate or to hope for salvation through politics, and therefore they do not write disguised tracts or propaganda. But I hope Cowley does not mean that he would want them to. On any other ground, it would be very hard to show that the New Criticism has damaged the work of these practitioners of it.

Both Jarrell and Cowley give the quarterlies full credit for their achievements, and both are careful to qualify their criticisms so that they are, if read carefully, informed and not unfriendly strictures. But both pieces have been seized upon gleefully, by those who have always suspected the quarterlies, as giving the "inside story" on the harm they are doing. One is sorry to see the New Illiterates encouraged in their contemptuous dismissal of the New Critics and New Fictionists. The New Fiction is a figment of Cowley's imagination, and the New Criticism does not exist as a definable entity; but the New Illiteracy does exist, and threatens to dominate the publishing business.

III

Since I have kept insisting, while I defended the quarterlies, that I do not think they are perfect, you may have wondered what I consider their real defects to be. At the risk of belaboring the sadly obvious, I will therefore mention briefly what are, in my opinion, some of their worst faults. First, most important, and most obvious, their editors are limited in taste and knowledge, and subject to every kind of error. Sometimes they fail to recognize talent; more often they are taken in by the spurious. Their native tendency to error is increased by special handicaps: Usually they do the editing as a part-time job, teaching or doing other work in addition, and usually they have inadequate clerical and business assistance, so that much of their time is taken up by routine matters. The quarterlies do not have advisory boards of specialists to report on manuscripts, as do the learned journals; nor do they have separate editors for the various divisions—poetry, fiction, articles, reviews, and so on—as do commercial magazines. Instead they have from one to three editors, usually, who divide up all the work. These editors are always rushed and harried; they have to deal very rapidly with unsolicited manuscripts, which come in at the rate of at least three hundred to five hundred a month, and are nagged by the fear that they will therefore overlook a promising writer or fail to recognize a new kind of achievement: they cannot take the time to write as many letters of encouragement and advice as they would like to; and they are left with insufficient time to devote to the actual editing of accepted manuscripts. To add to the pressure, they are usually trying to do some writing of their own.

In addition to these practical difficulties, there is the larger problem of attempting to carry out any editorial policy or program; for a quarterly editor has much less control over what gets written than a commercial editor. Writers for the quarterlies are fiercely independent, as they should be, and resent any undue editorial interference. The editor has to choose his regular contributors and then let them write pretty much as they please; he is likely to find himself publishing much that he does not entirely agree with or perhaps even approve of. I do not mean that the editor is or should be merely passive: He can exert a good deal of influence by encouraging certain kinds of writing and discouraging others, he can solicit and commission work, and occasionally he can get just the writer he wants to deal with the subject he wants at just the time he wants. But his control even over the process of book reviewing is limited and sporadic. He tries to select from the flood of new books those he thinks especially important and especially appropriate for his magazine to review. (Usually, he will give most space to poetry, criticism, philosophy, and other kinds of "unpopular" writing that will not get much attention elsewhere.) He then tries to find a suitable reviewer, but often without success: The reviewer who knows most about the book may be unable to write in a manner suitable to the quarterlies' audience, or may be overly influenced by a personal relationship to the author, as friend or enemy, or may be tied up by other commitments, or may amiably accept the job and then postpone it for years or forget it. The most general difficulty, and one that is insuperable, is that the best-qualified reviewers are often so busy with their own projects that they are understandably reluctant to take time out for reviewing. Since the quarterlies normally publish rather long reviews of a very limited number of books, the operation of all these factors may make the choice of books look capricious or haphazard.

Aside from the defects I have mentioned—those produced by the fallibility of the editors and made worse by the mechanical difficulties inherent in understaffed organizations—I think that the chief faults of the quarterlies are the result of their isolated and insulated situation. Since they are noncommercial and published at a deficit, they cannot begin to pay their contributors enough to live on, so that writing for them has to be an avocation rather than a profession. Since their audiences are extremely small and scattered, there is not a healthy relation between writers and readers. As I have noted, the number of readers is much greater than the circulation figures would indicate, since most copies go to libraries. But people who read magazines in libraries have no stake in them and are less likely to trouble to express themselves to authors or editors than are subscribers, who have, so to speak, made a small investment. Thus library readers, though much better than no audience at all, are not entirely satsifactory; only when the audience makes its reaction known can there be a sense of community between writers and readers. For these reasons, the quarterly writers feel "alienated," and some of them, in defensive reaction, speak like oracles because they are afraid nobody is listening, or say outrageous things in the hope of producing *some* response. They tend to react violently against the low standards of the commercial world; if they are unduly severe on minor writers, as Jarrell complains, this is because they are aware that writers of minor or no talent are acclaimed as "major" and "great" every week in the *New York Times Book Review.*

The quarterlies are sometimes guilty of romanticizing and dramatizing their plight and seeing themselves as the happy few, the saving remnant, doomed but gallant aristocrats defending the old order against the howling mob, or bearers of the true faith hiding in the catacombs of an alien civilization. Such dramatic posturing is usually unconscious and does harm only when it leads the writers to assume an absolute distinction between unpopular art, to which all virtue is attributed, and popular art and mass culture, which is taken to be entirely worthless. But the quarterlies are fairly vigilant against this kind of self-righteousness, and they are far more ready to allow merit to the commercial world than the commercial world is to allow even good intentions to them.

The only effective remedy for these defects would be to make the audience for the quarterlies larger and more responsive, and the quarterlies are constantly seeking ways of doing this. Modern techniques of cheap reproduction and effective distribution have made more good music and painting available, in recent years, to more people than ever before in history; and, through paperback books, good literature and criticism have been distributed to a similarly expanding audience. There should be some way for the quarterlies, or their equivalent, to participate in this expansion and reach this new audience. The paper-back book-magazines—in book form so that they can be distributed and displayed through exactly the same facilities as the popular books—have attempted to do precisely this. They have had some success in reaching the audience—*New World Writing* announced with its seventh issue that it had printed a total of one million copies, and the circulation of the others apparently has been comparable—but they have not been able to maintain a very elevated literary standard while doing this. The trouble is that they depend almost entirely on bookstore and newsstand and drugstore sales rather than subscriptions, and hence need something sensational to attract the casual reader; and since they are commercial ventures they are subject to pressure to keep expanding their sales rapidly. The two earliest, *New World Writing* and *Discovery,* went under in spite of what seem to a quarterly editor staggeringly large sales. *Anchor* and *Evergreen* reviews, backed by publishers of "prestige" paperbacks aimed chiefly at college bookstores, operated on a higher level but made an unashamed "sales pitch," usually based on some current semi-intellectual fad: Zen or the San Francisco School or *Lolita* or Beckett or Ionesco. (The one exception to the preceding generalization is the *New American Review,* which has survived since the mid-sixties without undue commercialization.)

Many years ago R. P. Blackmur (in an essay reprinted in *The Lion and the Honeycomb*)[4] described the economy of the American writer and suggested that the serious artist would have to look for help to the universities and the foundations. He was right: The foundations have helped writers a good deal, sometimes using the quarterlies as agents, and the universities have become large-scale patrons of serious writers, established and aspiring. All this is a kind of artificial stimulation, as is the very existence of the subsidized quarterly addressed to an audience far too small to support it. If, say, one-tenth of the three hundred thousand people who subscribed to *American Heritage* at ten dollars a year (in 1986 it was twenty-four dollars) had enough interest in literature to subscribe to the quarterlies they would be healthier and better and happier magazines. Unfortunately, they cannot appeal through being both expensive and patriotic, like *American Heritage* (superimposing the image of the Cadillac upon the covered wagon), nor can they offer the social cachet and glamour that helps other arts such as music, opera, and dance to meet their deficits, nor the element of gambling—speculating on futures—that helps sell paintings. (*Poetry* magazine has managed to use some of these appeals, together with that to civic pride, in its annual fund-raising dinners; but this is a special case.)

Apparently the quarterlies produce no "consumer's image"; they contribute nothing predictable to a coffee table in the way of atmosphere, and therefore are not likely to be bought for any purpose other than reading.

Unless someone discovers a way to bring to the Mohammed of the quarterlies not a mountain but a least a small hill of an audience, it appears that they will have to continue with their serious make-believe: trying to operate as if their contributors were professional men of letters and their audience mostly intelligent general readers, and they themselves part of the commercial world. Thus they will try to keep alive the ideal of a profession of letters operating with dignity and integrity at the center of a unified culture. This is an ideal and not a reality; it is grotesquely at variance with the facts; and the quarterlies keep it alive only by a kind of hothouse cultivation. But if the climate is unfavorable, we must have hothouses or lose some valuable flowers; and someone may yet discover how to change the weather.

The Criticism of Allen Tate

Like Jonathan Swift, Allen Tate means to vex the world rather than divert it; he hopes to break through the reader's complacent indifference, make him aware of his predicament, and force him to take sides. Since I assume that Tate achieves his purpose, and that most readers will already admire him or dislike him, I shall spend no time in general praise of his career. Tate is, as a critic, essentially a polemicist, an aggressive and sometimes truculent warrior who for more than twenty years has conducted a skillful defensive action. Believing that the best defense is an offense, he has given no quarter to any in whom he detects, under whatever disguise, allegiance to the Enemy—the reigning tyrant, Positivism. Although I do not come to praise Tate, I am not attempting to bury him, for the corpus of his criticism here displayed[1] is still fresh and lively. But the appearance of this collection, together with many other omens, does seem to mark the end of a campaign. The cause that Tate champions has probably won as much territory as it is likely to obtain without a change of strategy; and it is time now for a consolidation of gains, a check of casualities, a regrouping of forces. In the hope of aiding in this necessary task, I shall devote my review to analysis of the ideas and assumptions upon which his criticism is founded. There is plenty of comment on Tate, but most of it is controversial and partial; a reasonably objective attempt to define

Although this chapter is early (1949), belongs so much to its time that I have not tried to detach it by revision, and is incomplete in that it does not cover the essays written after Tate's conversion to Roman Catholicism (collected in *The Forlorn Demon*, 1953, and *Essays of Four Decades*, 1969), it seems to me still essentially valid. Tate, with his usual candor and generosity, wrote at the time, "You have, of course, put your finger on the fundamental trouble." For me, it was the beginning of a lifelong and much-treasured friendship and of my connection with the *Sewanee Review* and later with Sewanee itself.

the basic convictions underlying the various essays should, therefore, serve a useful function.

First, a note on the contents of *On the Limits of Poetry.* Tate is a severe critic of his own work, and he has collected here only a small part of this critical writing. Specifically, the book contains five essays not published before in book form, and most of the contents of Tate's two previous volumes of criticism (three pieces from each of them are omitted). The essays are arranged in five sections. Those in the first concern the relation of literature to society, and define the functions of literature and criticism in an age dominated by Positivism; the fourth group consists of essays similar in approach, but dealing with the special problems of Southern society and literature. The pieces in the second division are general discussions of the nature of poetry and, more briefly, of fiction. The third section is composed of extended interpretations and evaluations of particular poets; the final group consists of shorter comments, written originally as reviews, on individual poets. The new essays reveal no important change in Tate's views, though they do seem to indicate a certain broadening of interest. In "A Reading of Keats," for example, Tate approximates "total" criticism, and of a Romantic poet; in "Techniques of Fiction" he deals with the novel; and in "The Hovering Fly" he ventures farther than usual into aesthetic theory. In the latter two pieces he substitutes for his usual blunt directness a more subtle and tentative style, which is even, at times, reminiscent of Virginia Woolf. But, with these minor differences, the new essays fit naturally into place beside the old. Tate's criticism is remarkably homogeneous; his basic principles and methods have remained unchanged, as far as I can tell, from his first essay to his latest. In discussing his work, I shall therefore ignore chronology.

Tate's approach to criticism is refreshingly modest. Criticism, he holds, is a form of literature, since it tells us the meaning and value of concrete experience; but it is definitely not autotelic: Its purpose is "the protection of that which in itself is the end of criticism"—creative writing. The function of criticism is "to maintain and to demonstrate the special, unique, and complete knowledge which the great forms of literature afford us" (8). It must instruct the reader in "the exercise of taste, the pursuit of standards of intellectual judgment, and the acquisition of self-knowledge" (66). Its function, in thus creating a proper audience for imaginative writing, is highly important, especially in times such as the present; but it is distinctly subordinate. Tate's criticism fits his own definition: It is intended to educate the reader and guide him to an understanding of literature, and especially of modern poetry. To achieve this purpose, the negative task of preventing the audience from misunderstanding literature through expecting too much, or the wrong things, of it is now most urgent: "On reading my essays over, I found that I was talking most of the time about what poetry cannot be expected to do to save mankind from the disasters in which poetry itself must be involved. . . . Lessing says that poetry is not painting or sculpture; I am saying in this book, with very little systematic argument, that it is neither religion nor social engineering" (xi).

For the most part, Tate aims at the limited objective of destroying popular misconceptions that distort or prevent the reception of poetry among its potential audience. Since he emphasizes this corrective function, he does not elaborate his positive demonstration of the value of literature, which is developed mostly by implication. All criticism, Tate believes, is limited and partial: There "are all kinds of poetry . . . and no single critical insight may impute an exclusive validity to any one kind" (75). The critic "is convinced that the total view is no view at all, the critic not being God, and convinced too that even if (which is impossible) he sees everything, he has got to see it from somewhere" (149). And his own criticism, he points out in his preface, is particularly unsystematic and incomplete: Most of his essays are occasional, controversial, and comparatively brief; hence they represent opinion rather than any fully developed theory. In the face of this disclaimer, to discuss Tate in terms of general principles may seem unfair or foolish. Yet even negative criticism must proceed from a coherent intellectual position if it is to be valid; and permanent value will depend upon the presence, by implication at least, of a satisfactory positive theory.

I

The central theme in Tate's criticism of society may be stated simply: the "deep illness of the modern mind," which he labels *Positivism,* has deprived modern man of tradition and of the religion upon which tradition ultimately depends. Positivism (scientism, pragmatism, instrumentalism), assuming that all experience can be ordered scientifically, reduces the spiritual realm to irresponsible emotion, irrelevant feeling. Regarding action as an end in itself, and concerned only with practical results, it substitutes method for intelligence. It interprets history in terms of abstract concepts of natural law and quantitative differences (the historical method instead of the historical imagination); ignoring the concrete particularity of history, it compels no choice, no imaginative identification. Thus Positivism destroys tradition and cuts man off from his past.

Against the Positivist spirit, Tate asserts the existence and value of tradition and of the individual intelligence. With T. E. Hulme, he assumes "a radical discontinuity between the physical and spiritual realms" (4); "it is contrary to the full content of our experience to assume that man is continuous with nature" (308). Only the traditional religious attitude is true to man's total experience. The form of society depends ultimately upon religion, for "the social structure depends on the economic structure, and economic conviction is still . . . the secular image of religion" (316–17). Tate illustrates through a horse metaphor, much like Ransom's image of the World's Body: The Positivist sees only one half of the horse, the Irrationalist (Symbolist, Mystic) sees the other half; the religious imagination alone is aware of the horse as he really is. Abstracting the rational, predictable aspects of experience, and forgetting the other half of man's total experience — the concrete, unpredictable qualities that constitute the traditional awareness of evil — Positivism worships the false absolute of omnipotent human rationality. A society dominated by this demi-religion, which falsifies the nature of man and ignores its own failures, says Tate (invoking the concepts of *hubris* and *nemesis*), is "riding for a crushing fall," and it "will be totally unprepared for collapse" (308). A traditional society depends upon a true religion of the whole horse.

The essence of tradition, Tate believes, is a harmony between man's moral nature and his economics, between his way of life and his way of earning a living. This harmony can best be achieved in an agrarian society: "Traditional property in land was the primary medium through which man expressed his moral nature; and our task is to restore it or to get its equivalent today" (303). Modern man has lost not only the religious imagination with its Christian mythology but also the historical imagination, which, since the Renaissance, has furnished substitute myths through which men have dramatized themselves as Greeks or as Romans of the Republic; he is therefore unable to form any imaginative version of himself. Tate interprets the "Game of Chess" section of *The Waste Land* as a symbol of the "inhuman abstraction if the modern mind," deprived of both kinds of imagination: "It means that in ages which suffer the decay of manners, religion, morals, codes, our indestructible vitality demands expression in violence and chaos; it means that men who have lost both the higher myth of religion and the lower myth of historical dramatization have lost the forms of human action; it means that they are no longer capable of defining a human objective, of forming a dramatic conception of human nature" (301).

Tate upholds Regionalism as one aspect of tradition. Dismissing the "picturesque regionalism of local color" as a by-product of literary nationalism, he defends true Regionalism: "that consciousness or that habit of men in a given locality which influences them to certain patterns of thought and conduct handed to them by their ancestors" (286). Its opposite is Provincialism, whose horizons are geographically larger but spiritually smaller; Regionalism is limited in space but not in time, whereas Provincialism is limited in time but not in space. The provincial man "cuts himself off from the past, and without benefit of the fund of traditional wisdom approaches the simplest problems of life as if nobody had ever heard of them before" (186). Provincialism is increasingly our ideal; in our secular Utopianism we think that we should "save" others with the gospel of world Provincialism, for we have forgotten the nature of man.

Tate's comments on the South constitute his most extensive specific application of these general ideas. Although the ante-bellum South was a traditional society, it failed, for two main reasons, to produce great literature. First, because it was an aristocracy (which is, like plutocracy, class rule), and its best intellectual energy therefore went into politics; second, because of slavery—not that slavery was immoral, but that the Negro was alien. "All great cultures have been rooted in peasantries," but the Negro was not a good root; the "white man got nothing from the Negro, no profound image of himself in terms of the soil" (273). Considering Southern society generally, Tate finds the chief cause of its downfall in the lack of an adequate or appropriate religion. An agrarian economy, the South had "a non-agrarian and trading religion that had been invented in the sixteenth century by a young finance-capitalist economy" (316), and Southerners developed no philosophy or body of doctrine of their own. This failure of the South to possess a "sufficient faith in her own kind of God," and not the Civil War ("the setback of the war was of itself a very trivial one" [321]), is responsible for its ultimate spiritual defeat, its present conversion from Regionalism to Provincialism.

Although I do not intend to quibble about specific points, and I certainly do not wish to revive extinct controversies, I feel that two general difficulties in Tate's view of society should be mentioned. In "Humanism and Naturalism" (*Reactionary Essays;* not reprinted in this collection), Tate argued that the Humanism of Babbitt and More "is obscure in its sources; it is even more ambiguous as to the kind of authority to which it appeals." The Humanists make literature a substitute for philosophy and religion; their Socratic method yields no absolutes, and ultimately they pursue morality for morality's sake. Tate concludes: "There should be a living center of action and judgment, such as we find in the great religions, which in turn grew out of this center. The act of 'going into the Church' is not likely to supply the convert with it. Yet, for philosophical consistency, this is what the Humanists should do. . . . The religious unity of intellect and emotion, of reason and instinct, is the sole technique for the realization of values."[2]

With his usual candor, Tate makes no secret of the fact that he is himself unable to accept religious faith;[3] his own attitude would seem to exemplify what he calls, speaking of John Peale Bishop, "our modern unbelieving belief"—the "attempt to replace our secular philosophy, in which he does not believe, with a vision of the divine, in which he tries to believe" (247). He is more logical and consistent than the Humanists in stating that the traditional view of human nature and the traditional society that embodies it are based ultimately upon religion, that religion is the core of the problem. But it is hard to see why Tate's criticism of the Humanists does not apply essentially to his own position. Lacking belief himself, he cannot derive authority for his values from religion or find any positive way of realizing them. In another essay not included in this volume, "Liberalism and Tradition" (*Reason in Madness*), Tate defends himself against such criticisms. Workability and truth, he points out, are not identical; belief is not to be confused with potentiality of fact: Whether a traditional society is possible in the future is a question of fact, but that moral unity in such a society is "the highest good that men can seek to achieve"[4] is an imperative of reference. Similarly, the traditionist may believe that modernism is false without having, necessarily, any special positive beliefs; appealing to history, he is convinced that "man needs absolute beliefs in order completely to realize his nature," even though he himself, affected by the mental climate of his time, cannot accept absolutes (206). But even the non-Positivist reader will ask (as does Tate in the Humanism essay) what can be done to attain these desirable values; and he will find no adequate answer. "Being from all salvation weaned" like the moderns in his poem "The Cross," Tate is, I think, driven unwillingly to set up false absolutes; and the attempt to posit moral unity and traditional society as absolute imperatives of reference is foredoomed to failure; for they can derive sanction and workability only from religion. Religion cannot take its sanction from tradition and moral unity considered as absolutes, although this seems to be Tate's conception; to strive to achieve a society in which belief will be possible is to begin at the wrong end. I am afraid that Tate's comment on the Humanists applies equally to his own social criticism: "The truth of their indictment, negatively considered, cannot be denied. But this is not enough" (113).

II

In literary criticism, according to Tate, Positivism dominates academic historical scholarship and sociological (he has in mind primarily Marxist) criticism. Critics of both these schools subscribe to the Doctrine of Relevance, which "means that the subject-matter of a literary work must not be isolated in terms of form; it must be tested (on an analogy to scientific techniques) by observation of the world that it 'represents.'"[5] Assuming that literary works are not existent objects, but are expressive of substances beyond themselves, the Postivist cannot discuss the literary object in terms of its specific form; he can only "give you its history to tell you how he feels about it" (56); he is either naturalistic or impressionistic. Refusing to judge, Positivists deny their moral nature and intelligence; substituting for them the historical method, they dissolve the literature into its history. The historical scholar defends himself by the hypocritical pretense that his work is a preparation for future criticism, just as Positivist social planners ask us to look for reference not to the past, but to the future. Against these trends, Tate asserts the necessity of intellectual and moral responsibility toward both past and present: "We must judge the past and keep it alive by being alive ourselves; and that is to say that we must judge the past not with a method or an abstract hierarchy but with the present, or with as much of the present as our poets have succeeded in elevating to the objectivity of form" (60).

Although Tate has occupied himself mainly with demonstrating that poetry is not what the Postivists variously take it to be—history, emotion, false science, propaganda, religion—he has always maintained positively that its true value is cognitive, that it gives us a unique, true, and complete knowledge (e.g., 8, 47, 95, 113, 250). Usually, he rests his case upon simple assertion, with little explanation. The only systematic exposition of his theory of poetry that I have been able to discover is that in his early essay "Poetry and the Absolute."[6] Since his later remarks are more comprehensible in the light of this explicit statement, a brief summary of it will perhaps be useful. Both poet and philosopher, Tate argues, strive to construct a "portrait of reality" that will be absolute; but the poetic absolute, being "a function of subject-matter in interaction with a personality," is not single and unchanging like the metaphysical; it is capable of infinite re-creations. The poetic absolute is achieved, created, in terms of form. The poet may come to terms with his experience through contemplating it in the created absolute of art; he constructs the possibility of this kind of absolute experience first of all for himself, but if the perceptions are perfectly realized, presented free of the disturbance out of which they have sprung, the poem will provide the same absolute experience for others. If, on the other hand, the poem is not completely realized, it presents an inferior and mixed experience like that of ordinary life; it may even increase the disturbance normally connected with such experience and do moral damage. Romantic poets produce poems that are absolute only in the sense that they have no connection with the practical, relative world:

> But Donne created a permanent focus of emotional reference out of the disorder of feeling started in him by frustrated love. He did not wish to discover an escape from emotion. . . . The world of "The Funeral" is a section of the known world. . . . But there is a particular quality of the poem that makes it wholly unlike the portion of the knowable world for which it stands; as a portion it is complete, it is finite. There is nothing beyond it; while in the current of ordinary experience the last consequent is always a fresh antecedent; the practical world of science has no dimensions, no frame, no form. "The Funeral" has form — completeness, finality, absolutism. And it is great art because its absolute quality is created out of the perceptions not of an easy, imaginable world, but of the accepted, common-sense world. (42)

In the absolute poem, any original ulterior motive is absorbed and implicit in form, not explicit and didactic; only if the poet can accept his experience without too much intermediary rationalizing — which is not so much interpretation of experience as rejection of it — can he come to absolute terms with it. "For the perfectly realized poem has no overflow of unrealized action. It does not say that men ought to be better or worse, or as they are; it has no ulterior motives" (44). The bad poem confronts the reader with the problem the poet should have solved for him; there is a diffusion of interest beyond the margins of the poem, and some extra-aesthetic activity is demanded. But great poets are absolutists; there is nothing beyond their poetry. Donne found the "ultimate value of experience to be its ordered intensification; and this is the sole value and meaning of poetry. He found this meaning in absolute form" (45). This absolute quality, Tate concludes, explains the necessity for poetry: If the need of the mind for absolute experience could be satisfied adequately in ordinary experience, this experience, metaphysically defined and classified, would be sufficient; but only sentimentalists hope for a world absolute of this sort. Art alone provides absolute experience.

Perhaps Tate decided that the term *absolute* was misleading, for he does not use it in his later comments on the nature of poetry. These comments are, in other respects, entirely consistent with the earlier essay; in fact, two of the new essays in this collection seem to indicate a curiously specific return even to its terminology. "Techniques of Fiction" defines the "completeness of presentation," "fullness of realization" achieved by Flaubert, through which the novel caught up at last with poetry; the distinction is between "getting it [the original purpose] all inside the book and leaving some of it irresponsibly outside."[7] In "The Hovering Fly," the conclusion is that "we shall not know the actual world by looking at it; we know it by looking at the hovering fly" (156; the fly, of course, symbolizes Art).

This aesthetic is obviously, in a sense, art for art's sake, and Tate does not disclaim the inevitable label. Discussing the kind of knowledge gained from poetry, he remarks:

> It is not knowledge "about" something else; the poem is the fulness of that knowledge. We know the particular poem, not what it says that we can restate. . . . I have expressed this view elsewhere in other terms, and it has been accused of aestheticism or art for art's sake. . . . There is probably nothing wrong with art for art's sake if we take the phrase seriously, and not take it to mean the kind of poetry written in England forty years ago. Religion always ought to transcend any of its particular uses; and likewise the true art for art's sake view can be held only by persons who are always looking for things that they can respect apart from use (though they may be useful), like poems, fly-rods, and formal gardens. (250)

This defense of poetry as knowledge, through an effective controversial technique, seems ultimately dubious, for it depends on a semantic shift: Tate's *knowledge,* which is about itself, proves nothing, explains nothing, and "has no useful relation to the ordinary forms of action" (113), is certainly not *knowledge* in the Positivist or any ordinary sense. But the important point is that Tate seems to mean by *knowledge* precisely what he earlier termed *absolute experience:* the contemplation or vision or revelation of absolute truth sought usually in philosophy and religion. And this goes beyond art for art's sake; it suggests life for art's sake. In asserting that art, and only art, gives us this absolute knowledge, Tate seems to be doing (much more subtly and intelligently) what he takes others to task for: making art a substitute for religion. In order to understand Tate's scale of values, however, we must examine his comments on the relation of art to society.

III

Although Tate regards genuine poetry as autotelic and unconcerned with action, he attributes to it an important, if indirect, moral and social function. Poetry is above morality, but it assumes its existence: "a mind without moral philosophy is incapable of understanding poetry. For poetry, of all the arts, demands a serenity of view and a settled temper of the mind, and most of all the power to detach one's own needs from the experience set forth in the poem" (342–43). Poetry belongs to the realm of contemplation, which is an end in itself, and beyond—though not unrelated to—practical ethics: "Perhaps the act of contemplation after long exercise initiates a habit of restraint and the setting up of absolute standards which are less formulas for action than an interior discipline of the mind" (317). Thus demanding and encouraging contemplation, poetry has the indirect psychological function of counteracting over-emphasis on the will: "Poetry finds its true usefulness in its perfect inutility, a focus of repose for the will-driven intellect that constantly shakes the equilibrium of persons and societies with its unremitting imposition of partial formulas. When the will and its formulas are put back into an implicit relation with the whole of our experience, we get the true knowledge which is poetry" (113). As this quotation implies, Tate sees the social effect of poetry as essentially conservative: Poetry is "the instinctive counter-attack of the intelligence against the dogma of future perfection for persons and societies"; it "tests with experience the illusions that the human predicament tempts us in our weakness to believe" (340).

Tate is, however, much more interested in the effect of society on poetry than in the effect of poetry on society. His view is, with some qualifications, deterministic; and its most extreme embodiment is the concept of the "perfect literary situation." The perfect literary situation occurs when a tradition, a culture, is breaking up; the "poet finds himself balanced upon the moment when such a world is about to fall" (209). The world order can then be assimilated to the poetic vision, "brought down from abstraction to personal sensibility." In such an age the clash of powerful opposites "issues in a tension between abstraction and sensation"; the poet is able to fuse sensibility and thought, perceive abstraction and think sensation. "Only a few times in the history of English poetry has this situation come about, notably, the period between about 1580 and the Restoration" (204). From the similar age in New England emerged two great talents, Hawthorne and Emily Dickinson; and the recent Southern renascence sprang from another such transition, on a lesser scale, as the South changed from traditional Regionalism to Provincialism (281). Poetry "probes the deficiencies of a tradition. But it must have a tradition to probe" (208). The poet criticizes his tradition, puts it to the test of experience, compares it with something that is about to replace it.

The perfect literary situation is obviously not by any means the perfect situation for society as a whole; great art is produced not by traditional societies, but by the breakup of such societies. With his usual candor, Tate makes this conflict of values perfectly explicit; speaking of the moral aspect of Emily Dickinson's poetry, he says that it is "a magnificent personal confession, blasphemous and, in its self-revelation, its honesty, almost obscene. It comes out of an intellectual life towards which it feels no moral responsibility" (213). "In Miss Dickinson, as in Donne, we may detect a singularly morbid concern, not for religious truth, but for personal revelation. The modern word is self-exploitation. It is egoism grown irresponsible in religion and decadent in morals. In religion it is blasphemy; in society it means usually that culture is not self-contained and sufficient, that the spiritual community is breaking up. This is . . . the perfect literary situation" (208).

There would seem to be, in Tate's thought, a fundamental ambiguity, for his two goals—great art and a traditional society—ultimately conflict. And art is largely determined by society: Tradition provides its myths, controlling ideas, unification of sensibility, apprehension of total experience; yet for its greatest stimulation it requires the disintegration of tradition. Tate, however, frequently implies that the two goals agree, when he is discussing social questions or modern poetry. The two problems involved—primacy of values and literary determinism—he never considers directly. My impression is that the aesthetic value is primary for Tate (though he does not want to change society only for the sake of art); as to literary determinism, the inconsistency results from his double purpose: He wishes to defend modern poetry, and at the same time he uses its defects as a basis for condemnation of the society that produced it; the first motive leads him to minimize the relationship between literature and society, and the second to emphasize it. Hence Tate's attitude toward contemporary poetry is curiously ambivalent.

Modern poetry, as Tate sees it, is the culmination of tendencies beginning at the Renaissance, and manifest in poetry since the Restoration. The loss of traditional religious and moral unity and the spread of Positivism have led the public to expect poets to give them new systems of belief; the poets, forsaking their proper function, have misguidedly attempted to do so. In "Three Types of Poetry" Tate describes the "heresy of the will," positive and negative Platonism (i.e., roughly, allegorical or optimistic acceptance of science, and "romantic irony," which rejects it and becomes escapist), which has ruined most poetry for the last one hundred and fifty years; genuine poetry, in contrast, presents an imaginative vision of the whole of life, the vision itself being its own goal. In "Tension in Poetry" he puts essentially the same thesis into different terms, this time labeling the trouble the "fallacy of communication," which leads poets either to compete directly with science or to reject all claim to truth and reality. In technique, the two extremes manifest themselves as the Metaphysical (stressing extension, denotation) and the Symbolist (stressing intension, connotation); the greatest poetry is that of the center, achieving neither extension nor intension but *tension*. Since the Restoration, the dramatic instinct has survived best in lyric poets; for, lacking any epos or myth, any "pattern of well-understood behavior," poets are unable to write longer works successfully. "With the disappearance of general patterns of conduct, the power to depict action that is both single and complete also disappears . . . the dramatic lyric is a fragment of a total action which the poet lacks the means to sustain" (364). Modern poetry lacks *form,* in the larger sense in which Tate uses the term: "Form is meaning and nothing but meaning: scheme of reference, supporting symbolism that ceases to support as soon as it is recognized as merely that" (240). "In ages weak in form, such as our own age, theory will concentrate upon form, but practice upon the ultimate possibilities of language" (239). Our criticism, he remarks, is better than our poetry; the Elizabethans, in contrast, "wrote better than they knew." Having form in poetry, they concentrated in their (rudimentary) criticism upon propriety in language; we, lacking form, concern ourselves with it in criticism, but in poetry we try to compensate for deficiency in form by forcing language beyond its natural limits. The degeneration of public language provides further incentive for specialization of language: "Today many poets are driven to inventing private languages, or very narrow ones, because public speech has become heavily tainted with mass feeling" (76). Modern poets, because nineteenth century poets used subject matter badly, tend to be afraid of it and to try to do without it completely ("Poetry and the Absolute"). With the loss of tradition, of a common center of experience, specialization thus supplants a central view of life, and poetry becomes specialized aesthetic effects without formal limitations; distinctions of *genres* disappear; the arts tend to become geometrical and abstract. The novel, the least formal of the arts, takes the place of the epic and tragedy; lacking formal limitations and appealing to the ordinary sense of reality, it drives out the formal arts. The great problem of the modern poet is (since no substitute is ultimately satisfactory) to find a central source of form; and only Yeats, in Tate's view, has had much success in solving the problem. As John Peale Bishop represents, for Tate, the unsuccessful search for form, Hart Crane is the symbol of our spiritual life; his poetry "reveals our defects in their extremity" (235). Crane ends the romantic era; by "attempting an extreme solution of the romantic problem Crane proved that it cannot be solved" (237). He represents the narcissistic sensibility divorced from intelligence, relying upon "the intensity of consciousness, rather than the clarity, for his center of vision." This dissociation, because of our lack of an objective system of truth, a myth, a tradition, is characteristic of modern poets generally. (Again, Tate excepts Yeats, whom he seems to regard as a conspicuous exception to literary determinism, a great poet in spite of the defects of his age.)

Defending modern poetry against the charge of "difficulty," Tate asserts in one magnificent counterblast that the fault is not in the poetry, but entirely in the readers. The villain is Positivism, which, through modern education, has taught us that poetry is purely emotional; that reading, and education, are passive conditioning; that there is no such thing as intelligence or cognition. We are incapable of understanding *any* genuine poetry, not merely modern poetry: "If we wish to understand anything, there is only the hard way . . . we had better begin, young, to read the classical languages, and a little later the philosophers" (128). In a more temperate discussion, he distinguishes two types of misguided readers: the innocent reader, who lives in the past, and the social reader, who lives in the future; both have their heads buzzing "with generalizations that they expect the poet to confirm — so that they will not have to notice the poetry. It is a service that the modern poet, no less amiable than his forbears, is not ready to perform; there is no large scheme of imaginative reference in which he has confidence" (xv). Loss of tradition makes modern poetry available to a more restricted group than was poetry of the past; only to the proper reader, "the critical reader," who is aware of the present, not in terms of abstractions, but of experience. Tate's considered judgment seems to be that the difficulty of modern poetry, as well as its grave limitations and deficiencies, is real, but that it is the result of historical circumstances for which the poets are not responsible and which they cannot escape. The implied moral is that if we do not approve of the poetry, we must change the society that makes it what it is.

IV

Because Tate's criticism is intended as a corrective, a "reaction," and not as self-sufficient, many of his specific ideas and interpretations appear oversimplified or extreme when taken out of their controversial context. My concern has been not to dispute any such matters, but to determine, as precisely as possible, just what Tate's essential postion is. I do not know how completely these essays represent Tate's own philosophy; but they seem to reveal a fundamental inconsistency. Unable to accept religion (but convinced of its necessity), Tate is driven to set up art and traditional society (or the moral unity to be attained within it) as absolutes; the two agree imperfectly, and are unreconciled. Tate's literary criterion is a rigorous one: Most poetry lacks absolutism, and he is therefore occupied most of the time with explaining the failure of poetry in terms of its relation to society. Being a poet, he wishes to defend modern poetry (and the poetry of the past which is most like modern poetry); yet, largely on the evidence of the poetry, he condemns the society; and this dual purpose produces further ambiguities. Tate would probably say that only a Positivist would look to a literary critic for philosophy, and I hope that I have not appeared to do so; my point is only that the criticism would be more effective if the central ideas were clarified. Tate, who exhibits himself the self-knowledge he recommends, is aware that theorizing is not his forte; he omits from this collection the essays that deal most systematically with general ideas. I do not mean for a moment to suggest that Tate should be set up as aesthetician or philosopher, instead of continuing to do what he does so admirably; but I think that we need desperately, at this stage of our criticism, a satisfactory general theory. Even Tate's inconsistencies, however, are valuable; because of his honesty and refusal to compromise, they reveal "our defects in their extremity."

Tate's character as critic may be illustrated by a brief comparison to other critics. He is much like Yeats—from whom, apparently, he takes the key terms *abstraction* and *unity of being*—in his bitter hatred of science, which deprives him of religious faith; like Yeats, he undertakes his social and philosophical analysis with a motivation that I take to be basically aesthetic. Tate's general ideas, literary and social, are most like those of T. S. Eliot; the chief difference is that Eliot puts the position into explicitly religious terms and that his standard of values is therefore definite and unambiguous. Yvor Winters, like Tate, upholds a position ultimately religious without religious sanction, but otherwise there is little similarity. Tate is less rigid than Winters in literary judgment; he does not expect perfection, or criticize in terms of what *ought* to have been done. Winters is, of course, a moralist; and he regards action, conduct, as the goal; Tate exhibits on occasion an aristocratic contempt for the merely ethical. There is a strong Aristotelian element in Tate's whole philosophy: the highest good is the contemplation of absolute truth (for Tate, art), while practical ethics belongs to a lower realm; in aesthetic theory, *cartharsis* and *mimesis* can be detected; and Tate's mind seems to work in terms of extremes versus the mean (e.g., the two half religions versus genuine religion; poetry of positive and negative Platonism versus that of the center; poetry of extension and intension versus that of tension; the innocent and social reader versus the critical). In this emphasis on contemplation, not ethics, as the sphere of art, Tate is like Ransom, as also in the concept of poetry as knowledge. Ransom, however, is not so violently reacting against Positivism; his structure-texture formulation and many other aspects of his criticism are unlike Tate. Cleanth Brooks has tried to develop a critical theory similar to Tate's into a positive system; but it seems to me that one result of his excellent work has been to reveal certain contradictions more explicitly: for example, while maintaining the same kind of "historical fatality" in the relation of literature to society, he holds that much contemporary literature is great, while society is bad.

I do not wish to suggest that Tate's deficiencies in theory and logical inconsistencies (those I have pointed out; my interpretation cannot be entirely correct, and there may not be as many as I think) invalidate his criticism; many values, and those not the least important, are not dependent primarily on theory. In conclusion, I shall summarize what I take to be the chief permanent values of Tate's criticism. First, the essays aid one to understand Tate's own poetry: Not only do they define the kind of poetry he is trying to write, but they state explicitly most of the ideas and attitudes found in the poems. And Tate's poetry is so fine that this use alone would justify the essays (though I doubt that Tate would entirely approve). Second, the prose exhibits the same gift of language that distinguishes the poetry—the same concentration, imaginative power, boldness combined with restraint. Tate can sum up a whole indictment, a whole philosophy, in a sardonic sentence or a vivid metaphor. Yet the style is refreshingly simple and unpretentious, for he holds the sensible view that "critical style ought to be as plain as the nose on one's face; that it ought not to compete in the detail of sensibility with the work which it is privileged to report on" (x). Third, in the realm of ideas, his conception of history—the contrast of the traditional religious imagination, which sees the past as temporal and concrete, with the modern historical method, which sees it as abstract and detemporalized—is, with its corollaries and accompanying insights, his most important contribution. The bold simplification of reducing the enemy to Positivism, which is traced through its multiple metamorphoses, and the conception of poetry as the absolute are (whatever the difficulties involved) effective and valuable formulations. Finally, Tate's greatest virtue is one I have had almost wholly to leave out of account in this review. His analysis of specific poems are masterly: Their most remarkable feature is that they stress heavily the element of meter, rhythm, music, which most critics tend to neglect; Tate relates this element to the whole meaning and effect of the poem, and discusses it with an intelligence and sensitivity that are, as far as I know, unique. In reviewing contemporary poets, Tate is free of the note of envy or malice which so often mars reviews of poets by poets; he does not reduce his critical apparatus to a formula, as even such excellent critics as Ransom, Brooks, and Winters tend sometimes to do. These reviews, generous yet just and penetrating, are perhaps the soundest judgments we have; their only defect is a tendency to blame the society for all the faults of the poetry, and that is a defect compounded of generosity and polemic intent.

The final impression *On the Limits of Poetry* leaves is one of admiration for Tate's independence and common sense and avoidance of cant; for his stubborn honesty and candor; for his ideal of poise, integrity, and intelligence.

A Little Man Who Was a Writer: R. P. Blackmur

Hic Jacet Homunculus Scriptor was the epitaph Henry Adams composed for himself, and Russell Fraser suggests that it applies equally well to R. P. Blackmur, who identified himself with Adams so closely that he was never able to finish the book about him that he worked on all his life and intended as his major work. That Blackmur was a genuine writer—a major critic and a minor poet—is hardly open to dispute; that he was a small man, physically and psychically, *A Mingled Yarn: The Life of R. P. Blackmur*[1] provides abundant evidence. (He was not petty, and *small-minded* seems too severe; but no one could call him magnanimous.) More successfully than most literary biographers, Fraser reveals how the writing was related to the man's limited capacities, how the same pressures that left him emotionally stunted and distorted also drove him to write. Fraser never reduces him to a case history and wisely avoids diagnostic jargon (he will go only so far as to remark that his "handwriting was stingy—the Freudians would say it was anal"). After reading this book, a Freudian would say a lot more than that: Blackmur was a classic and extreme example of the anal type of severe neurotic, compulsive-retentive-obsessive-defensive-sadistic in character; without the sublimation he found in writing, he would probably have been a hopeless neurotic, unable to function at all. All the typical elements are there: a weak father for whom Blackmur felt only contempt and hatred; an overwhelming mother who lavished upon him all the love she had ceased to feel for her husband, self-sacrificial and grasping for affection. His relation to his mother was close indeed: He lived with her until he was twenty-six and thereafter wrote her every day. Fraser considers the possibility that he was a latent, and even briefly overt, homosexual; but he sensibly does not make much of it. As psychiatrists used to say, his libido was turned inward; Fraser confines himself to metaphors about

Narcissus. But it is no wonder that his relations with women were difficult and unsatisfactory.

These psychological generalizations are less interesting than the unique circumstances and specific details upon which they are based, and it is the richness of sharp detail (often gathered from interviews and unpublished letters) that distinguishes Fraser's book. A few examples will have to suffice. Blackmur, as presumably everyone still remembers, was a high-school dropout who became a full professor at Princeton and a revered and immensely powerful figure on the literary scene. What I had not known until I read this book was the full story of the private agonies and the constant conviction of failure that accompanied this external success. To be the child of a loveless marriage and the victim of an overcompensating mother who kept him at home for what should have been the first three years of school; to contend with near poverty, unhelped by a remote and ineffectual father who did not even try to work, while the mother supported the family by running a boarding house; to associate constantly with Harvard students in the boarding house and in the bookstores where he chiefly worked, while always aware that he had neither the money nor the academic qualifications to attend Harvard—all this would make anyone a little peculiar, and it sounds as gloomy as a Russian novel. As Fraser tells it, however, it is entertaining and often funny as well as sad.

Aside from his mother, his first and only real love appears to have been Tessa Gilbert, an appetizing beauty: "She had heard that Cleopatra washed her hair in myrrh and frankincense—a potent aphrodisiac, according to her sources. Myrrh and frankincense were not to be had, so she washed her hair in cinnamon and nutmeg. The trouble was it made her smell like apple pie." Tessa was always eating chocolates if she wasn't eating ice cream; she "lived in her body and rejoiced the world. The body was Richard's torment, and he defined the alienated man"; he looked like "someone who hadn't had enough to eat from the time he was a baby" (43). These polar opposites went together for three years; then she finally refused to marry him. On the rebound (though, given Blackmur's temperament, it was a long, slow rebound, taking four years), he married Helen Dickson, "totally the wrong wife for him." Helen was a painter, competent, practical, and humorless. "'Why are you always laughing?' she asked Tessa reproachfully. Helen had a baleful look like the girl in the fairy tale, Jack Wheelwright used to say. 'When she opened her mouth, toads fell out'" (69). Richard, thinking as always in literary terms, found that Tessa, his Molly Bloom (somehow also Maud Gonne), would not say Yes and that Helen, his Georgie Yeats, unveiled no visions with her psychic powers but only a trace of poltergeists. The marriage was marked by "quiet sadness and resignation," and the pattern of Richard's early years—"the woman who toiled and the stay-at-home husband"—was repeated as Helen supported them (by painting murals for the WPA and teaching ballroom dancing at night) while Richard stayed at home and wrote. The marriage rapidly went bad, Helen complaining "to anyone within earshot how Richard wouldn't sleep with her." Helen had affairs, but continued to live with Richard, even after they were divorced in 1951; being around the two of them was "like an Ingmar Bergman film." Whatever Richard's sexual peculiarities—his friends said that his attachment to his mother "led him to repress his sexual desires except perhaps once a year, when they would explode in a sadistic fashion"; he "was tense with women as they confronted him with a sexual possibility," and one such said that dancing with him was "like dancing with a steel cable of the Brooklyn Bridge" (69), the tension dropping only when a woman was safely married to a friend—the more important and even sadder fact is that he was contemptuous of women and cruel to them in the presence of others, while at the same time he needed them. "What he couldn't dispense with, he couldn't abide"; and he treated the women to whom he formed attachments in his later years very badly indeed.

Although Fraser tries to be fair and realistic, he does exhibit some notable biases. His description of Princeton, and particularly of its English department, is wholly from Blackmur's point of view. Because I knew most of the people involved (though from a graduate student, or worm's eye, perspective; I left with my Ph.D. just before Blackmur arrived), I feel obliged to protest that they were not the dim pedants or shifty rascals they appear as in this book. The most distorted portrait is that of Allen Tate, who brought Blackmur to Princeton as his assistant, and was supplanted by the cuckoo he introduced into the nest. Tate was no politician: I heard him deliver "A Rose for Emily," which accused traditional scholars of trying to preserve literature as a decaying corpse, to the English Club; there was no discussion; everyone tiptoed out as at a funeral. But Tate was certainly not the bigot and malicious gossip he appears as here. (Fraser's "evidence" for the first epithet is a letter of 1933; for the second, the word of a close friend of Blackmur who later studied with Tate.)

Fraser seems to have interviewed Tate just once, when Tate was seventy-eight; from this interview he takes Tate's generous assertion that Blackmur was "our best American critic" and repeats it as if it were an authoritative statement of consensus, while dismissing everything else Tate said as malicious gossip. Now, what concerns me is not the question of whether or not Blackmur deliberately sabotaged Tate at Princeton in order to get his job. What matters is that Fraser throughout the book systematically denigrates Tate as a person, a teacher, and a critic. This may be quite unconscious, a consequence of the natural impulse to exalt Blackmur. But it seems to me to lead to serious distortion and falsification in terms of biography and of literary history.

Fraser begins by calling Blackmur "a great man," though he soon qualifies this by calling him an "equivocal hero" and professing his willingness to bear witness to "the hokum that went with the greatness." To his friends and students at Princeton, "he came to represent a hero of our time." But the book reveals Blackmur as small in every sense, a canny and parsimonious Scot obsessed with getting ahead and gaining security, shifty in money matters and getting maximum mileage from everything he produced (e.g., republishing the same essays over and over). There were stories of his "unscrupulousness and dirty academic politics"; he was not above "using brass knuckles when he had to, or sacrificing a friend to save himself"; he displayed an "excess of charity" toward those in the seats of power. Lincoln Kirstein spoke of the "hideous overcompensating" for his early poverty that marked the later years, called him "a joyless man, incapable of pleasure, a sexually bedeviled man who didn't like his own body"; he "attacked literature as if it were a piece of property and he played with the property, oblivious of what it stood for" (62). When he gave literary advice, he was paid for it. He was shifty about money matters, not conscientious about returning advances, fulfilling contracts, reading manuscripts. Worst of all, he was something of a fake and charlatan, pretending to knowledge—especially of languages—that he did not really have. Fraser concedes this and seems to recognize its importance: "He understood how different language traditions entailed different perceptions of reality. This meant that translation entailed falsification. So the word was sacrosanct. All of New Criticism reduces to these formulations. Understanding so much, he let his criticism depend on translation." The mistakes, he says, "weren't decisive. But by not reading his authors in the original, he forfeited linguistic purity, and that was decisive." (250). In his later years he made circular puns in Latin and "got the Latin wrong. He ran on about writers he hardly knew—like Novalis"; he took advances for books on seminal thinkers and never began writing them; his "style grew prolix, and sickly shining like the paintings of Douanier Rousseau" (256–57). Every year he proposed to the English department that all freshmen be required to take a year's course in the novels of Trollope. He opposed inviting Faulkner to Princeton.

Allen Tate, in contrast, though physically not large (except for the head), and certainly not without his faults, was large-minded, generous, and open-handed. From his earliest years he displayed a high-minded concern for the Republic of Letters which transcended his own interests, and he was prodigal of literary advice and help to hundreds—perhaps thousands—of aspiring writers. From his fellow Fugitives (especially Ransom, Warren, Brooks, Davidson) to Hart Crane and John Peale Bishop through Lowell (who literally camped in his front yard all summer) and Berryman, through succeeding generations down to the latest beginners, poets (and critics and fiction writers, too) found in him a warm and sympathetic friend who understood each new work instantly, saw what was good and what not so good about it, and was prepared to offer practical help through writing prefaces, recommendations, or doing whatever was needed. Tate's enormous correspondence, as it gradually appears, and Robert Buffington's biography, when it finally reaches completion, will show him to be the great master of this kind of unpaid practical criticism (which must be larger in bulk than his published criticism). His only rival, to my knowledge, is the early Ezra Pound; Tate never did anything quite so spectacular as Pound's revision of *The Waste Land;* but he might well have been capable of it had opportunity offered.

Tate behaved toward Blackmur with his usual generosity, offering him praise and encouragement both in letters and in published reviews, for both his poetry and his criticism, recommending him for fellowships, and getting him the job at Princeton. His suspicion that Blackmur had knifed him in the back at Princeton made no difference to his attitude toward Blackmur's work: he published it in the *Sewanee Review* and promoted and praised it at every opportunity. I mention all this not to criticize Blackmur for not being Tate, but to correct the prejudice against Tate that appears frequently in *The Mingled Yarn.* Fraser cannot even allow a student who took classes with both Tate and Blackmur at Princeton to say that he "much preferred Tate, . . . missing in Richard 'a unified and powerful critical methodology'" without adding the undercutting comment that "this will be matter for praise or blame, depending on how you value the importance of a unified methodology" (202).

Fraser's attitude toward the New Criticism seems ambivalent and confused. He quotes Tate's statement (made orally, at a symposium) that Blackmur "probably invented what we call the New Criticism in the United States," describes Tate as Blackmur's "fellow New Critic," and says Tate and Blackmur created the New Criticism between them (196, 272). At the same time he calls Tate the "least New Critical among the New Critics" because all his life he "was bemused by ideas," and he notes that Blackmur as early as 1941 renounced New Criticism: "The New Critical mode, his one greatest achievement, showed as illusory now. 'It is plain,' he wrote, 'that we never do in fact understand literature solely by literary means'" (193, 175). But no early New Critic ever asserted that we did (except possibly in a moment of polemical excess); Eliot and Tate were always at particular pains to make this clear. Fraser seems bemused by the myth of New Criticism as a coherent school, with its emblem a critic in a vacuum, peering myopically at an equally isolated poem. Even Blackmur's famous dictionary, with him from the first, spoils the purity of that picture; the outside world was never banished, only put temporarily in the background. In his genealogy of the New Criticism (a term, by the way, that I would abolish if I could), Fraser does not even mention Eliot and I. A. Richards, and this seems significant: They were the strongest immediate influences on the fledgeling New Critics, and they both were obviously involved with the world outside literature.

Blackmur was, Fraser makes clear, a complete skeptic, unable to believe in anything beyond the value of art; in his unpublished fiction and journals Wilde and Pater are prominent, and Fraser terms him "the strayed reveler out of the Mauve Decade." Art was his religion, and he tries to make of it a "rival creation" that will "alter that actual life." In this notion that language creates another world he parts company with Eliot and Tate; and in conceiving of the critic as prophet or sage or artist or priest of art — as he does increasingly in his later essays — he diverges even farther. In their pretentiousness, self-indulgence, and pseudowisdom, these later pieces were often embarrassing to admirers of his earlier work.

Resistance to Fraser's attempts to attach the label of "our best American critic" to Blackmur should not make us lose sight of the fact that Blackmur at his best was a magnificent critic. The early pieces on Cummings, Stevens, Pound, Eliot, Yeats, James; some of the writing on Adams and on the nature of criticism; parts of *Anni Mirabiles* and other late pieces such as "Lord Tennyson's Scissors" and "Between the Numen and the Moha" — these are still alive and permanently valuable. But there are many American critics who seem obviously superior. Allen Tate, for one (as I have already hinted), and Lionel Trilling and Cleanth Brooks, in their very different ways — all these are clearer and better writers, far more penetrating in dealing with ideas, and more reliable and stimulating in the interpretation of particular works. (And there is, of course, Eliot, who began it all, and continued to think of himself as an American critic in spite of his expatriation).

As Fraser's Shakespearean title suggests—"The web of our life is of a mingled yarn, good and ill together"—everything about Blackmur is mixed and double. At his best a wonderfully suggestive critic who could make the reader understand and feel how language works in poetry perhaps better than anyone else, at his worst he was ignorant and pretentious, relying on complacent ironies and incantatory formulas. The yarn of his life, too, was more mingled than that of most writers. He was so clearly an emotional cripple who *had* to write that we are thrown back into meditations on the relation between psychic damage and compensating gifts, the wound and the bow. To my knowledge nobody has formulated the relation satisfactorily—certainly not Freud or Trilling or Edmund Wilson—but its existence cannot be doubted. ("I wonder what hurt him into writing?" a novelist once asked me about another; certainly that way of putting it applies to Blackmur.) Fraser handles this well, without oversimplifying or pontificating; as always, though, it is easier to see the connection between the writer's horrendous early life and his limitations than between these circumstances and his peculiar gifts. Naturally enough, Fraser's writing is somewhat gnomic and involuted—what other style could a disciple of Blackmur possibly have?—but fortunately more open-textured, informal, and humorous. Like Blackmur, though, Fraser often mingles his yarn compulsively, making style a defense and refuge; every statement is followed by a qualifying one, which, though often witty, comes to seem both predictable and evasive. "Elevating the status of language, he hid the world as immediately experienced by an ersatz world of his own devising. Or you can say that he made his world golden." "He wasn't a charlatan, but his critics weren't wholly off the mark" (251).

Fraser, who was a much younger colleague and friend of Blackmur's during his last nine years at Princeton, seems to try hard to present both sides—so much so that it becomes almost a tic, every agent being double, every yarn mingled. Very properly, he makes his portrait of Blackmur as favorable as he can while preserving truth and candor; but it does not leave you feeling that you wish you had known him. This book takes a worthy place on the rapidly growing shelf of literary biographies of the forties and fifties; it has none of the intimacy and poignance of Eileen Simpson's *Poets in Their Youth* or the exuberance of James Atlas's biography of Delmore Schwartz or Saul Bellow's fictional version. But Blackmur was hardly an exuberant person, and intimacy was not a possibility. Given the limitations of his subject, Fraser manages remarkably well: His book is consistently interesting and entertaining.

Cleanth Brooks and the Responsibilities of Criticism

In *A Shaping Joy,* Cleanth Brooks remarks that the New Criticism for most people "vaguely signifies an anti-historical bias and a fixation on 'close reading.' The New Critic would seem to be trapped in a cell without windows or door, staring through a reading glass at his literary text, effectually cut off from all the activities of the world outside—from history and science, from the other arts, and from nature and humanity itself."[1] In this caricature, the New Critic is responsible to no one and nothing except his own perverted obligation to be ingenious; oblivious of larger human concerns, he works his little rhetorical machine to discover—or produce—ambiguity, irony, paradox, and other such effects.

If Brooks as critic may be said to have a characteristic method, it is that of demonstrating that a formula or generalization is inadequate because it will not fit all the complex facts of the individual case. Applying this method to Brooks's own work, we observe immediately that his recent books, at least, are not limited to close reading, for one (*The Hidden God*) deals explicitly with the religious implications of literature and the other two (*William Faulkner: The Yoknapatawpha Country* and *A Shaping Joy*) are, in their different ways, richly historical. In the later volume, he protests against being typed "as the rather myopic 'close reader,' the indefatigable exegete," and affirms mildly, "In fact I am interested in a great many other things besides close reading" (231). It is not that Brooks has changed—"I am not conscious of any fundamental change in my critical principles and what follows is no palinode," he says in *A Shaping Joy*—but that the stereotype that made him the archetypal New Critic never did correspond to the facts. "The New Criticism" was from the beginning an unfortunate and misleading label; only insofar as it meant "the first really adequate criticism"[2] did it ever make sense. In *A Shaping Joy*, Brooks suggests "structural or formal" to designate his emphasis on the work rather than on the reader or the writer. These labels are unquestionably better than "New Criticism," but have their own misleading associations: Brooks's "structuralism" has little in common with that of recent anthropologists and linguists, and his "formalism" is neither that of the Czech or Russian schools nor that Aristotelian version once copyrighted by the University of Chicago. At any rate, though Brooks continues to maintain that close reading is the critic's primary obligation, in these later books he deals more explicitly and at greater length with the other things he is interested in.

Far from being the irresponsible aesthete or technician that his opponents used to represent him as (in the polemics of literary journals and seminar rooms), Brooks is, I propose to argue, distinguished among critics precisely by his strong sense of responsibility. (This is not his only distinction: Aside from such obvious gifts as perceptiveness, imagination, and intelligence, his critical integrity, his sense of proportion, and his instinct for the centrally human are rare qualities indeed. But responsibility is primary.)

To whom, as Brooks sees it, is the critic responsible? I suggest that, judging from his practice, we might put the priorities in this order of ascending importance: to his readers or other audience; to his authors, whether living or dead; and to whatever standards of truth he believes in. For Brooks, the kinds of truth invoked most often are those of fact, especially linguistic and historical, and of religion in the basic ontological sense of awareness of human nature and experience as complex, contradictory, and mysterious.

With respect to his audience (and both meanings of "respect" are appropriate), Brooks has always seemed to think of his criticism as simply an extension of his teaching, exactly the same in nature and purpose. All the pieces in *The Hidden God* and most of those in *A Saving Joy* were originally lectures; they differ from those written first as essays only in having a slightly more open texture. It appears never to have occurred to him to think of his criticism as autotelic; assuming its role to be obviously ancillary to that of literature itself but nevertheless vitally important, he has been concerned chiefly with its practical effectiveness upon his audience—mostly students and teachers, with some general readers. Through collaborative textbooks and editing, as well as through reviewing, lecturing, and criticism proper, Brooks has devoted himself single-mindedly to the aim of improving this audience's understanding of literature and hence of its powers of discrimination. Teaching is more conducive than most professions to vanity and petty tyranny: The analyst has his analyst, the preacher has his God; but the teacher has only his students to keep him humble, and students are not often in a position to be as effective as the other agencies mentioned. An excessive confidence in one's own righteousness is also one of the occupational hazards of criticism: from Rymer down to Leavis, Winters, and (descending steeply) John Simon, there have been some critics who have seemed to writers to stare "tremendous! with a threatning Eye" like fierce tyrants in tapestry. In the face of these combined temptations, Brooks's modesty is conspicuous and unusual. The myth one sometimes encounters of him as presiding with self-satisfaction over an Age of Criticism that he has helped to create could hardly be more remote from reality.

True collaboration—the kind that produces something different from what either collaborator could do separately—requires a difficult self-abnegation and openness. Few manage it successfully even once. But Brooks has collaborated brilliantly not only with Warren, in their great series of pioneering textbooks, but also with numerous others; *Understanding Drama,* with R. B. Heilman, and *Literary Criticism,* with W. K. Wimsatt, may be singled out as especially impressive. In giving his time to these collaborative textbooks, Brooks has been willing to be almost anonymous in order to achieve his purpose. His work as an editor of periodicals and various other books, his tireless lecturing and reviewing, and his service as U.S. cultural attaché in England (by common consent, I understand, the best one ever) all show the same self-effacing concern for the good health of the literary audience.

The personal qualities of courtesy and tact (in addition to modesty) are, I would suggest, what has enabled Brooks to establish the relation to his audience that has made him so effective as a teacher-critic. Like W. H. Auden—another natural teacher—he has also the gift of simplification, of reducing complex problems to their essentials. (This gift, together with Brooks's unpretentiousness, is probably responsible for the illusion encountered now and then that his kind of criticism is easy to practice.) His devotion to literature is, in a sense, purer than Auden's: Whereas Auden's mind is often willingly violated by ideas, Brooks always rigorously brings the reader back to the complexity of the literary work itself, and leaves him confronting its inexhaustible richness. To return, however, from this tempting bypath to the quality of tact. In this context, tact means primarily knowing when to stop—a talent notoriously lacking in many of Brooks's imitators—but also being able to provide information and direction without condescending. Like courtesy (which, in this context, has the full traditional Christian meaning it has in Chaucer and Spenser, and in more recent interpretations by such writers as Charles Williams and C. S. Lewis), tact is based on respect for other persons—for their dignity, integrity, and value. Whether these qualities are inborn or infused by grace, they also require an inner discipline. They are, obviously, humane qualities, the very opposite of the kind of bloodless formalism or mechanical ingenuity attributed to the New Critic by popular mythology.

The same personal qualities lie behind the second kind of responsibility demonstrated by Brooks, that toward his authors. Some critics do not hesitate to instruct their authors (living or dead) and show them the error of their ways. F. R. Leavis, for example, at his best excels in discriminating between the good and the less good; at his worst he seems to take special satisfaction in showing where authors went wrong and why their later careers were so much inferior to their early work (James, Eliot, Auden). Brooks seems to feel that this would be presumptuous. The critic's function, as he sees it, is to improve the reader, not the author (though the aspiring author may well be also an educable reader). Thus he usually begins his analysis with the tacit assumption that whatever the author has done is right; if it seems wrong, the probable fault is in the reader's understanding, which is enlightened and corrected through Brooks's patient analysis and interpretation. It is not that Brooks is uninterested in evaluation: If his hypothesis that the work is good will not stand up under analysis, he abandons it, and he can both demolish bad work with gusto and make fine discriminations between degrees and kinds of goodness. But his primary dedication is to helping the reader to understand as fully as possible why good literature is good.

If it is no part of the critic's responsibility to correct or guide his author, or to cut him down to size, then for what is the critic responsible to the author? Primarily, as Brooks sees it, for respecting the integrity of his works and defending them against violation, and for reading these works in the right way and thus helping to provide him with the right kind of audience. Ransom long ago remarked that Brooks was our best living "reader," and this distinction seems generally conceded even by opponents. The essential secret is to be found, I think, in his personal attitude. To revert to previous terms, this attitude may be described as exhibiting a kind of metaphysical tact. One feels that Brooks never claims to pluck out the heart of the mystery of art. He does his best to explain, and he is in no doubt about the legitimacy and importance of his enterprise; but the reader never feels that Brooks is inclined to set up his version as exclusive and complete truth, or to substitute it for the original work. The poem, he always remembers, is more complex and more permanent than the critic; and life is larger and more mysterious than either. Hence Brooks always appeals finally to a standard beyond literature: truth to experience. His firm sense of limitations, of an order of priorities and significances, of man's creatureliness and morality, is (I suppose) ultimately religious. In this respect (as in many others) Brooks stands in strong contrast to his only serious rival as "reader," F. R. Leavis. Leavis is like Brooks in seeing criticism as simply an extension of teaching, in antipathy to the dominant culture, and in advocating a humane critical discipline as remedy. But Leavis's rigid insistence on exclusive possession of the total truth, with consequent feelings of persecution and tendencies to the messianic, are utterly unlike Brooks. Perhaps it is not without significance that Auden, Eliot, and Tate, who share Brooks's freedom from such attitudes, have similar religious allegiances; their religious convictions appear to restrain any hubristic or dogmatic inclination.

Insofar as "close reading" is a method, it has been well learned; reasonable competence in it seems fairly common. True excellence is, however, extremely rare. Brooks's academic epigones often seem like the sorcerer's apprentices: they know how to work the machine but do not fully understand it, so that finally the machine takes over. It was Brooks's distinction that he, not the machine, was always master. In adapting and synthesizing the theories of other critics for pedagogical purposes and reducing them to a practical method, he never forgot that the method was a dynamic one of balances and tensions between opposing qualities, and that it had to be operated by a responsible human being. There is a similar contrast in style. Brooks's writing is always alive, sensitive, and lucid; he seeks no meretricious charms and maintains a proper decorum; but he is without a trace of the pomposity, oversolemnity, and excessive display of method that mar the writing of many of his imitators.

It is clear in retrospect that the "autonomy of the poem" was primarily a *machine de guerre*: a battering ram with which to shatter the excessive historical emphasis then prevailing. It is obvious enough that Brooks did not really mean to insulate the poem permanently from history and other contexts. But, insofar as it inculcates respect for the integrity of the literary work, the slogan is still useful and far from obsolete. It is amusing to see Brooks, in *A Shaping Joy,* having to reprove Joyce critics (who pride themselves on their sophistication and extreme modernity) for practicing old-fashioned biographical interpretation.

If there is one author for whose work the critic shows a special affinity and deep affection, and particularly if it seems a case of literary first love, then the critic is likely to feel a very powerful kind of responsibility to him. For Brooks, this first and best-loved poet, without much question, is William Butler Yeats. There are many other favorites.

Eliot, Ransom, Auden, and—especially of late years—Joyce always produce a response of particular warmth. Warren obviously holds a very special place in Brooks's admirations and affections, and both his poems and his novels have been discussed with exceptional flair and conviction. Faulkner, too, has been increasingly a favorite; the books on him are a labor of love as well as intelligence. But I feel little hesitation in suggesting that, early and late, the greatest master of all has been Yeats.

Is it not true that the critic tries (consciously or not) to make himself into the ideal reader of this best-loved author? Perhaps this whole notion is romanticizing on my part, but it seems to apply to Brooks and Yeats. Setting aside as irrelevant the uncorrupted but illiterate "A Fisherman" and the beauties whose ignorant ears are flattered in other poems, "A Prayer for My Daughter" gives what may be the best picture of Yeats's ideal reader. How does Brooks square with the picture? Well, he is, as we have seen, notably learned in courtesy and, in the Yeatsian sense, he thinks "opinions are accursed"; he is without intellectual hatred and has a "radical innocence" rooted in the interior discipline of custom and ceremony.

The title of *A Shaping Joy* comes from one of Yeats's essays, in which he describes the joy that the hands and the tongue of the artist feel in the exercise of his craft, while "with his eyes he enters upon a submissive, sorrowful contemplation of the great irremediable things." "That shaping joy has kept the sorrow pure, as it had kept it were the emotion love or hate, for the nobleness of the arts is in the mingling of contraries, the extremity of sorrow, the extremity of joy." Brooks's subtitle is *Studies in the Writer's Craft,* and the "mingling of contraries" to which Yeats refers is central to Brooks's conception of literature. The first essay, "The Uses of Literature," puts it briefly and explicitly. In answer to Randall Jarrell's complaint that the New Criticism made readers too self-conscious and his advice that they should instead read naturally, for pleasure, Brooks points out that most people do not know how to read, that intensity and effort are not opposed to pleasure, and that literature is concerned primarily not with pleasure but with a kind of knowledge.

In a time when many hanker after newer and fancier critical models, when textbooks are full of "relevant" propaganda against pollution and for minorities, of New Journalism, science fiction, and rock and pop lyrics, it is salutary to come back to the integrity of Brooks's position, with its utter unconcern for fashion and the topical. He has kept faith, in Yeatsian terms, to "the Muses' sterner laws." Literature, he says, is "not generalizations about life, but dramatizations of concrete problems—not remedies designed to solve these problems but rather diagnoses in which the problems are defined and realized for what they are. A formula can be learned and applied, but the full, concrete, appropriate response to a situation can only be experienced. Literature is thus incurably concrete—not abstract."[3] Those who demand relevance—and hence ultimately demand that literature be propaganda—assume "that the themes of literature are generalizations to be affirmed rather than situations to be explored." But the knowledge to be gained from literature is self-knowledge and knowledge of the world conceived in human terms: that is, dramatically.

This discussion has taken us imperceptibly across the threshold of our third kind of responsibility, that to ultimate standards of truth. The qualities we have stressed so far are humane and personal: courtesy, tact, integrity, innocence (in the etymological sense). Brooks has also an eighteenth-century sense of human limitations and respect for tradition, as well as an old-fashioned reticence about himself that makes it a little embarrassing to spell out these personal attributes. Nevertheless, we must go so far as to designate him scholar and gentleman, a phrase hardly to be used nowadays without irony, but applying to Brooks so precisely that it cannot be avoided. Gentleness and mildness (sometimes deceptive) are conspicuous characteristics of the man, as is respect for his opponents even in vigorous controversy. While exposing the errors and pretensions of individual scholars, he has demonstrated his faith in scholarship by his own excellent practice, especially in his Faulkner books and his collaborative editions of Milton's early poems and the Percy letters.

As has often been pointed out, moral and religious assumptions were implicit in *Understanding Poetry* and *Understanding Fiction,* as well as in *Modern Poetry and the Tradition* and *The Well Wrought Urn:* questions that seemed aesthetic or rhetorical turned out to be at bottom moral. It has also been observed that much of the history and other material that was theoretically excluded from these books was actually smuggled in and taken account of, at least tacitly. But what was handed out under the counter was not (as some said) crypto-fascism, snobbery, or other vicious doctrine, but a traditional respect for facts (especially linguistic and historical) and for the complexity of human nature and experience, as against simplifiers of all varieties. Brooks's most frequent critical "strategy," as we noted earlier, is that of showing that a stereotyped or partial response to the literary work is inadequate. It is true that the implications go beyond literature: When the reader is shown that simple and abstract interpretations do not do justice to the literary work, he is likely to be suspicious of simplistic and abstract explanations of human experience in other realms—in politics or religion, for example. But Brooks's concern is with the nature of truth, and his conviction is that truth—at least that most important kind with which literature deals—is never simple or easy; but that to learn the truth about himself and his world is man's basic need. Human experience is seen as complex and contradictory, involving the recognition of evil and hence of duality (indicated by such theoretical devices as ambiguity, irony, and paradox); the point of view is not explicitly or specifically religious, but grounded in the tradition of Christian humanism. Man is seen as weak and limited, guided by inherited patterns, by instinct and emotion far more than by reason. Truth is seen as real and absolute, though forever exceeding the comprehension of the individual; as multiform, and perceived by other faculties as well as by reason. This credo is not set forth positively, however, but becomes apparent by implication as the converse is held up for doubtful scrutiny: that man is naturally good and rational, per-fectible and progressing, needing only such external aids as political and social planning can provide to remove the evil that comes entirely from outside himself; and completely in charge of his own destiny. Brooks is not, however, concerned with the writer's beliefs or philos-ophy as such, but rather with the nature of the world he presents; not with what the poem says, but with what it is. Such qualities as wit, ambiguity, irony, paradox, complexity, and tension are valued for more than aesthetic reasons, however; they are indexes to the view of reality—of man and truth—in the work. They are, therefore, not really aesthetic or rhetorical, but—since they are modes of apprehending reality—ontological or, in the broad sense, religious. If students now seem less impressed than they used to be by the goal of maturity of in-sight, as opposed to sentimentality, this may reveal more about the students than about the doctrine.

The notion of Brooks as pure aesthete has never been plausible to anyone with even a slight acquaintance with his career. His profound respect for, and deep concern with, history, especially in its relation to literature, are increasingly apparent in the later editions of *Understand-ing Poetry,* in his books on Faulkner, and in *A Shaping Joy;* he has also practiced the more "scientific" varieties of literary scholarship in his early linguistic treatise (to be discussed shortly) and his edition, still in progress, of the Percy letters. But he has always insisted on a firm distinction between the literary work considered as art and its use as historical document, case history, sermon, or sociological or moral tract.

Important among the third category of critical responsibilities—

fundamental, in fact—is the English language itself. Brooks seems to think of this as a tradition in the literal sense, a heritage passed into his stewardship to be cherished and improved, if possible; if not, preserved; and handed on to succeeding generations. This attitude is the opposite of the apocalyptic one now so fashionable. Brooks is—in this respect as in others—concerned not only with the present, but also with the past and future; and his sense of the present is thereby greatly enriched. His attitude toward the language is similar to Eliot's, for which the *locus classicus* is the famous passage in "Little Gidding" in which the "dead master," echoing Mallarmé, states the poet's function as "to purify the dialect of the tribe." Another parallel is the letter of the Russian poet Iosif Brodsky asking for readmission to the Soviet Union: "Language is a thing far older and more inescapable than the state. I belong to the Russian language. As regards the state, the measure of a writer's patriotism is not, I think, a loyalty oath pronounced upon some high public platform, but the way in which he writes the language of the people among whom he lives."[4] The notion of the critic as owing a similar allegiance to the language itself, and as helping the author and the reader to keep faith with it, is fundamental to Brooks's criticism.

Brooks's concern with language was shown early in his one linguistic publication, *The Relation of the Alabama-Georgia Dialect to the Provincial Dialects of Great Britain* (1935). This treatise has recently enjoyed a curious revival, figuring as one of the *bêtes noires* in J. L. Dillard's important book *Black English*. (Brooks thus reappears as culture villain, a role he used often to play when the New Criticism was being attacked. Perhaps it is his clarity and definiteness that make one so inoffensive a tempting target.) Brooks holds, to put it very briefly, that Black and White English are the same in the dialect he is studying, and that it derives from the provincial dialects of southwestern England. Dillard attacks him for failing to recognize the uniqueness of Black English and its true derivation from Africa, and by implication for racial prejudice. Actually, Brooks is admirably scientific in this study, very clear about his sources and methods. Insofar as any motive is apparent, it would seem to be to remove Southerners' sense of inferiority about their language by showing that it is not a corrupt or slovenly version of Standard English, but derives from older or regional forms that are equally legitimate. Presumably he saw the conclusion that black and white speech are identical as favorable to black self-respect; in any case, it was decreed by his sources. There are additional sources for Dillard to use, and Brooks's work may now be partly superseded; but it is not racism that prevents him from anticipating

Dillard's thesis that the black forms derive from Africa and the white from the black. At any rate, the treatise is evidence of Brooks's deep interest in language and his technical competence (within self-imposed limits) in linguistic study.[5]

In *A Shaping Joy* Brooks stresses the fundamental importance of language. He draws an audacious parallel between Joyce's use of cliché in the "Nausicaa" episode of *Ulysses* and Adolf Eichmann's banality (as observed by Hannah Arendt); in both cases, debasement of language makes possible dehumanization. "When the very means for registering value are as coarsened and corrupted as Gerty's, how can one hope for honesty, decency, charity, or any of the other virtues on which any healthy civilization is founded?" And he suggests that Joyce's parody may be therapeutic: "To peel off the dead skin and callosities from the language—even if this seems to be done simply for the fun in it—is not merely to remove dead tissue. It could mean exposing once more the living fibres of the imagination so that men might once again see who they are and where they are." For the Nazis, evil became banal: "People who are sensitive and fully aware of what they are doing and whose responses to the world about them, including their responses to other human beings, are fresh and individual, are simply incapable of this kind of wickedness." The death of language, he argues, is a serious matter indeed, and "one of the uses of literature is to keep our language alive—to keep the blood circulating through the tissues of the body politic. There can scarcely be a more vital function." Discussing Eliot, he remarks that "a poetry that can deal with the clutter of language in an age of advertising and propaganda restores to that degree the health of language."[6] Brooks's most extensive treatment of this theme, however, is an essay published in the *Sewanee Review* in 1971, "Telling It Like It Is in the Tower of Babel."[7] Ours is a time, he says, "in which language is systematically manipulated by politicians, advertisers, and publicity men as it has probably never before been manipulated. I am concerned with what is happening to our langauge. But I am, of course, even more deeply concerned with what is happening to ourselves. The two concerns cannot, in fact, be separated. If you debauch a langauge, you run a grave risk of debauching the minds of the people who use it" (137). Ranging widely over contemporary examples from the verbal smog poured over us by the media to the religious press, Brooks comments: "Language is important, and debased and corrupted language accounts for the currently lamented failure in communication. More even than that—for the failure in self-knowledge. We shall have difficulty in identifyng our true selves if we lack the language of meditation and self-analysis" (146–47).

But let us return to *A Shaping Joy* for further examples of the importance of language and of fact in Brooks's criticism. As Brooks recurrently distinguishes close reading from its perversion, symbol-mongering, it becomes clear that irresponsibility with regard to language and fact is one of the distinguishing characteristics of the latter. Thus he observes that the blind trust in even so great an author as Faulkner is misplaced, and he shows that Faulkner misused the word *equinox* in one passage. Symbol-mongering "magnifies details quite irresponsibly; it feverishly prospects for possible symbolic meanings and then forces them beyond the needs of the story."[8] Courteously but firmly, Brooks demonstrates the foolishness of some such readings. The view of Gide, Sartre, and others that "Faulkner's characters make no decisions at all and are merely driven and determined creatures" Brooks characterizes as "nonsensical"—the result of not reading closely enough. In fact, as he shows, though Faulkner does not often dramatize "the agony of choice—the process by which the character actually arrives at his decision," he does dramatize the character's "sustaining of a choice"—as when Bayard, in "An Odor of Verbena," maintains the decision against every pressure. Brooks's analysis of Joyce's "Clay" is especially helpful because the story has been a favorite of symbol-mongers who have nevertheless often missed the point—not through reading too closely, but through not reading closely enough, or with enough responsibility to the integrity—the total meaning—of the story. It is the "ruthlessness" of the dedicated symbol-monger that Brooks finds horrifying; his determination, for instance, to find significance in Maria's name, or in her witchlike profile, though unable to show how such significance would contribute to the total meaning of the story. Brooks himself reads the story in basic human terms, stressing the pathos of Maria's situation (though it is presented unsentimentally) and refusing to be drawn into speculation about the significance of every detail. His discussion of *Ulysses* provides the same contrast between symbol-mongering and close reading that is informed by Brooks's kinds of responsibility. Brooks agrees with the general thesis of R. M. Adams (in *Surface and Symbol*) that "some parts of *Ulysses* are merely surface and have no symbolic reference" (68). But he proceeds to show, with courtesy, that Adams has failed to see many symbolic patterns that are really there. He finds, characteristically, that part of the trouble is linguistic, part is religious, and part is characterological or dramatic: In all these areas, previous critics have not known enough (e.g., about *dogsbody*) and have failed to see the intricate patterns that Brooks is able to clarify. With erudition balanced by tact and his usual instinct for centrality, Brooks elucidates the way that the dog symbolism expresses the central meaning of the book. Reading closely, he argues against many a facile symbol-monger that Bloom and Stephen do not communicate. "To argue that since an atonement is desirable it must occur takes the intent for the deed. In fact, it does more: it makes an assumption about the author's intent that cannot be supported by the author's text" (83). And Brooks concludes that even though *Ulysses* is, as Adams has shown, many other things, it is still primarily a novel. It is refreshing to see him insist, quite properly, against Joycean interpreters who think of themselves as the very tip of the avant-garde that they really must not commit the nineteenth-century error of interpreting the novel in terms of the author's biography.

How does Brooks relate literature to religion? Although his own position is clearly that of orthodox Christianity, he is scrupulous not to suggest that Christian writers are likely to be better than the un-blessed. As in so many other matters, he takes his basic text from Yeats. In this case, the necessity of the Vision of Evil to the poet. Yeats was "no utopian activist" and "expressed rather caustically his lack of be-lief in progress, which he called the sole religious myth of modern man" (100). Brooks observes that "up to our time at least all great poetry reflects a mixed world, a world of good and evil, and that the good which it celebrates can be seen in full perspective only by means of the shadows that the good itself casts. Though as decent men we are committed to try as hard as we can to make this a better world, some of us are disposed to think that the struggle with evil, in one form or another, is probably destined to go on for a very long time" (100). The basic attitude is that made familiar to us by Eliot and Hulme (and Baudelaire before them); but it is very much Brooks's own. He is especially good on Milton, remarkable among critics in keeping his humane central focus, without wandering off into history of ideas or amateur theology on one side or purely aesthetic analysis on the other. He is as unaffected by Eliot's hostility to Milton's verse and personality as by Empson's hostility to Milton's God. Interpreting the Fall in *Paradise Lost,* Brooks is much less interested in playing with theological paradoxes of the *culpa felix* than in working out in human and dra-matic terms the consquences: These are unpleasant and very real, how-ever hard prelapsarian life may be to imagine. Brooks stresses that evil is not just a concept to be glibly manipulated by theologians, but a dreadful and ugly reality; and that its entrance into human life (in Mil-ton's archetypal situation) is tragic. The modern reader is too ready to assume "that Milton as a renaissance humanist couldn't really have be-lieved that Adam could have been happy to continue in paradise, that

Adam's moral development required his sowing his wild oats, and that Milton was really on Lucifer's side unconsciously if not consciously. The real remedy for these misconceptions is to read the poem itself" (365).

Brooks is also especially good on Marlowe's *Dr. Faustus*. He compares it to Eliot's *Murder in the Cathedral* and Milton's *Samson Agonistes:* In all three, the question is whether the middle functions viably to unite the beginning and the end—a question primarily aesthetic but also religious. The essay is too complex for summary; comparisons are made also to *The Countess Cathleen, The Hamlet,* and *Heart of Darkness;* the conclusion is that *Faustus* does constitute a unity, and that its protagonist, though fallen and damned, retains admirable qualities: "Faustus at the end is still a man, not a cringing wretch. The poetry saves him from abjectness. If he wishes to escape from himself, to be changed into little water drops, to be swallowed up in the great ocean of being, he maintains to the end . . . his individuality of mind, the special quality of the restless spirit that aspired. This retention of his individuality is at once his glory and his damnation" (380).

He remains similarly humane and undogmatic in discussing so mundane a topic as the Southern temper, though the religious implications are clear. With Peter Taylor's "Miss Leonora When Last Seen" as the principal text, he concludes that the Southern writer "respects a mystery lying at the heart of things, a mystery that at some level always evades the rational explanation, a reality that can be counted on to unpredict prediction. . . . He finds human beings wonderful in their courage and generosity, but also wonderful in their 'orneriness' and folly. He is continually fascinated by the teasing mixture of elements that is man" (214).

The Hidden God is Brooks's most extended discussion of the religious significance of literature. Of the five writers considered, only one—Eliot—is explicitly Christian; on the other hand, he and all the others except Hemingway (Yeats, Faulkner, and Warren) are among those listed as special favorites of Brooks's. Clearly, then, Brooks chose for discussion (as, indeed, his title suggests) not writers who profess adherence to Christian doctrine, but writers who are among our greatest and with whom he felt a special affinity. He begins his essay on Faulkner by disagreeing with a critic who calls Faulkner "profoundly Christian," and calling him rather "profoundly religious"; he is Christian only in the sense "'that his characters come out of a Christian environment, and represent, whatever their shortcomings and whatever their theological heresies, Christian concerns; and that they are finally to be understood only be reference to the Christian premises."[9] Faulkner's criticism of secularism and rationalism is considered through his treatment of the theme of discovery of evil as initiation into the nature of reality. "That brilliant and horrifying early novel *Sanctuary* is, it seems to me, to be understood primarily in terms of such an initiation. Horace Benbow is the sentimental idealist, the man of academic temper, who finds out that the world is not a place of moral tidiness or even of justice. He discovers with increasing horror that evil is rooted in the very nature of things" (25). It is not the sensational corncob rape or the murder that most disturbs him. "What crumples him up is the moral corruption of the girl, which follows on her rape: she actually accepts her life in the brothel and testifies at the trial in favor of the man who had abducted her. What Horace also discovers is that the forces of law and order are also corruptible." And he sums up Faulkner's attitude thus:

> Man is capable of evil, and this means that goodness has to be achieved by struggle and discipline and effort. Like T. S. Eliot, Faulkner has small faith in social arrangements so perfectly organized that nobody has to take the trouble to be good. Finally, Faulkner's noblest characters are willing to face the fact that most men can learn the deepest truths about themselves and about reality only through suffering. Hurt and pain and loss are not mere accidents to which the human being is subject; nor are they mere punishments incurred by human error; they can be the means to the deeper knowledge to the more abundant life.
> (43)

If asked which is Brooks's best single book, I should vote (not without hesitation, because each book attempts something quite different from the others, and all of them will endure) for *Faulkner: The Yoknapatawpha Country* as exhibiting most fully all of Brooks's mature virtues and as most helpful to the greatest number and variety of readers. Brooks has here quietly and unobtrusively managed to do what others have debated endlessly about: bring about a happy marriage of the historical with the aesthetic approach. He knows the life Faulkner writes about intimately; but he buttresses his personal impressions by meticulous scholarship. Similarly, he uses the writings of psychiatrists to check his own interpretation of Faulkner's more peculiar characters (e.g., Vardaman, Addie, Benjy). He finds Faulkner, as man and artist, extremely sympathetic; but he maintains a firm distinction between the man and the artist, and he manages never to use either as a stalk-ing-horse for his own opinions. The book is a marvel of conciseness and imaginative tact; both a handbook to Faulkner and the most profound and comprehensive interpretation.

What is immediately impressive is the precision and thoroughness of his reading; again and again he corrects the errors, distortions, or partial interpretations of other critics—though with his usual courtesy, he relegates most of these corrections to the notes. In discussing *Light in August*, for example, he shows how inaccurate it is to say, as many commentators do, that Joe Christmas is lynched. The point is important because it distorts the role of the community (which Brooks properly emphasizes in this novel, as throughout Faulkner) and relates to that favorite theme of the symbol-mongers, Joe as Christ symbol—a theme that Brooks finds of little or no significance. Brooks is in general vastly better than anyone else on Faulkner's treatment of religion, his attitude toward nature, and his representation of blacks—all vitally important to *Light in August*.

His discussion of *The Sound and the Fury* is notable because, instead of focusing on the matter of technique, as he would if he were a stereotypical New Critic, Brooks stresses the different conceptions of love implied by the four sections and the different kinds of time as related to them. "Benjy's idiocy and Quentin's quixotic madness are finally less inhuman than Jason's sanity. To be truly human one must transcend one's mere intellect with some overflow of generosity and love."[10] "Benjy represents love in its most simple and childlike form. . . . Quentin is really, as his sister knows, in love with death itself. In contrast with this incestuously Platonic lover, Jason has no love for Caddy at all, and no love for anyone else" (327). In contrast to the popular reading of this novel and others as quasi-allegorical—a legend of the South—Brooks reads it in basic human terms: "The basic cause of the breakup of the Compson family—let the more general cultural causes be what they may—is the cold and self-centered mother who is sensitive about the social status of her own family, . . . who feels the birth of an idiot son as a kind of personal affront, who spoils and corrupts her favorite son, and who withholds any real love and affection from her other children and her husband" (334). As this quotation suggests, Brooks's explanations are often psychological, in a sensible and undogmatic way, and he buttresses them by citing psychologists from Jung to Rollo May. Whether one calls it psychological or dramatic or merely humane, his approach makes more sense, finally, of the technique, too, than any other; but the technique comes last. Sociologizing and symbol-mongering are different ways, Brooks says in his first chapter, of "evading the central critical task: to determine and evaluate the meaning of the work in the fullness of its depth and amplitude." It is a task that Brooks does not evade, but carries through magnificently.

In discussing *Absalom, Absalom!*—which he considers the greatest of all the novels—Brooks focuses on the theme of innocence: Sutpen's tragic innocence about the nature of reality. This is not shared by the community, but is "peculiarly the innocence of modern man," rationalistic, cut off from the past, believing that hard work and planning can accomplish anything. "The only people in Faulkner who are 'innocent' are adult males; and their innocence amounts finally to a trust in rationality—an overweening confidence that plans work out, that life is simpler than it is" (308). In one of the most brilliant essays in *A Shaping Joy,* Brooks compares Faulkner's treatment of American innocence in this novel with that of James in *The American* and Fitzgerald in *The Great Gatsby.*

Brooks understands Faulkner's appreciation of the homely mule as well as the chivalric horse, and of the virtues associated with each; he understands the nature and dominance of puritanism as against the cavalier myth, and the importance of the plain folk or yeomen as against either planters or white trash. One feels that he understands almost everything about Faulkner, and that much of the time he is the first critic to do so. His characterization of Faulkner's world is masterly:

> Its very disorders are eloquent of the possibilities of order: Joe Christmas's alienation points to the necessity for a true community, and the author's dramatically sympathetic delineation of Joe's plight may be said to point to the possibility of that true community. It is difficult to think of an author whose basic assumptions are farther from the currently fashionable world of the absurd. For Faulkner's work speaks ultimately of the possibilities and capacities of the human spirit for finding and embodying meaning. (368)

To conclude, let me repeat my paradigm of the critic's responsibilities as I think Brooks sees them; or, to put it another way, let me describe Brooks's work as a model of responsible criticism. He is responsible to the reader for treating him tactfully and courteously. But because he takes him seriously as a human being, he also treats him with a certain rigor and strictness: He insists that the reader confront *all* of the literary work, and will not allow any evasion or easy cut. He enforces the Muses' sterner laws after he has made these ladies as seductive as possible. Second, he takes his authors as serious artists, and he respects the complexity and integrity of their works. Moreover, he responds to these works not only through the "fascination of what's difficult," but also as a human being, with love. (As Auden once remarked, love is another name for intensity of attention.) Finally, his criticism respects language and historical fact, elucidating them and preserving them against distortion; and it deals responsibly with the full complexity of human nature and experience as they are manifest in the work of art. Political, moral, and religious issues are recognized and explored; but no abstraction or simplification is allowed to be a shortcut or an escape route from contemplation of the whole work. Brooks's criticism embodies a high, noble, and strenuous view of art and of human nature. It will remain useful and inspiring (to use a word that might make Brooks wince) for a very long time to come.

Robert Penn Warren as Critic

Since Warren is far better known as poet and novelist than as critic, and since he insists repeatedly in interviews that he is not a critic, why should he be discussed as such? Although he has published only one collection of criticism, *Selected Essays* (1958), he has written numerous highly influential essays and introductions throughout his career, and as half of the corporate entity Brooks and Warren he has exerted even more influence through editing the *Southern Review* and the great text-books *Understanding Poetry* and *Understanding Fiction.* If there was such a thing as the New Criticism, he must have been a founding father; yet in most respects he was and is the very opposite of the mythical New Critic. Nobody was ever farther from being a mandarin or a pure aesthete: His primary concerns as critic have always and undisguisedly been moral, historical, and even patriotic. A New Dealer who has never recanted, he has always been involved with political and social questions—for example his *Segregation* (1956) and *Who Speaks for the Negro?* (1965)—and has written much about American history: first the biography of John Brown (1929), then *Remember the Alamo!* (an account of early Texas history, meant for children but much to be relished by adults), then *The Legacy of the Civil War* (1961), and most recently *Jefferson Davis Gets His Citizenship Back* (1980). In this work, as well as in his editing of selections from Melville's and Whittier's poetry and of collections of essays on Faulkner and Katherine Anne Porter, in his many introductions, and in his *Homage to Theodore Dreiser,* Warren is a careful, thorough, and highly competent historical scholar as well as critic.

Although he says he has no critical sense and does not enjoy the process of writing criticism as he does that of writing poetry or fiction, he has never belittled the importance of criticism: He has simply given the other activities priority—and who could wish him to do otherwise? Nevertheless, his achievement as critic is substantial and valuable, and it is appropriate to put the spotlight on him in this role, in spite of his disposition to linger in the wings. My intention is to touch briefly on his whole career, but to spend the most time on the *Selected Essays* and the more recent, and rather neglected, *Democracy and Poetry* (1975). First, however, a few words about *Understanding Poetry.*

When it was published in 1938, *Understanding Poetry* was neither a manifesto nor a profession of critical theory but a practical textbook designed to answer a specific need. It was the first, but by no means the only, alternative to the historical-biographical approach, which was widely felt to be inadequate because it did not teach students to read. I. A. Richards's *Practical Criticism* (1929) had shown that students in the Cambridge Honours School, presumably the flower of the existing system, were helpless when confronted by new poems of whatever period. Brooks, in an essay published in the *Sewanee Review* in 1981, says that Warren introduced him to *Practical Criticism* at Oxford in 1929–30 and they discussed it and Richards's other work. As Brooks suggests, many of the characteristic doctrines implied in *Understanding Poetry* derive, at least in part, from *Practical Criticism:* the dangers of stock responses, message-hunting, sentimentality, preferring smooth and regular meters; the importance of context and tone; the values of tension, irony, inclusion as against exclusion. But the motive of Brooks and Warren was not to inculcate any doctrine: Instead they wished to remedy the reading deficiencies they had observed in their students at Louisiana State University and elsewhere.

When I began teaching at the University of Wisconsin in 1940, we used, together with various other texts, *Reading Poems* by Brown and Thomas. That Brown and Thomas were members of the Wisconsin department was one reason we used this text rather than *Understanding Poetry,* but *Reading Poems* also contained much more modern poetry and more material about revision and was a much handsomer book. *Reading Poems* was not an opportunistic or meretricious imitation of *Understanding Poetry* but a response to the same needs felt by Brooks and Warren; and there were many other responses. Of the three varieties of freshman English from which the Wisconsin student could choose in democratic freedom, one was Language in Action, using a textbook of the same title by S. I. Hayakawa, who was later to attain fame as a U.S. senator. Here the dominant emphasis was on language and its use in different types of speech and writing; the semantic analysis was based on the theories of Korzybsky, somewhat rationalized and combined with others. Most intensively in this course, but also in the other two, the aim, made urgent by the war, was to enable students to spot propaganda and, through discriminating among the various uses of language, to read and write more effectively and responsibly. Many people thought this the most important function of English studies.[1]

When I arrived at Vanderbilt in 1946 (after four years in the military), I taught *Understanding Poetry* and *Understanding Fiction* for the first time, and found them wonderful but strenuous. They provided all students and teachers with an approach that was vital and humane; in this sense Brooks and Warren's doctrine and method were democratic rather than elitist (as New Criticism has often been charged with being). Nor did it seem revolutionary: I have always thought that the continuity of this approach with the oral tradition of good teaching in many times and places has been much underrated. Good teachers have always emphasized close reading of the text, with careful attention to tone and to all the devices of rhetoric, and they have tried to help students see how the work is related to their own experience.[2] I was fortunate enough to have several first-rate teachers, all the way from high school through graduate school, coming from various backgrounds but mostly innocent of contact with anything that could be described as New Criticism. The professor from whom I learned most as an undergraduate, though, a former Rhodes scholar named J. E. Norwood, certainly knew the work of Richards, Empson, Eliot, probably Leavis, and maybe Winters, as well as the whole earlier history of criticism. (This was before 1938; perhaps it is worth noting that Norwood was no more a pure aesthete than Brooks or Warren: His favorite of recent critical works was Babbitt's *Rousseau and Romanticism*.) He introduced critical awareness to the classroom in a manner not unlike Brooks and Warren, and he introduced me to the critical matrix out of which they grew. *Understanding Poetry* and *Understanding Fiction* thus seemed to me to be far more traditional than revolutionary, in preserving the best of the pedagogical tradition and making it available to new and larger groups. *Modern Rhetoric* (1949) made this continuity clear; it had remained obvious at Vanderbilt, partly because of Donald Davidson's reconciliation of the Brooks-Warren approach with greater rhetorical and historical emphasis in his widely used freshman English text (*American Composition and Rhetoric*) and in his own influential teaching, which emphasized the relation of poetry to music and to folk traditions as well as to society.[3]

In the postwar situation, when the universities were flooded with intelligent and mature students who had sketchy academic preparation, the need for teaching them how to read was even more urgent than it had been, and the missionary impulse to teach them also how to cope with the special difficulties of modern literature was strong.

The Brooks and Warren textbooks were properly demanding, exciting, and provocative to teachers and students: I can remember many a desperate and exasperated debate, as I rushed from Vanderbilt's postwar housing with fellow instructors just out of the military, through the smoky Nashville dawn to an eight o'clock class, over what on earth the correct answer to one of the questions appended to poems or stories might be. Some of them I still wonder about. They made you work and think!

Warren's central theme, from "Pure and Impure Poetry" (1942) to *Democracy and Poetry* (1975), is that poetry exists not in some purely aesthetic realm but in the everyday world of experience and change, which it interprets and which it can affect. Let us consider *Selected Essays* with this theme in mind.

In "Pure and Impure Poetry" Warren argues against the ideal of pure poetry, showing the value of impurity from the contribution of the ironic and irreverent figure of Mercutio to *Romeo and Juliet* to the fundamental importance of irony in the *Divine Comedy,* with its conflicts between human and divine conceptions of justice; and he elaborates the same thesis at much greater length in the long study of *The Rime of the Ancient Mariner.* He insists that poetry does have meaning and is related to the real world of history: There is the repeated image of the poet as earning his vision by submitting it to the fires of irony. In every essay Warren is exploring a writer who is like himself and is defining themes that are like those of his own novels and poems. This is criticism as self-definition, self-discovery. To put it another way, we might say that in each essay Warren explores certain possibilities of himself as writer, masks of the self, personae in Pound's definition. This is plain in the essay on Coleridge, a romantic-philosophical poet whose main theme is the sacramental One Life of man and nature, with the violation of this communion through Original Sin and its restoration through love and repentance; and whose secondary theme is the crime against the Imagination and the final restoration of unity. (In the most general terms the *Ancient Mariner* is "about the unity of mind and the final unity of values, and in particular about poetry itself.") "A Poem of Pure Imagination" is an essay in definition, all as relevant to Warren's work as to Coleridge's. As in "Pure and Impure Poetry," the critic argues for the unity of experience ("I cannot admit that our experience, even our aesthetic experience, is ineluctably and vindictively divided into the 'magical' and the rational, with an abyss between") and hence for a definition of art as impure, involved with history on the one hand and ideas, philosophical and religious on the other.[4]

The splendid essay on *Nostromo* defines the philosophical novelist, in terms that obviously apply as much to Warren as to Conrad, as not "schematic and deductive," but "willing to go naked into the pit, again and again, to make the same old struggle for his truth"; and as one for whom "the very act of composition was a way of knowing, a way of exploration." Conrad's central theme is the relation of man to the human communion, he says, and Faulkner's basic theme is similar — recognition of the common human bond, with the only villains those who deny that bond. Another variation of the theme is apparent in the title "Love and Separateness in Eudora Welty." Frost's theme of the relation between fact and the dream resembles Conrad's, and the title "Irony with a Center" suggests another dimension of irony, which may be purely destructive, the corrosive intellect when pure Idea; but, when held in balance, irony makes for inclusiveness and richness in art. The Wolfe and Hemingway essays define certain kinds of naturalism, together with a romantic anti-intellectualism, that Warren seems to be exorcising in himself.

As we shall see, the essays on Melville, Faulkner, and Porter in *Selected Essays* were elaborated later. The next big cluster of critical activity for Warren was 1970–73, when he published the Melville, Whittier, and Dreiser books, the long Hawthorne essay, and the two-volume American literature textbook (with Brooks and R. W. B. Lewis). Many of these studies are more social in emphasis than the earlier ones, but Warren has always been mainly a moral-philosophical critic: As this second cluster makes very clear, the aesthetic criterion was never primary in Warren's mind.

Homage to Theodore Dreiser, published in 1971 on the centennial of Dreiser's birth, begins with Warren's poem. The prose text begins: "The career of Theodore Dreiser raises in a peculiarly poignant form the question of the relation of life and art": His fiction is so much like his life that we are tempted to think him a mere recorder. "What is wrong with this way of thinking is, of course, that it does not account for the fact that, in one sense, art is the artist's way of understanding — of creating even — the actuality that he lives." Dreiser was the first important American writer from across the tracks; even those who were poor, like Whittier, or had little formal education, like Twain and Melville, felt themselves inheritors of the civilization they had been born into. But Dreiser is the immigrant, "the outsider, the rejected, the yearner, and that fact conditions the basic emotions and the basic power of his work." It may be "reasonably guessed that the germ of his philosophy, like that of Herman Melville, lay in the early disaster of the father. And if a secret drama of Melville's work is the search for the father who died after failure, a secret drama of Dreiser's is the rejection of a father who, after failure, lived." The father may have been afraid of success, or had fallen in love with failure and with the rigid religiosity in which he had taken refuge. The son's admiration of the superman probably resulted from reaction against the father more than from the influence of Nietzsche, Machiavelli, and Darwin. Dreiser was not a novelist of manners, but of "the metaphysics of society"; but he could never separate the aesthetic dimension from the sociological (as Proust did): He saw art merely as an instrument to satisfy his grossest aspirations. His attitude toward the Gilded Age and the robber barons was ambivalent, like that of Twain, whose *Connecticut Yankee* is also a revolt against the sentimental medievalism of Charles Eliot Norton or of Henry Adams, who said the only thing he wanted in life was to be made a cardinal. But for Dreiser "part of the wisdom of the unillusioned man is to recognize that even more redemptive than illusion is the pity for illusion; and, at this point, we see how, for Dreiser, naturalistic insight is akin to Christian charity." Warren argues that Dreiser's power and compassion are known only through his control, "by the rhythmic organization of his materials, the vibrance which is the life of fictional illusion, the tension among elements, and the mutual interpenetration in meaning of part and whole which gives us the sense of preternatural fulfillment"—in short, by his art. The book is a fine example of historical-biographical criticism not neglecting the aesthetic dimension, yet it is about as far from New Criticism or aestheticism as it is possible to get.

Both in the *Selected Essays* essay, written in 1945, and in the later "Reader's Edition" (1970) of his selections from Melville's poetry, Warren admits that Melville is uneven—did not "master his craft" in some sense—but explains and defends his poetry. The book, obviously a labor of love, contains, in addition to the long introduction and several hundred pages of selections, 102 pages of notes on the text. The most brilliant passage in the introduction entails the comparison of Whitman and Melville as poets of the Civil War, defining Whitman as essentially ritualistic, while Melville is seen as dramatic and ultimately tragic.

Whittier, perhaps Warren's most unlikely book, defends this rural (not "peasant") abolitionist (and hence idea-ridden) poet. This selection of his poems with a long introduction (1970) demonstrates the primacy of nonliterary motives in Warren's criticism: His moral concern and social and political interests, together with his fascination

with American history, make him sympathize with this almost inde-
fensible writer. The volume rehabilitates this most virulently anti-
Southern of American writers, the abolitionist Quaker who was a half-
educated, trashy, popular, propagandistic, and moralistic poet, and it
says all that can be said for him and for his poetry. (One is tempted
to add, like the advertising men, "and more.")

Hawthorne, in Warren's long essay of 1973 in the *Sewanee Review,*
shares the central theme, both in life and works, of isolation: He
yearned to be "a man in society," to learn "the deep, warm secret" by
which other people seemed to live but which somehow eluded him.
But "unconsciously—literally, out of the unconscious—a writer may
find the meaning and the method which later, consciously, he may
explore and develop; that is, in writing, a man may be discovering,
among other things, himself. To have intuited this truth was one of
Hawthorne's most brilliant achievements. But the truth, once intuited,
was one that he could rarely bring himself to contemplate for long.
. . . The work that reveals may also be used to conceal." In Hawthorne's "emotional involvement with the violence of the New England
past is some feeling that in that violence there was at least a confronting of reality, which was lacking in the doctrines of Transcendentalists,
Brook Farmers, and Unitarians, and in Emerson. . . . If there was
violence and cruelty in that older society there was also, in that very
fact, a sense of reality and grim meaningfulness." (This last sentence
obviously applies to Warren as much as to Hawthorne.) *The Scarlet
Letter* was "hell-fired," Hawthorne said; and when he read it to his
wife, she went to bed with a grievous headache. Emerson, when asked
what he thought of the novel, murmured "Ghastly, ghastly." (Warren
quotes Henry James: "Emerson, as a spiritual sun-worshipper, could
have attached but a moderate value to Hawthorne's cat-like faculty of
seeing in the dark.") Warren sums it up:

> Even nature . . . cannot be taken simply. The forest is a haunt of evil
> as well as of good, and the wishes of the heart may be wicked as well
> as benign. . . . Man is doomed to live in a world where nature is denied
> and human nature distorted, and—most shatteringly of all—in a world
> where love and hate may be "the same thing at bottom," and even vice
> or virtue may represent nothing more than what Chillingworth calls "a
> typical illusion." But men must live by the logic of their illusions, as
> best they can. . . . That is their last and darkest "necessity." What com-
> pensation is possible in such a world comes from the human capacity

for achieving scale and grandeur even in illusion . . . and from the capacity for giving pity.

Warren's introduction to *Katherine Anne Porter: A Collection of Critical Essays* (1979)[5] is one of his finest essays—perhaps second only to that on *Nostromo* and, like it, revealing much about Warren's own aims and ideals as a writer. There is an apt comparison to Faulkner: "Both regarded the present as a product of the past, to be understood in that perspective, and both, though repudiating the romance of the past, saw in it certain human values now in jeopardy, most of all in jeopardy the sense of the responsible individual, and at the same time man's loss of his sense of community and sense of basic relation to nature." This is part of Porter's deeper theme, "the conviction that reality, the 'truth,' is never two-dimensional, is found in process not in stasis. All this gives the peculiar vibrance and the peculiar sense of a complex but severely balanced form to all the stories." She reveals inner tensions and complexity of motives, but "never confounds the shadowy and flickering shapes of the psychological situation with vagueness of structure in the fiction itself." She has the gift of "touching the key of feeling," but never exploits it: "Certainly, she never indulges in random emotionality; she knows that the gift must never be abused or it will vanish like fairy gold." "And always feeling appears against a backdrop of two other factors, the strain of irony that infuses the work (even though the writer knows that the exploitation of irony is as dangerous as that of feeling) and the rigor of form. The writer has some austerity of imagination that gives her a secret access to the spot whence feeling springs. She can deny herself, and her own feelings, and patiently repudiate the temptation to exploit the feeling of the reader, and therefore can, when the moment comes, truly enter into the heart of a character. One hesitates to think what price may have been paid for this priceless gift." "One feels that for her the act of composition is an act of knowing, and that, for her, knowledge, imaginatively achieved, is, in the end, life." "If a deep stoicism is the underlying attitude of this fiction, it is a stoicism without grimness or arrogance, and though shot through with irony and aware of a merciless evil in the world, yet capable of gaiety, tenderness, and sympathy, and its ethical center is found in those characters who . . . have the toughness to survive, but who survive by a loving sense of obligation to others, this sense being in the end, only a full affirmation of the life-sense, a joy in strength. . . . Like all strong art, this work is, paradoxically, both a question asked of life and a celebration of life; and the author knows in her bones that the more corrosive the question asked, the more powerful may be the celebration."

As a critic Warren unobtrusively subordinates himself to his subject: He perhaps lacks that minimum arrogance required for him to appear as a professional critic. But he always shows a deep conviction of the importance of literature and of criticism, and he is always reasonable, humane, and moral. He is not exactly a reluctant critic, or a critic in spite of himself, because he takes such obvious satisfaction in championing favorite writers against neglect and misinterpretation. He is not detached, remote, balanced, judicial; instead he is involved, often a passionate advocate, convinced of the worth of his subject and its value to society. The role grows out of teaching, as Warren conceives of it, and like a good teacher he advocates the writers and principles he believes in. He is at the opposite pole from judicial critics like Yvor Winters and F. R. Leavis, and he takes none of their relish in negative criticism.

He does not try to be funny often: He displays only an occasional sardonic and wry wit. Instead he is serious, responsible, and democratic, spelling out for the common reader exactly what he means. The contrast with such other critics as Jarrell, the early Eliot, Leavis, Winters, sometimes Empson and Tate—all of whom are often ironic, oblique, allusive, enigmatic, giving the reader a sense of belonging to an inside group—is marked. Perhaps Warren's most unusual quality is that he is so openly patriotic and openly concerned with American politics, society, and history, though never confusing his categories. Except for Conrad and Coleridge, all his criticism deals with American writers.

Democracy and Poetry (1975) may be taken as a critical last testament and valediction, for Warren said in 1977 that he had sworn never to write another line of criticism of any kind. More significantly, however, it may be taken as a credo, reaffirming Warren's lifelong and passionate commitment to both democracy and poetry and undertaking the tricky and perilous task of defining and reconciling the two. (The analogy that comes to mind is the task in Christian theology of explaining how the persons of the Trinity are both three and one.) Warren is committed absolutely to both poetry and democracy in its American manifestation: He remains an unashamed patriot, while being fully aware of the worst that can be said about the present state of the Republic and its history (e.g., he comments devastatingly on Nixon's taped remark that "the Arts you know—they're Jews, they're left wing—in other words, stay away"). He knows how much nonsense has been written on the subject (from MacLeish's attacks on the Irresponsibles to Hillyer's attacks on the Bollingen Award to Pound, not to mention innumerable Marxist and other sermons); and yet he confronts this most treacherous of all questions about poetry and is determined to make his beliefs explicit without sacrificing honesty or realism. If his position is sometimes more passionate profession of faith than impartial argument, it is an utterly serious redefinition and rededication. One is tempted to say, against the facile propagandists, that there is no connection between art and society (or, specifically, poetry and democracy). Certainly such a response is much easier than to say precisely what the connection is. Auden put this denial in its most extreme form ("If not a poem had been written, not a picture painted, not a bar of music composed, the history of man would be materially unchanged"), but most modern critics have been ironic, oblique, or skeptical about the relation of art and society.

In attempting to write a Defense of Poetry for our time, Warren argues that poetry is "a nourishment of the soul, and indeed of society, in that it keeps alive the sense of self and the correlated sense of a community." Poetry, he continues, "helps one to grasp reality and to grasp one's own life." He is not willing to distort or simplify reality, to "demote science, the purest expression of the love of intellectual beauty, to the role of a scullery maid or to deny the special, and in an economic sense primary, role of technology"; and he flinches "from those who, like Henry James, would assume art to be the justification of all life." (On the other hand, one is obliged to note that Warren's solution seems primarily for the artist; it is for the reader only insofar as he participates in the experience [and discipline and labor] of the artist, just as his notion of democracy is based on the willingness of the common man to change, to strive to realize his potentialities and work to redeem himself.) "I am not suggesting that in an ideal use of free time a man would take up finger painting or raffia work. What I do suggest is that art obviously provides the most perfect example of self-fulfilling activity, the kind of activity of which gratuitous joy in the way of the doing is the mark, and in which the doer pursues the doing as a projection of his own nature upon objective nature, thereby discovering both the law of the medium . . . and his own nature. A man need not create art in order to participate, with varying degrees of consciousness, in the order of experience from which art flows." Warning very effectively of the trends toward passive consumerism and isolation in our society, Warren argues that poetry is "a sovereign antidote for passivity. For the basic fact about poetry is that it demands participation." Hence it is a model for, and an agent in, the creation of the self, which is possible only in a community. Poetry can achieve this because it embodies a total and unifying experience: Its form "embodies the experience of a self vis-à-vis the world, not merely as a subject matter, but as translated into the experience of form. The form represents uniqueness made available to others, but the strange fact is that the uniqueness is not be be exhausted: the 'made thing' does not become a Euclidian theorem any more than love is exhausted by the sexual act." Hence it can heal our psychic divisions and impoverishments: "The self has been maimed in our society because, for one reason, we lose contact with the world's body, lose any holistic sense of our relation to the world, not merely in that there is a split between emotion and idea but also because perception and sensation are at a discount." Rhythm, Warren argues, "—not mere meter, but all the pulse of movement, density, and shadings of intensity of feeling—is the most intimate and compelling factor revealing to us the nature of the 'made thing.'" In all the arts "we can envisage a structure out of time as well as experience the sequential rhythms in time. And when we experience the contrast and interplay of rhythms of time and movement with those of non-time and stasis—that is, when we grasp a work in relation to the two orders of rhythm and both in terms of felt meaning—what a glorious *klang* of being awakens to unify mind and body, to repair, if even for a moment, what Martin Buber has called 'the injured wholeness of man.'" This is a memorable statement of the function of art because it includes both poles, the formal-aesthetic and the emotional-psychological, and unites them in an implied religious conception. But why should I try to embellish what Warren has said so well?

Warren proceeds to argue that "historically a strong and high art is to be associated only with societies of challenging vigor." However, such societies have often been antidemocratic. Warren points out that democracy is a recent development, historically, for in earlier societies the laborers were not regarded as persons at all; but the poetry of such an elite order did develop the conception of selfhood, and he cites the examples of Greek epic and tragedy. To debate this much-vexed question of the relation of high art to the success and vigor of a society is tempting; but Warren's central point seems all too plausible: A society that, like ours, seems to be losing both its vigor and its concept of the self is likely to lose its capacity to produce great art as well. Or, to put it more positively, art can help to prevent this from happening and can thus be valuable to the society as well as to individuals. Although it is incomplete and vulnerable, Warren's is an honest and serious attempt to confront such questions, and it is worthy to stand in the great line of defenses of poetry with Sidney's and Shelley's.

Although Warren has, as he insists, never been a critic in the sense of developing and defending a fully articulated critical theory, he has produced a large and varied body of criticism and thereby has exerted an enormous influence. From the beginning his criticism has been impure in the sense that aesthetic motives and criteria have never been primary or unmixed in it; and his chief polemic has been directed against all doctrines of purity. As we have noted, the moral basis of Warren's criticism has always been unconcealed, though he has argued against any division between moral, aesthetic, and social. Consider, for example, the conclusion of his long study of the *Ancient Mariner:* ' "If poetry does anything for us, it reconciles, by its symbolical reading of experience (for by its very nature it is in itself a myth of the unity of being), the self-divisive internecine malices which arise at the superficial level on which we conduct most of our living."

However much he shrinks from the role, then, Warren has been extremely influential as a critic. From my point of view, his influence has been very salutary, for he has helped to keep us aware of the moral, dramatic, and emotional texture of literary art and its closeness to the gritty unpredictability of reality. His emphasis has often been philosophical, but he has been steadily less interested in critical theory and in aesthetic evaluation. He has been a very effective advocate for neglected writers both of the past (Melville as poet, Dreiser, Whittier, etc.) and of the present (through innumerable blurbs for first novels and favorable reviews of works that seem fated to a hostile reception, such as Dickey's *Zodiac*). His generosity of spirit and his love of his country and its history have been exemplary for us all.

Two Doctors for Critics: René Wellek and Randall Jarrell

René Wellek

Both meanings of *doctor* are relevant: For many years Wellek has been both a teacher and an intellectual physician for critics, theorists, and historians of literature. Most Americans who aspire to criticism have learned from him, and many of us feel that literary studies would be in a healthier condition if we had learned more. His role has been unique and indispensable. As a critic of critics, he has striven not to propagate any dogma in terms of which other dogmas are to be judged, but rather to remind those who practice criticism that their vision of the truth is partial, their assumptions and methods not forever valid but limited and imperfect. Against all varieties of parochialism, patriotism, and dogmatic complacency, he has maintained the rigorous ideal of literary criticism, theory, and history as distinct yet indissoluble, and as part of a common culture, a potential European intellectual community. His principal aim has been, with this ideal in mind, not to accept some doctrines and reject others, but to reconcile and synthesize the various doctrines in the hope of arriving at a consensus, if not on answers to ultimate questions, at least on which approaches are likely to be most fruitful. Wellek not only upholds this ideal but, happily, exemplifies it: a genuine polymath, widely and deeply read not only in the literatures of a dozen languages, but also in their philosophy and history, and, most comprehensively of all, in their criticism and scholarship, he does not let his central concern for literary theory become exclusive, but practices and discusses equally the other two disciplines of literary history and criticism of specific works. He is academic in learning, poise, and rigor, but without the academic vices of dullness, superficiality, and pretentiousness; he has a shrewdness and common sense and skepticism that do not desert him in dealing with complex abstractions or seas of facts.

Concepts of Criticism,[1] which was edited by Stephen G. Nichols, Jr., as a tribute to Wellek on his sixtieth birthday, contains fourteen essays, three of them new and the others published originally in widely scattered books and periodicals between 1946 and 1962. There are also a complete bibliography of Wellek's writings and a brief introduction by Nichols. The essays are very much worth preserving: Some of them develop, with more detail and documentation, ideas presented briefly in *Theory of Literature* or other works; some expand and bring up to date Wellek's analyses of various controversial matters; and some break new ground. Since the essays are not revised, there is a good deal of repetition in the book; but most of it seems justified because the same issues are seen in different perspectives in different essays. This varied context also explains many points that Wellek's earlier treatments may have left in some obscurity: for example, the Russian formalists and the Linguistic Circle of Prague who keep turning up in *Theory of Literature* like King Charles's head, to the incredulous bafflement of most American students. In the present volume these exotic references are seen to be justified on the ground that Wellek was himself a member of the Prague circle for many years and thus speaks from first-hand knowledge, and, more importantly, that the references are a part of Wellek's demonstration that the "New Criticism" is not provincial or eccentric but is part of a world-wide movement.

The heart of the book is the three famous essays on the concepts of Baroque, Romanticism, and Realism; the first two of these, which first appeared in the late 1940s, are now brought up to date by extensive postscripts. Protesting against the extreme nominalism and pragmatism of many scholars, Wellek defends the use of such "period terms," though he wishes to reexamine and define them most scrupulously. His position is remote from a naïve traditionalism or a Teutonic worship of abstractions; in command of the facts, he is easily a match for the "tough-minded" scholars who would abolish the terms, while in philosophical awareness and dexterity he is clearly their superior. To simplify drastically, his basic contention is that we cannot talk meaningfully about literature in its historical or theoretical aspects without using such concepts, because, whatever the difficulties of definition, they do point to distinctive and massive phenomena. To despair before the complexity of the task and simply abandon the terms is, he suggests, an evasion of responsibility. In "Romanticism Re-examined," the new essay on this topic, Wellek puts the case even more strongly than in his first treatment: His conclusion is:

> I prefer not to be called "the champion of the concept of a pan-European Romanticism." I would not be understood [as] minimizing or ignoring national differences or forgetting that great artists have

created something unique and individual. Still, I hope to have shown that in recent decades a stabilization of opinion has been achieved. One could even say (if we did not suspect the word so much) that progress has been made not only in defining the common features of romanticism but in bringing out what is its peculiarity or even its essence and nature: that attempt, apparently doomed to failure and abandoned by our time, to identify subject and object, to reconcile man and nature, consciousness and unconsciousness by poetry which is "the first and last of all knowledge." (221)

There are also several very penetrating surveys of recent trends in criticism, American and European, with the kind of wide-ranging synoptic view that only Wellek can give. One of these, "Philosophy and Postwar American Criticism," is specially noteworthy as an example of the kind of thing Wellek, with his philosophical training and aptitude, is uniquely qualified to do. Wellek does not avoid commitment; he knows that complete impartiality and objectivity are impossible and meaningless goals. On the last page of the book, for instance, after describing other approaches, he says: "It still seems to me that formalistic, organistic, symbolistic aesthetics, rooted as it is in the great tradition of German aesthetics from Kant to Hegel, restated and justified in French symbolism, in De Sanctis and Croce, has a firmer grasp on the nature of poetry and art" (363–64). But his principal effort is, as we have seen, toward synthesis and reconciliation. This approach is rare, since most critics whose range of learning is comparable to Wellek's use it to buttress a doctrine of their own; and it is immensely useful. Wellek is keenly aware of the larger world outside the literary one, of the relation of literature to philosophy and other modes of discourse, and to the other arts, and of the relation of literary study to other disciplines, both in and outside the academy. By precept and example, he shows the importance of wide and deep learning, of philosophical and historical training and awareness, of rigorous definition of premises, aims, and methods. American literary students, misled by our British cousins, are all too prone to dismiss these as Teutonic requirements that do not apply to cultivated and artistic souls. But Wellek will not let us evade our responsibilities in any such fashion. There is an important sense in which the special virtue of his work may be called moral: He practices and teaches a discipline of humility among the prophets, aesthetes, and hanging judges who sometimes dominate the critical scene.

In this respect, as in most others, Wellek is at the opposite pole from F. R. Leavis, whose famous exchange with Wellek in the pages of

Scrutiny[2] makes a comparison specially appropriate. Enough has been said about Leavis's many virtues and the valuable services performed by *Scrutiny;* I shall take awareness of these for granted and look at the other side of the picture. When he refused, in the 1937 exchange with Wellek, to formulate or examine the assumptions on which his criticism proceeded, and rejected Wellek's formulation of the norms in terms of which his evaluations seemed to be made, Leavis revealed plainly enough that he did not really believe in all the talk of "assumptions" and "norms"; his conviction was simply that his values were true and all others false. In short, his doctrine was not only absolutist but essentially religious, held as not only true but necessary for salvation; and it was sometimes hard for believers to avoid the *reductio ad absurdum* of concluding that there was no salvation outside the Cambridge English Tripos under Leavis. Literary values are taken as the only serious ones, and Leavis's special scorn has always been directed at those who suggest that other values may be even more important, from the frivolous Oxonians who took religion or scholarship or history seriously to C. P. Snow and his concern for science and the relief of human suffering. The Leavisites, however, constantly smuggled in other kinds of values without recognizing or examining them. In the 1937 debate Leavis refused to admit that his judgment of Shelley was partly moral and intellectual; he insisted that it was purely literary, based on "completeness of response" and "immediate sense of value"—and because thus intuitive and nonintellectual, not subject to challenge. This appeal to "sensibility," while obviously containing a measure of truth, was essentially an evasion; it was never satisfactory as an escape from intellectual questions, though Leavis's expert polemics sometimes made it seem so. Its effect was to substitute a kind of taste-snobbery for the class-snobbery the Leavisites justly attacked; but the taste-snobbery was equally vicious, for the slight margin of free will (taste can be improved by discipline and cultivation) allowed lack of taste to be identified not only with error but with wickedness. A further consequence of the refusal to examine assumptions is that Leavis and his disciples were influenced by all sorts of extraliterary and only partly avowable motives, such as a bitter hatred of Oxford, of the upper class, of "Bloomsbury," of scholars, and of most living poets and novelists. The Leavisites saw themselves as revealing a conspiracy among these groups which dominated the academic and literary "establishments"; hence their posture was that of iconoclasts and at the same time guardians of the true tradition, outposts of lonely virtue, the happy few in a world going rapidly downhill. Whatever elements of truth there may have been in this myth, nothing could be more dangerously flattering to the ego; it has the fatal seductiveness of all reductions of truth to a single doctrine and discipline, providing answers to all questions except those that are dismissed as unimportant.

The moral effect of Wellek's doctrine is precisely opposite: Where Leavis offers a temptation to pride, Wellek gives the critic a lesson in humility. One must choose among imperfect alternatives and be aware of the premises and consequencs of the choice, Wellek says again and again; no approach is perfect and no reader ideal, and therefore the critic must strive to be conscious of his assumptions and motives and methods, must seek philosophical and historical perspective. Leavis, on the other hand, would separate literary theory and history from criticism and would deny them any real significance; obviously he thinks the critical approach is the *only* way to deal with literature: The ideal reader is the critic, and vice versa, and it is dangerous for the critic to know too much of theory or history. Wellek, in contrast, insists that all three approaches are indispensable, and that they are distinct but inseparable. His ideal is a collaborative one, and sometimes he seems to hope for more disinterested collaboration than is ever likely to take place; but the ideal is as healthy morally as it is rigorous intellectually. His influence on critics and scholars has been wholesome, clarifying, and inspiring; long may it flourish and increase!

Randall Jarrell in His Letters

These are wonderful letters,[3] fully as good as I hoped they would be. Witty, often brilliantly perceptive, often touching, usually funny, they have many of the best qualities of Jarrell's criticism and his novel, *Pictures from an Institution.* They bristle with ideas while they also show great freshness and openness to experience.

Precocious and prodigious though his intelligence was, Jarrell retained both a child's curiosity and a child's cruelty. (Or a cat's, for there was something feline in the way this great cat-lover toyed with his prey; and there was often an element of *Schadenfreude* in reading him.) At the same time, this most formidable of critics professed an abhorrence of criticism and a suspicion of the intellect, and as a poet his great subjects were pity, and nostalgia for childhood. It is the strangeness of this combination that has always made Jarrell fascinating to me, though also disturbing and enigmatic.

I have the impression that Jarrell is read and enjoyed more now than the other New Critics. (It is a fitting irony that Jarrell, who spent much of his time attacking criticism, and especially those kinds now regarded as New Critical, should inexorably wind up in this pigeonhole. But it is a sad irony that Jarrell, who yearned so desperately to be remembered as a poet rather than as a critic, should be suffering the fate he feared: a poet of talent, a critic of genius, seems the verdict of even his greatest admirers.) Some of the reasons for this preference are obvious enough: Jarrell as a critic, as these letters show once more, is more readable, more entertaining, more often witty or amusing than his peers. He is less concerned than they are with attempting to formulate principles or conclusions of general validity. His specialty is subverting any such effort and undermining the whole critical enterprise. He flatters the reader's prejudices by making him the final judge, superior to critics, and, rather than trying to educate the reader's taste, urges him to read for pleasure alone.

This attitude allows Jarrell to express both sides of his nature: On the one hand he exalts the natural, the simple, the spontaneous (also the naïve, the childish, sometimes the sentimental), in a kind of romantic primitivism; on the other, he expresses his aggressions by attacking with savage glee both his rivals and the critics from whom he springs. There is a definitely Oedipal tinge to this dichotomy: He loves the maternal, emotional, poetic side of himself and others and directs his hostility toward the masculine, paternal, intellectual side; symbolically, he strikes the father dead. As these letters reveal, Auden was the earliest and most conspicuous of these father figures: Jarrell's first publication was a review in 1934 of Auden's poetry; he wanted to write his master's thesis and eventually a book on Auden, and Auden's influence on him both as a poet and as a thinker was obviously enormous. Yet the two long essays about Auden that he did publish were, though very brilliant, essentially demolition work, destroying the foundations of Auden's reputation. The changes of attitude and rhetoric in Auden's poetry were, as Jarrell described them, all for the worse, and the stages of his ideology from Freud to Paul were increasingly incoherent. Something of the same pattern may be seen in his relation to Allen Tate, who helped extensively to get Jarrell published and recognized and was repaid by remoteness tinged with hostility. Ransom and Blackmur, too, were personally kind and helpful to Jarrell. With Tate, they were, of course, leading figures of the Age of Criticism that Jarrell made his reputation by attacking and repudiating. The hand that fed Jarrell was likely to get bitten.

On the pleasanter side, though, Jarrell's relations with Robert Lowell are revealed in these letters as one of the most gratifying of literary friendships. Each was the other's best critic, and the credit ledgers were at last pretty evenly balanced, Lowell's concern for Jarrell's posthumous reputation balancing Jarrell's generous help to this younger friend (and rival). "Child Randall," Lowell's epithet for him in *History,* is perfect, with its allusions to to *King Lear* and Browning ("Childe Rowland to the Dark Tower Came") and its suggestion that Jarrell was both an heroic and ambiguous quester and a perennial child. Lowell's "Appreciation," published in Jarrell's *The Lost World* and elsewhere, is the definitive summing up of Jarrell's life and work, his "noble, difficult, and beautiful soul." As Lowell rightly observes, "eulogy was the glory of Randall's criticism," and this comment puts in perspective what I have said of its negative aspect.

These letters, edited and annotated lovingly by Jarrell's widow, Mary, are described as an "autobiographical and literary selection." She chose some 400 of about 2,500 letters available to her, ranging from Jarrell's senior year at Vanderbilt in 1935 to his death in 1965. The letters to his first wife during his service in the Air Corps (1942–46) are especially interesting. Jarrell established his reputation as the leading poet of the air war in his *Little Friend, Little Friend* (1945) and *Losses* (1948). As the letters make clear, Jarrell served as a ground instructor in the United States; he washed out as a pilot, was never sent overseas, and was never in combat. But the letters show, as he repeats stories told to him by participants in battle, the kind of imaginative empathy that makes him fully deserve his reputation as a war poet. (He is especially good at representing a carrier pilot's experience, though he never saw a carrier.) There are sidelights on many episodes of some importance in literary history, from Ransom's leaving Vanderbilt to backstage views of Blackmur and Berryman at Princeton (the editor suggests that these are contributions to the history of "the American 'Bloomsbury Circle' of the fifties" [xiii]); Fiedler and Fitzgerald at the Indiana School of Letters; the Salzburg Seminar; the poetry consultantship at the Library of Congress; and faculty controversies and feuds at Greensboro. There are interesting letters to people ranging from Hannah Arendt (to whom he confesses, "Indeed I *don't* read Greek—it's a wonder I can read English. In my earlier lives I couldn't read anything, but just sang songs so that people put gold bracelets on my arms or threw big bones at me" [342]) to B. H. Haggin, Edmund Wilson, Elizabeth Bishop, and Marianne Moore. Not surprisingly, the most revealing letters are those to the women he loved: the wartime letters to his first wife, Mackie; the series to Elisabeth Eisler, the Viennese woman with whom he fell in love at Salzburg in 1948; and the letters to Mary, his second wife, from 1951 on. The love for the last two women intertwines amusingly with Jarrell's light-hearted but dead-serious and long-lasting love affair with the German language, memorably described in the poem "Deutsch Durch Freud."

The letters are not quite an intellectual autobiography, because too many topics are untouched; but there are some brilliant pages of this. Lowell called Jarrell a "radical liberal"; for some periods, in some sense, he was certainly a Marxist, and in this respect he sharply differed from his Southern peers. (The sense that Auden was a lost leader to Marxists was certainly part of Jarrell's animus against him in the Auden pieces.) Probably because of their similar political backgrounds, as well as their common anticriticism stance, Jarrell found Leslie Fiedler very congenial: "I like Fiedler—he's very intelligent and much more restrained and pleasant than what he writes. All in all I had rather a sense of how lonely you are when you come out on the side of life and risk-taking and thinking works of art are live and mysterious and unaccountable; on the side of everything that can't be institutionalized and handled and graded by Experts. Most academic highbrow people really do go along with the critical abstract categorizing mind, not the artist's" (329). On the same grounds, he liked Karl Shapiro.

One of the sad aspects of Jarrell's life is that he meant to write books on Auden, on Hart Crane, on Eliot (a psychoanalytic study), and on Saint Paul; he worked on both the Auden and Eliot ones over many years, and wrote extensively, yet was never able to bring either to completion. Perhaps one reason is that, aside from his progress from Marx to Freud and his enduring myth of childhood, he seems to have formed no central core of belief or conviction.

Jarrell, who majored in psychology (shifting to English in his second year of graduate work) and never hesitated to diagnose others, has no claim to immunity from psychological speculation; and his letters provide a rich field. The nostalgia for childhood and the compulsive destruction of father figures have already been mentioned. He seems to have felt like a motherless child not just sometimes, but constantly, though his letters to his mother are lost. The addressing of Mary as "Big Sister" and the absorbing of her into the Elektra myth are striking (303–4, 313). But his psychological peculiarities are much less interesting than his common and generous humanity. Not long before the sad story of his last days began—depression, separation from Mary with divorce intended, a suicide attempt (though his actual death seems not to have been a suicide)—he wrote to Adrienne Rich: "If you believe in happiness and have ordinary good luck you really can be happy a lot of the time—but most people of our reading-and-writing sort have conscientious objections to any happiness, they'd far rather be right than happy. It *is* terrible in our time to have the death of the world hanging over you, but, personally, it's something you disregard just as you disregard the regular misery of so much of the world, or your own regular personal aging and death" (436). Considering what the future held for both Jarrell and Rich, this sensible observation seems touching indeed.

Of recent collections of letters, only Flannery O'Connor's rival these in consistently high level of interest and entertainment.

Two Women Critics: Helen Vendler and Ursula Le Guin

Our First Woman Critic?

It is curious that no woman so far has become a major literary critic. True, major critics are at least as rare as major poets or novelists; but at least a few women have been numbered in the latter categories for two hundred years. It is true, too, that we have had excellent woman journalist-critics and scholar-critics. But in the whole galaxy of modern criticism no female star has yet appeared.

Why this should be so is a mystery to me. If one of the critic's functions is to exhibit a sympathetic understanding of the artist and a maternal solicitude for him, women might be thought to have some native advantage. If the critic's other principal function — to judge and place his artists, and to support his judgments by theoretical formulations — is thought of as masculine, however, then the ideal critic must be that mythical creature, the androgyne. At any rate, women would seem psychologically at least as well equipped as men for the critic's role.

Helen Vendler's *Part of Nature, Part of Us: Modern American Poets*[1] may well mark the advent of our first major woman critic. Vendler has published three excellent historical books, each of more than specialized interest: a study of Yeats's *A Vision* and its relation to his later plays, an analysis of Stevens's longer poems, and a reading of George Herbert's poems. The present volume, collecting her essays and reviews dealing with modern American poetry, will go far toward establishing her reputation as a critic of the contemporary. Some of these pieces were written for the larger audience of the *New York Times Book Review, The New Yorker,* and the *Atlantic,* others for the smaller and more specialized one of the literary quarterlies. Vendler writes in a manner well calculated to satisfy both audiences: Her style is lively, entertaining, and humane, with the boldness in generalization, the exactness of metaphor, the conciseness in summing up a poet, and the deadly accuracy in locating defects, that delight both the common reader and the expert.

In a time when much criticism seems increasingly academic and autotelic, self-generating and self-absorbed and perhaps self-destructive, it is a relief to find a critic who conceives of her work as having a definite and humane purpose. This is the old-fashioned middleman (middleperson?) function of introducing and explaining poets to readers who might otherwise find them difficult, intimidating, or unsympathetic. These pieces, Vendler observes, "urge the simplicity, naturalness, and accessibility of the poems they consider, to the neglect, perhaps, of the difficulty, perculiarity, and density of those same poems" (ix). Whatever its limitations, the happy result of this strategy is to make the reader want to go immediately and read, or reread, the poets for himself—a result not contemplated by much currently fashionable criticism. Rather than describe poetry from any regional, historical, or ideological perspective, she prefers "to focus on poets one by one, to find in each the idiosyncratic voice wonderfully different from any other." But these voices are also, as her title says, echoing Stevens, "part of nature, part of us," and she tries to explain "what common note they strike and how they make it new" (x). She is the same kind of critic as Randall Jarrell, who said the critic should be "an extremely good reader—one who has learned to show to others what he saw in what he read" (115)—and her discussion of Jarrell is one of her most brilliant.

In accord with her denial of theoretical pretension or any systematic framework, the arrangement of the volume is based entirely on chronology. The pieces are presented in the order of the birth dates of the poets they discuss, from Stevens (1879) to Dave Smith and Louise Glück (both 1943). The longest chapters (each made up of several separately published pieces) are those dealing with Stevens, Lowell, Rich, and Merrill; two omnibus reviews conclude the volume.

Obviously, a volume so made up is affected by the luck of the reviewer's draw and other random factors, and it would be foolish to expect balanced coverage of "modern American poets." Nevertheless, some preferences are clear from the choice of poets discussed as well as from what is said. First, she does not like poets who are relatively traditional in form and diction. Theodore Weiss she responds to tepidly, trying to decide what is the matter with him; Richard Wilbur, Anthony Hecht, Daniel Hoffman, William Meredith—for example—are never mentioned. Second, she does not like religious poets. (This may seem odd in one who has written an excellent book on George Herbert; but that book attempts to demonstrate that no religious beliefs or sympathies are required to appreciate Herbert.) As she sees it, Eliot's career after *The Waste Land* was all downhill, and so was

Auden's after the thirties; once they succumbed to religious belief, their poetic development was subverted (or, as the *Scrutiny* critics used to say, inverted). Later poets are praised for not subscribing to these "falser poetic consolations" (236). Lowell, however, developed in the right direction, away from religion: "reading the complete Lowell is rather like seeing Dostoevsky grow up to be Chekhov" (158).

These preferences do not amount to deliberate literary politics: the reader does not feel that Vendler is trying to make him enlist under the banner of Stevens against Eliot or to convince him that the only strong poets are those who strike their poetic and heavenly fathers dead. But a definite position does emerge: The dominant poetry of our time is the "poetry of deprivation." This poetic tradition (or antipoetic antitradition) appears most fully in Stevens and Lowell, and Vendler's chapters on these two poets (constituting almost a third of the book) are certainly among her best. The previously unpublished "Stevens and Keats's 'To Autumn'" is perhaps the most brilliant single piece, though it follows the unpromising model of reading the poems in relation to the poet's psychology—a model generally producing dismal results, but handled by Vendler with such tact, insight, and sensitivity that it works beautifully. "Stevens recognized, I think, that Keats's ode is spoken by one whose poetic impetus arises from a recoil at the stubble plains; the method of the ode is to adopt a reparatory fantasy whereby the barren plains are 'repopulated' with fruit, flowers, wheat, and a providential goddess" (28). This goddess "reappears in innumerable guises in Stevens' work, but is more often than not maternal. . . . Keats's season is an earth-goddess whose union with the sun makes her bear fruit; the sun, his part in procreation done, departs from the poem as the harvest begins. . . . Finally, when she becomes herself the 'soft-dying day,' she is mourned by creatures deliberately infantine. . . : these creatures are filial forms, children grieving for the death of the mother. Stevens, I believe, recognized these implications and brought them into explicitness" (26–27). Discussing the role of feeling in Stevens, she argues that "we must ask what causes the imagination to be so painfully at odds with reality. The cause . . . is usually, in Stevens' case, passionate feeling, and not merely epistemological query" (40). Most of the best poems spring from "castastrophic disappointment, bitter solitude, or personal sadness." In "The False and True Sublime," she traces Stevens's "slow lifetime's acquaintance with the human less" after his beginning with "rapturous praise of the inhuman more"; though he wondered in his last months whether he had lived a skeleton's life, "Better a skeleton's life than a deity's, we could answer, the skeleton being at least a part of the human less" (15).

In discussing Lowell she similarly relates the poetry to human feeling: She quotes Lowell as saying that he would like critics to describe him not as violent or comic but as "heartbreaking" (165). Although her approach remains biographical, she protests oversimplifications of the relation between life and art: "We cannot go behind the art: the illusion that we can is art's most compelling hallucination" (156). Lowell's later poetry is better than his earlier not because it is closer to experience but because it is better written. Lowell, she argues, is "in no sense a religious poet as the phrase is commonly used; those who dislike him find, above all in the later verse, a relentless trivializing of life, . . . which seems to rob existence of ardor, transcendence, and devotion" (157). She follows Lowell unflinchingly into his final nihilism and concludes by paralleling him with Stevens: " 'Not to console or sanctify,' says Stevens, speaking of the aim of modern poetry, 'but plainly to propound.' The plain propounding—of things thrown in the air, alive in flight, and rusting in change to the color of dust—if too severe, for some tastes, is to others profoundly assuaging. We are lucky in America in our poetry of old age: Whitman's, Stevens's, and now Lowell's" (173). (It is noteworthy that Eliot and Auden are not included in this honorific list.)

Vendler finds the elegiac line of poetry of deprivation, of loss and poverty, in most of the poets she discusses, including the only two Southerners, Warren and Jarrell. I would argue, however, that this "bleak cheatedness" (365) is not a central aspect of Warren, and that, though she denies any regional perspective, the poetry of loss seems to flourish chiefly in the Northeast. A. R. Ammons (whose poetic world is Northern, despite his Southern origin) she praises as the latest exemplar of the tradition: His poetry is "deprived of almost everything other poets have used, notably people and adjectives" (330). "It is a severe poetry, attempting the particularity of Hopkins with none of what Hopkins' schoolmates called his 'gush,' trying for the abstraction of Stevens without Stevens's inhuman remove from the world of fact, aiming at Williams' affectionateness toward the quotidian without Williams' romantic drift." If he can succeed he "will have written the first twentieth-century poetry wholly purged of the romantic" (335). "The voice reasonable in loss is one Ammons; the eviscerated Ammons, doggedly writing down the weather day after day, is something else, Beckett-like, hard on himself as ice" (369). "He has changed the 'we' of poetry from the high philosophical mode ('We live in an old chaos of the sun') to the mode of refugees caught together in a bad time" (371).

There are, of course, other ways of seeing the contemporary poetry scene than in these terms of "poetry of deprivation." For many of us, Eliot and Auden loom as central figures, Lowell's progress seems more complex and dubious, and less impoverished poets seem more interesting now. But all of us are glad to have this view of the ruins, this presentation of the chroniclers of loss and this demonstration of their common humanity.

Science Fiction's Queen of the Night

Ursula K. Le Guin established her reputation as the best living writer of science fiction with *The Left Hand of Darkness* and "Nine Lives" in 1969 and confirmed it with *The Dispossessed* in 1974. (Both the novels won both Hugo and Nebula prizes, awarded by science fiction fans and writers respectively; and the story is one of the most widely admired and reprinted of all science fiction stories.) In 1972 the last volume of her *Earthsea* trilogy won the National Book Award. She has, then, full title to speak as queen of the realm of fantasy, which she describes thus: "Those who refuse to listen to dragons are probably doomed to spend their lives acting out the nightmares of politicians. We like to think we live in daylight, but half the world is always dark; and fantasy, like poetry, speaks the language of the night."[2]

Unlike real queens, however, Le Guin has no interest in maintaining borders or increasing her territories at the expense of other states. Instead, she dedicates herself to getting science fiction out of its self-created ghetto (or psychiatric ward for permanent adolescents) and fantasy out of the nursery, and naturalizing both in the Republic of Letters.

The Language of the Night: Essays on Fantasy and Science Fiction moves toward this goal. It is part of the book's attractiveness that Le Guin does not presume to present herself as critic; instead she has allowed Susan Wood (whose editing is devoted and very intelligent) to assemble the book from addresses, reviews, introductions, interviews, and essays written by Le Guin over the past decade or so. Partly because of this variety and unpretentiousness, partly because of the candor, seriousness, and penetration with which Le Guin speaks of her own work, but mainly because of the pleasure of seeing a first-rate mind at work on these matters, I should say that this is the most attractive introduction to science fiction yet to appear. There are, of course, good histories by Brian Aldiss and James Gunn, and plenty of useful textbooks; but the audience I am thinking of consists of mature and sophisticated readers. Many such readers, I suspect, are convinced that science fiction can appeal only to the immature, the semiliterate, and the weird; this book explains and demonstrates better than any other the special attractions that the genre may have for a civilized and humane mind. Science fiction buffs—the compulsive and often exclusive readers of the genre—should respond to her pleas for a breaking down of the walls to let the wider world of fiction in, and for discrimination among science fiction products according to the same criteria employed for the rest of the bookstore or library. For both groups, the book should be a civilizing and ecumenical influence, strengthening the sense of common humanity.

Although Le Guin is suspicious of definitions, categories, and boundaries in the world of fiction, she makes the necessary demarcations well. Whereas the mainstream or "absolute" novel (as she prefers to call it) presents reality "as expressed and transfigured through art," science fiction or fantasy presents "a personal variation on reality; a scene *less* real than the world around us, a partial view of reality." But "by that partiality, that independence, that distancing from the shared experience, it will be new: a revelation. It will be a vision, a more or less powerful or haunting dream. A view in, not out. A space-voyage through somebody else's psychic abysses. It will fall short of tragedy, because tragedy is the truth, and truth is what the very great artists, the absolute novelists, tell. It will not be truth, but it will be imagination" (22).

She calls science fiction "a modern, intellectualized, extroverted form of fantasy." The "unique aesthetic delight of science fiction," she says, lies "in the intense, coherent following through of the implications of an idea, whether it's a bit of far-out technology, or a theory in quantum mechanics, or a satirical projection of current social trends, or a whole world created by extrapolating from biology and ethnology" (203). Hence the criterion of intellectual coherence and scientific plausibility applies in science fiction with special rigor; the only other criterion is that shared with all fiction, stylistic competence.

She is very good on bad science fiction that escapes

> from a complex, uncertain, frightening world of death and taxes into a nice simply cozy place where heroes don't have to pay taxes, where death happens only to villains, where Science, plus Free Enterprise, plus the Galactic Fleet . . . can solve all problems, where human suffering is something that can be *cured*. . . . This doesn't take us in the direction of the great myths and legends, which is always toward an intensification of the mystery of the real. This takes us the other way, toward a rejection of reality, in fact toward madness: infantile regression, or paranoid delusion, or schizoid insulation. (205)

On the other hand, "the work of people from Zamyatin to Lem has shown that when science fiction uses its limitless range of symbol and metaphor novelistically, with the subject at the center, it can show us who we are, and where we are, and what choices face us, with unsurpassed clarity, and with a great and troubling beauty" (118).

Le Guin does not think much of extrapolation or prediction of the future as functions of science fiction. Her favorite analogy—and it strikes me as a very good one—for her own science fiction is to the "thought-experiments" of the great physicists, such as Einstein and Schrödinger. The purpose of both is to describe reality, the present world. "The future, in fiction, is a metaphor" (159).

Malafrena, in the context of her account of her development as a writer, is puzzling. The jacket blurb, which calls it "something new—a magnificent mainstream novel," is certainly misleading. It is not science fiction or fantasy, but neither is it mainstream or "absolute"; and it is definitely not something new. It is more like a historical novel than anything else, but it has neither the superficial attractions of the genre (adventure, sex, duels, picturesque language and manners) nor the more profound ones of interpreting historical characters and events.

A young man, Itale, leaves his home, Malafrena (in the imaginary duchy of Orsinia), to take part in the nationalistic revolutionary movement of the 1820s; he is eventually imprisoned, released after great suffering, and returns home to his childhood sweetheart, Piera. The central interest is in a sense historical: What would it feel like to be a young man in the 1820s willing to risk a secure and comfortable future for the sake of freedom and justice, and what was it like to be a young woman of the period? But these questions are muffled and absorbed in the universal question of what it is like to grow up at any time. History is scrupulously not violated; but it is not really used.

Why would Le Guin write such a novel now? My guess is that she did not—that this is early work. Describing her career in *Language of the Night,* she says that she wrote four novels set in Orsinia before she began writing science fiction, and all have remained unpublished. My reason for thinking that this is one of them is twofold: *Orsinian Tales,* also dating from this early period, uses the same method of precise location in time in the same imaginary country; and *Malafrena* reads like early or apprentice work, a five-finger exercise. It is emphatically not hackwork or juvenilia, but it has something of the feeling of a task well done. Le Guin is never less than competent, intelligent, and decent; but in this novel she is not much more.

Le Guin's first published story, "An die Musik," reprinted in *Orsini-*

an Tales, is exactly the same type of fiction as *Malafrena,* and set in Orsinia in the early nineteenth century. Yet it is a great story, because it deals with an idea Le Guin feels passionately about: in this case, precisely the one expressed in Schubert's song, that music is its own reward, transfiguring life's sorrows. Le Guin embodies this theme in the story of an imaginary composer whose life and feelings about his art are parallel to Schubert's.

What makes Le Guin a great science fiction writer is that this genre allows her to combine her serious and passionate interest in ideas with her ability to create real and believable characters. She understands this, and says, "Meanwhile, people keep predicting that I will bolt science fiction and fling myself madly into the Mainstream. I don't know why. The limits, and the great spaces of fantasy and science fiction are precisely what my imagination needs. Outer Space, and the Inner Lands, are still, and always will be, my country" (30).

PART · 4 *Fiction*

George Garrett and the Historical Novel

George Garrett's *Death of the Fox* (1971) and *The Succession* (1983) are such remarkable historical novels that they may be considered either a fulfillment of the genre or a repudiation of it. The term *historical novel* will not stand up under much examination. All narratives are historical in the sense that they must be placed in time and—even experiments in using the stream of consciousness and the historical present—must be retrospective. But a narrative concerned primarily with historical fact—with what actually happened—is not a novel, and poetry is closer to philosophy than to history, as Aristotle said. So what useful meaning can the term have? The question would seem one of degree or emphasis: Historical fiction is fiction in which history is important, in which the author lays claim to historical as well as poetic truth and the reader is kept aware of the historical aspect, conscious that the time of the action is distant from his own.

Of historical fiction thus simply defined we may distinguish two kinds. The first is that extremely popular form of entertainment in which the historical aspect is superficial, mainly picturesque and amusing or titillating. The costume romance places fictional characters against a backdrop of historical events and historical personages; but the central characters, insofar as they are real, are modern, and their doings bear at most a peripheral relation to the important events of the time. While this kind of fiction can be very attractive and sometimes informative, it rises no higher because the historical aspect has no meaning other than to provide the reader with escape (and perhaps the illusion that he is educating himself) and often to conceal the author's poverty of imagination in character and plot.

The other kind, which is much less common and much less popular, makes a serious attempt to interpret the historical aspect, to relate it to the characters and plot, and to render the "otherness" of the characters in their different time while also rendering their common humanity. *War and Peace,* by common consent, is the greatest such novel; but *War and Peace* interprets a time only a couple of generations earlier than that of the author, and one known to him not only (and not primarily) through written sources but also through legend, oral tradition, and memory. Allen Tate's *The Fathers* is a similar case, and so is Andrew Lytle's *The Long Night.* (Even *The Scarlet Letter, Henry Esmond,* and Sir Walter Scott's best novels, through remote in time, are set in the author's own country and draw on local associations and on oral as well as written sources.) Garrett's two novels are different: their settings are more distant in time and in a different country, and they are based on written sources exclusively.

Garrett thus meets the full challenge head-on, more completely and uncompromisingly than any other "historical" novelist I can think of. If all novels are historical, but some are more historical than others, Garrett's *Death of the Fox* and *The Succession* are historical in every sense compatible with remaining novels. His central characters are major actors on the stage of history and are so remote in time that there is little or no shared bond of genealogy, legend, or other common heritage between characters and readers. His fiction is based primarily on historical documents, not on memory and shared associations (though the places still survive, to be transformed by imagination; and Garrett has lovingly assimilated the topography of England and Scotland for this purpose).

The Succession, Garrett observes in his prefatory note, began as a study of the letters of Elizabeth I and James I. The impression made by his novels is, in solidity, authenticity, and immediacy, more like that produced by such great letter-collections as *The Lisle Letters* or *Children of Pride* than like that of other historical novels. But letters, except for a few fortunate collections enhanced by imaginative editing, are like literal translations; they are no substitute for reimagining and re-creating the whole.

Garrett, then, does not take any of the easy outs: His central characters are historical and are involved in centrally important historical events, which are followed meticulously in the novels. No liberties are taken with the facts: Garrett invents narrative detail but changes nothing and adds only what is plainly justified by analogy. Since the main characters are historical and the reader knows in advance what happened to them, there can be no narrative suspense. Garrett's position is the polar opposite of Scott or Alexander Dumas—no cloak and sword, rapid action, romance and suspense, quaintness and local color. The characters are always presented in depth, from inside. Although there is a great variety of perspectives, points of view, and kinds of interest in the different sections, the unifying attitude and tone are contemplative and meditative. Garrett's attitude toward the past is neither romantic nor debunking: He has a marvelous sense of ceremony, ritual, and pageantry, and of the immense significance of these things—and, of course, of religion—to the characters (in implicit contrast to moderns). The trials and executions are the most fully developed examples, though the conclusion of *The Succession* is perhaps the most impressive of all, with its picture of Christmas and of the whole cycle of the year at Elizabeth's court.

In Garrett's novels, we escape only in the sense that we do inhabit another world, fully imagined and realized. There is no explicit comparison to our own "real" world (though much implicit); Garrett never intrudes in his own person, but always speaks through the imagined mind of a "historical" personage or "ghost."

One mystery that the serious historical novel always points to is that of the relation between the individual and his times, or the individual and society. It is only in this sense that Robert Penn Warren will call his fiction historical: "Writing a story about an actual person and using him as a kind of model are really not the same. I don't pretend that Will Stark is Huey Long. I know Stark, but I have no idea what Long was really like." What interests him, he goes on to say, is how "individual personalities become mirrors of their times, or the times become a mirror of the personalities. . . . The individual is an embodiment of external circumstances, so that a personal story is a social story." His novels, he says, are not historical, because what he looks for is "an image, a sort of simplified and distant framed image, of an immediate and contemporary issue, a sort of interplay between that image and the contemporary world."[1]

These quotations define nicely the difference between Warren's fiction, which often appears to be historical (and is certainly concerned with history), and Garrett's two novels, which are centrally historical. Garrett does undertake to tell what Ralegh and James were really like (or how they may most plausibly be imagined, in accord with the facts). And, while obviously there are connections to the contemporary world, there are no contemporary issues that the reader feels are the central theme, and the connections are not explicit. On the other hand, Garrett is also concerned, like Warren or any other novelist, with his characters as unique individuals and not merely as mirrors of the times.

I

It is a curious coincidence that Garrett needed twelve years—close to the length of time Ralegh was in the Tower (1603–18)—to finish *The Succession* (1983) after *Death of the Fox* (1971); but no coincidence that they are in reverse chronological order, focusing on 1603 and 1618, respectively. *The Succession,* as we shall see, would seem to be motivated partly by the determination to be fair to James (who was, of course, responsible for the death of the Fox) and to the Jacobean era, thus complementing *Fox* and giving a balanced picture. In many ways, the two novels do certainly complement each other—the basic techniques and approaches are the same—and they are companion works, each dealing with characters and aspects of the age that the other does not. But each is also self-sufficient, and in many ways they are different.

To put it briefly, *Fox* is a tragedy, covering a short period of time— Ralegh's execution and the few days preceding it—with Ralegh's earlier life brought in through retrospection. In spite of the novel's length, there is a growing intensity, tension, and suspense as it proceeds to its foreknown conclusion; the focus narrows and sharpens. *Succession,* in contrast, is elegiac and sometimes nostalgic in tone; it has sixteen sections as against *Fox*'s nine, and multiple narrators (though usually not in first person) instead of *Fox*'s central intelligence dominating the other narrators. The time covered in *Succession* ranges from 1566 to 1626; though the primary action is the succession of James in 1603, we see throughout the novel the messenger traveling from Edinburgh to London in 1566 with the news of James's birth and the courtier who profited nothing from bringing the news of Elizabeth's death to James (from London to Edinburgh) but came into favor on the succession of Charles. The tone mellows into the concluding picture of the last Christmastide at Elizabeth's court.

Both novels are profoundly "historical," showing an easy mastery of an incredible amount of detail; but both are primarily works of imagination, to be judged by their success as novels, not by their historical accuracy. Yet Garrett's is a historically disciplined imagination: that of a modern man putting himself in the place of a historical character, as he must be; but doing so in terms of the historical background of that character, what his childhood was or must have been like, not with free-floating imagination unleashed. Garrett goes inside the minds of major historical characters (James and Ralegh, most notably and extensively, but also Queen Elizabeth, Bacon, Robert Cecil, and many others) as they confront major historical decisions. His is not only backstage, backstairs, or behind-the-scenes history, but main stage too. He does not come up with startling revelations or solutions to historical mysteries but with plausible and sensible interpretations of larger meanings.

Throughout both these novels there is the same unusual attitude toward religion that was apparent in *Do, Lord, Remember Me* (1965), Garrett's novel about a redneck revivalist and surounding grotesques in a small Southern town. Garrett presents Big Red's healing powers as real and Big Red as sincere, though also comic and corrupted; and he manages to sustain both attitudes at once. The mixture of the earthy and religious in these "low" characters is presented with nothing but sympathy. The complement of this attitude is the presentation of the priest in *The Succession* as he moves toward martyrdom; and Garrett manages to make this "high" religious character come to life just as fully as he did the low ones. (He does the same for Ralegh awaiting execution in *Fox.*) *Do, Lord* also anticipates *Fox* and *Succession* in using the technique of multiple narrators, with a correspondingly wide array of styles ranging from Big Red's brilliant and tormented rich allusiveness to the more limited minds of the others. But all are presented with a large compassionate acceptance and without a trace of condescension, while the novel is also continuously funny. (In this, it is at the opposite pole from *Fox,* which is in the tragic mode throughout, though not as grim and unrelieved as this statement would suggest, and *Succession,* which is not comic, though it is in some sense beyond tragedy.)

In *Fox,* Ralegh is a tough old soldier (among other things), no angel but decent, with many fine qualities (but enigmatic), a victim of circumstance but no whiner. In this, he is like the equivocal hero of *Which Ones Are the Enemy?* and Garrett's other stories of the postwar army: tough, competent, skeptical but not wholly cynical; finally overreaching himself and suffering a downfall. It is much harder to like James, the central character of *The Succession;* he is a winner, but a villain insofar as history has villains. But Garrett is at the opposite pole from making history a simple morality play; both books constitute a profound and continuing meditation on the meaning of time, memory, and history.

By presenting each segment as meditation or reverie by a specific character, as he remembers or dreams, Garrett can use neutral language, not noticeably modern or antique either. Thus he avoids the problem of archaic language—*gadzooks, egad, zounds*—one of the biggest stumbling blocks in the historical novel. But it is a real challenge to write like Ralegh or Bacon or Queen Elizabeth so that the reader is not shocked by the transition from their own prose to yours, and Garrett manages this with great success. It works partly because they were such good writers, and, when pruned of minor surface anachronisms, they do not seem at all dated or antiquated, but the "naked bone and sinew" of the language; and this is what Garrett seems to pattern his own prose on. The style, then, is not based on pastiche or fake antiquarianism, but on the solid middle ground of English. But having established this as basis, Garrett goes on to produce a great variety of individual voices and to write in very different styles according to the occasion.

As we have seen, Garrett employs multiple narrators, each of whom tells his story. Unlike the great exemplars of this technique, *Ulysses* and *The Sound and the Fury,* however, his novels do not attempt to reveal the stream of consciousness. Instead, they exhibit a great variety of levels of consciousness, from dozing reverie to full alertness and decision. Wisely, he avoids too much use of the first person, preferring to use third person (sometimes even second) and varying degrees of distance. The device of having ghosts appear who are "characters" in the manner of Overbury—a soldier, a courtier, a sailor, to describe authoritatively these aspects of Ralegh—is very effective. But Garrett is perhaps best on the characters the reader loves to hate: Bacon, James and his favorites (in *Fox;* James is seen differently in *Succession*), and Stukely, Ralegh's kinsman and betrayer.

Shakespeare is handled effectively and with restraint. It is plausible that Ralegh would not be overly impressed by his plays, preferring Marlow and Jonson, and of course he would not have known him personally, or wanted to. *Troilus* is certainly the right play to have performed to represent the Jacobean mood, and Pandarus the right character for the Player to act. *Fox* is wonderful on sailors, voyages, sea battles, and the like, and *Succession* on reivers of the Scottish border, players, messengers, and other low-life characters.

Ralegh was the perfect hero for *Fox* because he was enigmatic, skeptical, and tough-minded, and because he was many-sided, more man of action than poet. (No character in *Fox* is primarily a poet or artist of any sort.) But he was also appropriate because, in his writings, his central theme was the triumph of time and the meaning of time and history. Nothing could be more in keeping with this character, then, than to present him meditating over the meaning of time and history.

II

The Succession, as we have said, while the same kind of "venture into the imaginary past," as Garrett calls them, and while obviously so closely related to *Fox* that in many ways they are companion volumes, presenting complementary views of the same period, is in other ways quite different. For one thing, it covers a longer time: While *Fox* was dominated by the image of Ralegh on the eve of his execution in 1618, *Succession* ranges from the birth of James in 1566 to the succession of Charles I in 1625, though of course it is focused on the succession in 1603. (Both novels are focused on highly dramatic events that were, at the time, highly suspenseful; for it was by no means a foregone conclusion at the time either that James would succeed or that Ralegh would be executed. Although we know the historical outcome and therefore feel no suspense about what happened, we do feel suspense about just how and why it happened. And this suspense both novels satisfy, through the exercise of the informed or historical imagination.) More importantly, the novels differ in that *Succession* has no hero, as we have said; insofar as it does, the hero has to be James, the villain of *Fox.* *The Succession* shows us the sense in which we must say, however much we continue to dislike him, that his succession was a Good Thing.

Against all our impulses to write history nearer to the heart's desire, this prig, pedant, and spoiled boy is here understood and appreciated. Secretary Robert Cecil and others who were pro-James and appeared as villains in *Fox* are also seen in a different light here. Certainly one motive must have been to explore aspects of the age not covered in *Fox:* for example, the sovereign as concerned with larger problems than the fate of Ralegh, the Player (wonderful scenes here of playhouses, actors, taverns), the reivers of the Scottish border, the Catholic priest, messengers and spies of 1566 and 1603), and courtier of 1626 and 1575, and many others. (The succession of the novel's title is not only that of 1603 but also those of 1566, 1587, and 1626.) The book ends with a last glimpse of Elizabeth at Christmas, 1602–3, so that the final retrospective vision is that of Elizabeth's court, not James's.

The Succession is less obviously appealing than *Fox:* There is no fascinating and "romantic" central figure like Ralegh. The challenge, then, is greater: to make the reader, and the author, accept James and see the other side. The wisdom of acceptance is always rare and difficult, and it is perhaps especially unpopular and implausible now. It is much easier to say that any fool can plainly see that everything is absurd than to say that, in some deep sense beyond complacency, whatever is, is right. We will return to this point at the end; but before leaving *The Succession,* let us look at a few of its other remarkable qualities.

The novel begins with the dying queen in March 1603 and ends with

Christmas 1602–3, the last time the queen and court flourished. Garrett's account of this season includes the list of Christmas presents to the queen; with its description of the festivals, customs, ceremonies, and liturgies, it evokes the timeless cycles of the Church and of the land as against the ceaseless passage of time and what the Elizabethans called Mutability.

"Reivers" is wonderful: This world of the Scottish border is that of the ballads specifically, but that of feudal, anarchist societies in many times, in places everywhere from Sicily to the American West.

"Courtier 1626 (1575)" is Robert Carey, now Earl of Monmouth, writing Sir Ferdinando Gorges about his young protégé. He describes Elizabeth's visit to Kenilworth in 1575, when Leicester was her favorite (preceding Essex and Ralegh). (The Essex rebellion is covered in "Player: 1602," and the Essex trial and execution [1601] contrasted with Ralegh's.) Carey was the first to bring the news of Elizabeth's death to James; he got nothing from this, but profited from the favor of Charles when he was crowned in 1625. Thus the whirligig of time brings in his revenges.

Part of the appeal of bad historical novels is to the perennial yearning of the audience to be assured that the rich and powerful and historically famous are no better than they are, and to know the secrets of skulduggery in high places. In contrast, Garrett affirms the reality of heroism, courage, unselfish love, in his characters, while also affirming their common humanity. Both novels are acts of faith in the possibility of heroism, affirmations of the reality and validity of love and courage, honor and patriotism, of significance in history—all this while confronting the full reality of evil and apparent chaos. This is clearer in *Fox* than in *Succession,* which is essentially a Novel without a Hero, except to the limited extent that James can be called one. But however good a case the intellect may make for James, the heart's heroine remains Elizabeth, as in the long, nostalgic concluding scene of her last Christmastide.

Perhaps this is the real surprise of the books considered as interpretation of history: Instead of coming up with some new and startling thesis about Ralegh, some answer to the innumerable rumors and enigmas that surround him (e.g., concerning the School of Night), Garrett makes him at heart a thoroughly orthodox and, in his way, devout Christian. This is beautifully rendered in Ralegh's letter to his son: "Yet even without thinking of mysteries beyond understanding, we see how those whom we love are transformed. And being loved by another, we find that we ourselves have been somehow remade and restored. . . . If human love is a weak reflection, a wavering image of the light of infinite and eternal Love (to the extent that it is *caritas* and not the fevered fancy of our lust), then it may be that in the transformation of lovers, each one to the other, we are given a sign of hidden truth. . . . If so, then love has within it the power to transform all of creation, though none of us will ever see it, until Judgment Day brings us to life again."[2] This faith informs the whole extremely moving last section, in which Ralegh awaits execution, as it does the poems Ralegh wrote about his own death: especially the final couplets, "But from this earth, this grave, this dust, / My God shall raise me up I trust" and "Just at the stroke when my veins start and spread / Set on my soul an everlasting head." Similarly, in the letter Ralegh writes to his son, Ralegh concludes that the yeoman farmer is much better off than his father or grandfather—in other words, that the accomplishments of Elizabeth's reign were real, not illusory; that progress is possible and does sometimes occur and that history can be meaningful. (The whole long letter to his son meets the challenge successfully of writing in a style suggesting Ralegh's without producing a travesty of that style.) The scene of the last visit to Ralegh in the Tower by his wife on the night before his execution is beautifully handled; it is not sentimentalized or made to fit any clichés, but shows the reality of unselfish love and courage, as enacted by both Ralegh and Bess.

On the other hand, it is obviously impossible to know really just how people in the past felt and thought; even when they are quoted exactly, the words don't mean the same thing now as then. So pedantic sticking to the "facts" of history will not work. Thus the only method is Garrett's: To "make a work of fiction, of the imagination, planted and rooted in fact," as he said in the prefatory note to *Death of the Fox.* After mastering all the facts, soaking in all the details, he must imagine the novel, create it from scratch, but staying within the limits of what is not only possible but most probable historically. This will be the "imaginary past," as Garrett calls it in his note to *The Succession,* but faithful to the facts, and hence the past as conceived by a rigorously disciplined imagination.

As Garrett says, this is the "imaginary past" in the sense that it has to be imagined—there is no way of automatically reconstructing it (or them, for the past is not one but many, of course) from facts—but it is solidly based on a thorough knowledge of what historical facts and documents are available and, more importantly, of the writings (both literary and personal—e.g., letters) of the period. So this kind of historical novel is a kind of communal product, in a sense: not based on the limited scope of one man's imagination, but on the productions, fictional and real, of many people's minds: a kind of collective reality created by all of them together. (I am not suggesting that it is a Jungian collective unconscious; this communal product is conscious, too, and includes art.) It is at the opposite pole from fantasy, where the writer simply unleashes his imagination, with no regard for reality or possibility and no constraints. But it is finally dependent on the unifying imagination of a single author.

III

Although Garrett scorns the meretricious attractions of the conventional "historical" novel, this kind of deeper historical grounding has its own legitimate delights and satisfactions. Perhaps the chief is the deep sense of difference from the characters. Of course one feels primarily the sense of shared human nature, of common humanity, and this is never lost; but the characters are very different from transplanted moderns, and revealing this difference is one of Garrett's most difficult and rewarding feats. They have a different sense of time, based on the seasons and the church year; ceremonies and rituals are immensely more important to them than to us; they feel themselves to be far more intimately related to the past than we do. (It is difficult to express these matters abstractly, as Garrett never does: Garrett never mentions them and never calls attention to them; the reader gradually becomes conscious of them as the novel proceeds.) Thus without explicit comment, the reader enjoys what is in a sense escape, but meaningful escape— another world that is the same yet different, a comparison and contrast (but always implicit rather than explicit.)

But the final wisdom is that of acceptance, because the imagined world of the past is not simplified or distorted; neither prettied up nostalgically nor shown as inferior to the present (as in Eco's *Name of the Rose*); but revealed as essentially the same, yet different. (I am, of course, only repeating a Renaissance cliché, as in the title of Joseph Hall's *Mundus Alter et Idem.*) "Wisdom of acceptance" is a dangerous phrase, calling up visions of cosmic Toryism and Margaret Fuller accepting the universe. A better parallel is with the reconciliation beyond tragedy, in Shakespeare's romances or in the tragedies at the very end, when the bodies must be carried offstage and life must go on. *Fox* is, so to speak, the tragedy itself; *Succession* the moment beyond. Although in history nobody wins permanently (as Carey's story in *Succession* shows most explicitly), history does have meaning; there is something to say for winners as well as losers, and *Succession* says it. The attitude is ultimately a religious one, I suppose, and at the risk of pious platitude I have to say that the suggestion is that what thou lovest well remains (thinking of Pound rather than the Bible): This surely is the implication of the end of *The Succession* with its last long loving look at the last Christmas season of Elizabeth and her court. The theme is parallel to that of *Do, Lord,* which ends with the beatific vision of Howie Loomis, a most unheroic drunk old man, who sees his dead wife transfigured because he loves and accepts her wholly, choosing her over any heavenly vision:

> But I had to choose, you see. So instead I looked at her. The light of that place and shade too was on her. She didn't change and yet she was changed. What I mean is the light wasn't magic and it didn't wipe away any lines of scars. They remained. Yet they were beautiful. Even the scars were beautiful; . . . She looked at the place and smiled at it, and I looked at her and wept like a child, not for loss, but because the world was so large and so wonderful and we were both in it now and forever.
>
> Then the dream was gone and I was back in myself again, a drunk old man asleep on the floor. A drunk old man who had slept like a baby all night long.[3]

The Succession ends with a somewhat similar, though more communal and more inclusive vision of a Plowman (the fine tissue of allusions recalling, of course, the Piers Plowman of Langland's great satire, as well as the archetypal plowman. (His plow will be blessed on Plow Sunday, which marks the end of Christmastide, for the plowing race on Plow Monday with which the cycle of the year begins again.)

> Now still reeling a little and staring up into the sky lit with cold starlight. Fearful of nothing, not past or the future. Except for the certain knowledge that your head will be heavy and aching by daylight. And your laughter will have turned into such groaning as will arouse the laughter of others. But for now you are full of food and drink and gratitude.
>
> You believe you are full of love and charity also. And you can wish all the world, your friends and your enemies, nothing but well. Nothing but good fortune. Wishing the dead, from Adam and Eve until now, their rest in peace. And wishing the living, one and all, from the beggar in his hedge to the Queen in her soft bed. . . .
>
> And what is it she can be dreaming of now, as he, half dreaming, imagines her, that lady minted on his hard-earned coins, lady of ballads and of prayers in the parish church? Is there a place in her dream for this happy drunken plowman, mud of good English earth thick on his boots, out under the stars, who is wishing for her and the rest of the world, for the sake of our own sweet Jesus, a good night?[4]

Garrett's two novels belong to the exalted company of *Ulysses* and a very few other works that carry the novel form as far as it can go, exploiting all its resources and revealing new possibilities. They exhibit the novel operating at so high a level, with such variety of styles and perspectives, with such easy mastery of the "historical" aspect—of all details of time and place—and so deeply meditated in their study of the relation between the individual life and the history, that they are really something new. (In depth of learning and historical imagination, they belong in the company of Marguerite Yourcenar's *Memoirs of Hadrian* and Hermann Broch's *Death of Virgil*.) They are the finest historical novels I have ever read because they are not, in the conventional sense, historical novels at all.

The paradox is seen most clearly in the styles, which are not imitation Elizabethan or pastiche, but seem authentically of their period because they are first of all authentically modern. The discipline is somewhat like that of translation: As a poetic translation must be, to exist at all, modern poetry, and then be faithful to its original, so the historical novel must work first of all as a modern novel, and then maintain its fidelity to the historical past. These are nearly impossible demands; yet Garrett's novels are as fully historical as they are modern. They are, however, much more than acrobatic feats or displays of virtuosity: They are beautiful, profound, and deeply moving works of art.

A New Classic: Madison Jones,
A Cry of Absence

As we all know, a new classic is unlikely to be recognized as such very promptly: Freud's *Interpretation of Dreams* sold 351 copies in its first six years, and Wallace Stevens's first half-year royalties from *Harmonium* amounted to $6.70. With novels, however, it often happens that the serious work of art as well as the meretricious and ephemeral concoction will be hailed by the mass media and will even make the best-seller lists. We cannot but feel indignant, then, when a towering achievement like the present novel is saluted only by the odd and usually obscure reviewer. Although unqualified to do it justice, I feel obliged in this situation to attempt at least to call attention to its true stature. For *A Cry of Absence* (1971) is an authentic, pure, and deeply moving tragedy. Sophocles, Racine, Ibsen; in the novel, Flaubert, Hardy, Faulkner—these are the company it keeps and the comparisons it invites. In its dignity, integrity, and somber power it is a reproach to many of us for frivolity: for liking, for instance, such novels as Walker Percy's *Love in the Ruins,* so attractive and funny and entertaining, but finally so disappointing because incoherent and full of loose ends—things implausible or unexplained or meaningless. *A Cry* has, in contrast, the order and economy of the greatest art: There is no detail that is not essential, significant both in itself and in relation to the work as a whole.

Every event and gesture, every item of speech and dress, is, to begin with, precisely right in terms of place and time. Being very much about a particular time and place, *A Cry of Absence* may be described as historical and regional, though its central concerns are universal and timeless. The South in the midfifties (specifically 1957) was the kind of ambiguous and bloody ground in which tragedy flourishes: For one kind of right to be achieved, much had to be lost, and people on both sides deceived themselves and each other about their true motives and intentions. As a novel about Southern racial problems, *A Cry of*

Absence is the best thing since *Light in August*—though this is not, of course, what either novel is finally about. The subject of racial integration in the South is still a sensitive one (now, perhaps, even more sensitive in the North), and it is probable that a novel using these events as enveloping action could not have been written with success much earlier. One wrong note, even now, would take the novel out of the realm of art and into that of politics and sociology, or worse, of propaganda, inflamed self-righteousness, and partisan venom. But Jones's novel is a triumph of tact as well as integrity; there are no wrong notes, and every detail is fully dramatized and completely functional. Each one is necessary to the central action at the same time that it reveals the nature of the characters; each is historically typical, and each also functions on a symbolic or mythical level.

This spareness and economy of means makes the reader think of Greek tragedy, as does the action itself, as austere, powerful, and inexorable as any in Greek drama, and as evocative of both pity and terror. The book is full of suspense, too, in exactly the Greek way: not so much as to what will happen, since the pattern of external events is foreseen very soon, but as to how and why it will happen in terms of character. The basic pattern is much like that of *King Oedipus,* though the events are different: Like Oedipus, Hester assumes at the beginning that the criminal can have nothing to do with her, and she recognizes at last, after struggling long and painfully, that she is herself the guilty one. On the other hand, there are obvious resemblances to *Antigone* in the fact of dual protagonists (the novel is told partly from the point of view of Hester and partly from that of her elder son, Ames), in the conflict between family affection and duty to the state (as Hester sees it), and most of all in the *hubris*—more like that of Creon than of Antigone—which blinds Hester. Cam is her victim, as Haemon is Creon's. It is clear enough that Jones does not model his novel upon any single tragedy, but upon the Greek form in general. The basic structural divisions are similar to those of a typical Greek tragedy, but the correspondence is one of shape and total effect rather than of detail.

The book is divided into four parts, of which the first and last are substantially longer than the two middle ones in which most of the physical action takes place. Hester Cameron Glenn lives in her great-grandfather's house in Cameron Springs. She is proud of her family, her house, her town, and most of all of her younger son, Cameron (because he is like her family, "the epitome of them all"). When she hears of the murder of a black agitator, she assures her maid, Willodene, that the decent whites will see the murderers caught and punished. Ames (who resembles his father, from whom Hester has long been separated) becomes convinced that Cam is the murderer; but Hester refuses to believe in his guilt. Part two begins with a retrospect of Hester's childhood and marriage, to explain her self-deception. She sets herself in opposition to the white Northerners (led by the Delmores) who champion local blacks, and she resigns from the society for the preservation of antiquities when they refuse to commit themselves to the immediate replacement of the Confederate monument, blown up presumably by the blacks. She circulates a petition and otherwise agitates for the restoration of the monument. In the third part, Ames, at college, meets Libby Delmore; his feelings, mixed until then, are resolved by her injury in the bombing of the Delmores' house. Determined to force his mother to recognize Cam's guilt, Ames succeeds in doing so through tricking Pike Handley, who has been Cam's accomplice, into confessing to her. Finally aware of the alliance with Handley into which she has been forced, and aware at last of Cam's guilt, she encourages Cam to commit suicide. In the final part, Hester comes to recognize and admit her responsibility for Cam, and she takes her own life.

Hester Glenn is a heroine in the great mold, betrayed by what is false within both herself and her society; though what is false is, as always in tragedy, precisely the corruption of what is best. (Her name is surely meant to recall to us Hester Prynne, heroine of an earlier novel both regional and universal, who lives out the consequences of a sin that is both hers and her New England society's.) Hester is explained in both psychological and sociological-historical terms, and with a marvelous economy. She is proud of her family and of her own superiority, and she encourages this in Cam: "It was what all of her family had had—a just sense of their own excellence, their rightful place." Idealizing her family and romanticizing her childhood, she has driven her husand into deserting her: Maybe if my husband had been the man my father had been, she thinks at first. (Reared in a stern and self-righteous Presbyterianism, she cannot respect either her own church's new preacher or her husband's Episcopal leniency.) Under these circumstances, she romanticizes the past and idealizes Cam, partly for his resemblance to her family; hence she refuses to recognize the truth about Cam, her town, and herself until it is too late. After she has been driven by Ames to see Cam's guilt and to recognize at last that Cam is entirely her creature, that she has made him what he is, the "poor white" Handley says to her: "'Killed your own boy. That's really something. It ain't none of the old folks ever did come up to that.' He slowly blinked, but his lids seemed not even to interrupt the glare of triumphant hate in his eyes. 'Naw, Miss Hester. It ain't *nobody* you can look down on.'"[1] When she finally does accept the truth, she takes full responsibility:

> Whatever way she went would be the same, for this was where her fate had left her. The fate that her hands had made. Somehow had made. Hands that had shaped and guided a little boy and at last had turned a switch on him. Dangerous hands. "Somebody 'good' as you are, Miss Hester, other folks better keep their eyes open, hadn't they?" "Yes," was her silent answer now. But it was not only to others that she had been a danger. To herself, also: in the end her turn had come. For where was a way that she could change this self for another one? (274)

The double point of view, shifting from Hester to Ames and back, is complex but is the only possible one: We need to see Hester from inside, but we also need to perceive what she cannot perceive about herself and her relation to Cam; and this we see through the eyes of Ames, the rejected elder son. Although Hester is the protagonist, Ames is the Jamesian central intelligence, aware of everything that goes on, and in one sense his discovery of Cam's guilt and of Hester's relation to it, with his determination to make her recognize and admit both, constitutes the main action. Ames is thus not merely an observer; in fact, it is one of the triumphs of the novel that he takes on more life and body toward the end. Thus Jones avoids the pitfall of separating the percipient spectator from the central actor: Ames grows and acts as well as perceiving, and Hester suffers the last full measure of suffering self-awareness.

Cam is the only one of the central characters who is not fully realized; he remains somewhat dim and remote. Aside from his almost supernatural good looks and athletic prowess, we know little about him aside from the revelation of his cruelty, hatred, and pride. We see him chiefly through the adoring eyes of his mother, who makes him her compensation for all the deficiencies of her lost husband and of the modern world, raising him to be like the men she remembers from her childhood in what she thinks was a simpler and better world; and secondarily through the eyes of Ames, four years older and very different. Probably it would be inappropriate for Cam to be vividly realized on the human level, in any case: he is clearly sub- or superhuman. The fact that he, whom his mother associates with the unfallen childhood world of romance, chooses as his associates and accomplices the "white trash" that she scorns, reveals once more the folly (or *hubris*) of rejecting ordinary humanity. As character, Cam is less than human, though also godlike: His feet in their white tennis shoes are repeatedly described as shining, and his pitching is murderously accurate. But he is finally revealed as what his mother made him; her creature, and that only.

With the possible exception of Cam's shining feet, there is not a single obtrusive symbol in the book. The symbolic level arises from the historical and realistic—or, rather, it is as if the natural objects and events are seen into so deeply that they become transparent: for example, the fact that the original murder is committed by a "poor white" and an aristocrat together, and that the method is stoning (so that Ames, remembering Cam's cruelty to blacks and his pitching ability, is suspicious). The method also recalls the first Christian martyrdom, as Ames observes but his mother does not. But none of this is artificial or contrived; it is realistic and historically plausible.

The novel differs from many recent ones in that its fictional world is emphatically a moral one. And it is satisfying—aesthetically, intellectually, and morally—because it is complete and coherent: We understand finally exactly why Hester behaved as she did and how and why the tragic events took place. We behold this (in the ancient formula) with pity for Hester and with terror lest we also be betrayed by our best qualities and forced to confront our responsibility for evil done by others as well as, unwittingly, by ourselves. It is, in my opinion, a major work of art.

Two Southern Gentlemen as Heroes

The Last Gentleman Refuses to Retire

The Second Coming (1980) is Walker Percy's most appealing novel and perhaps his best. His last two novels before it were brilliant but somewhat gimmicky: in *Love in the Ruins* there was a science-fiction apocalypse, complete with a fantastic machine and warring survivors, and in *Lancelot* both allegory and a trickily indirect method of narration. In *The Second Coming,* his fifth novel, he returns to the mode of his first two, but carries it to a farther stage. The return and progression are literal in that *The Second Coming* is a sequel to *The Last Gentleman* (1966), Percy's second novel, and continues the story of the same central character, Will Barrett. More significantly, it goes beyond all the earlier novels in that it shows the hero undergoing a more definite and positive change: Will exorcises the *Hamlet*-ghost of his father, which beckons him to suicide, and finds rebirth and love through mutual need with a young girl who has escaped from a mental institution. At the end he is determined to pursue his quest both for love and for religious truth, as he thinks of his girl and looks at a foolish old Anglican priest:

> His heart leapt with a secret joy. What is it I want from her and him, he wondered; not only want but must have? Is she a gift and therefore a sign of a giver? Could it be that the Lord is here, masquerading behind this simple silly holy face? Am I crazy to want both, her and Him? No, not want, must have. And will have.[1]

To make so happy—or at least hopeful—an end convincing without evasion or compromise is no mean achievement. *The Last Gentleman* began with Will living in New York after dropping out from Princeton, working as a "maintenance engineer" and waiting for something to happen. What happened was his involvement with the Vaught family: the dying Jamie, his sister, Kitty, whom Will almost marries, and his brother, Sutter, suicidal doctor and pornographer. *The Second Coming* picks up Will some twenty-odd years later, after he has "made it" in every external sense. As a successful Wall Street lawyer, he has made much money and has married a rich wife; now, a widower whose "born-again" daughter is getting married, he has retired early to the beautiful resort country of North Carolina. He is an excellent golfer and has just received the local Rotary's man-of-the-year award for service to the community. As people keep telling him, he has picked up all the marbles. Nevertheless, as the novel begins, he is depressed, unwell (he keeps falling down), and contemplating suicide.

Although no reference is made in *The Second Coming* to *The Last Gentleman,* the two novels are plainly complementary. They show Will before and after he "settles down" and comes to terms with the practical world; or, in the language now debased by pop-psych, they show his two chief Identity Crises. To see the later Will in the light of the earlier novel is to understand him better, and to read the later novel as a continuation of the earlier is to experience a special satisfaction. Whereas he remained rather passive throughout *The Last Gentleman,* more spectator than actor, in this one he makes up his mind, commits himself, and takes action. His father's suicide, which was mentioned but not explored in *The Last Gentleman,* is a central theme here. Brooding over the hunting "accident" in which his father shot himself thirty-odd years before, and tempted by his ghost to despair and suicide, Will comes to a better understanding of himself and a rejection of his father. The argument of the father's ghost is that the only true Second Coming is the one he had: the coming of a shotgun blast in the mouth. But Will, crazy as he seems to the world and sometimes to himself, persists in looking for the biblical signs that will foretell the Second Coming and the end of the world.

There is nothing in this novel as dramatic as the end of *The Last Gentleman,* with Jamie's baptism and death and the suspense about Sutter's narrowly averted suicide, or as the hurricane and the multiple adulteries in *Lancelot.* The scene in the cave, when Will conducts his "scientific" experiment to determine whether or not God exists, is not very exciting because it can prove nothing as an experiment and its outcome seems predetermined by the symbolism (emerging from the dark cave into the greenhouse of the girl who nurses him back to life). On the other hand, the love scenes are the best of any in Percy. Allie (whose story alternates with Will's throughout the novel until they are united) is the daughter of Kitty, whom Will rejects in this novel as in *The Last Gentleman;* electroshock treatments for her mental breakdown have left her with little memory and a strangely innocent way of speaking. She and Will start over together, both crazy but creating together a sane world out of mutual need: He falls, she becomes expert in hoisting; she forgets, he remembers; she is innocent, honest, taking language literally and incapable of lying, he translates the speech of others for her and shares in the creation of a private, unsullied language for the two of them. It is a remarkable achievement for Percy to make so obviously mythic an anima figure nevertheless a real and immensely appealing person.

If this novel is in some ways more limited than its predecessors, it has a correspondingly sharper focus and sometimes greater depth. Percy has always been wonderful at rendering the precise nuances of language, gesture, clothing, and manners as they differ among different regions and different social classes and as they change with the times. The beautiful natural setting here — the expensive resort country in the mountains of North Carolina — is functional because it is inhabited now chiefly by wealthy retired people who have nothing to do but play golf and watch television. Part of Will's problem is, on the simplest level, that he has retired early and tried to content himself with this meaningless life. Having learned the folly of retirement, he has decided as the novel ends to practice law once more on a humble and local level, and he and Allie are bringing people out of the retirement homes to work with them in building old-fashioned good cabins. Their romance is not escapist, but involves a rediscovery of language and of the satisfactions of mutual aid, community, and mastering basic skills as well as the experience of passionate physical love.

This novel, then, manages without sentimentality or evasion to go beyond the existential discovery of the meaninglessness of modern life and the expectation of apocalypse. Some readers may feel that, compared with its predecessors, it is not disturbing or dramatic enough; others will compare the change in mood to that between Shakespeare's tragedies and his later romances, and will be grateful that any hope can decently be found. I do not mean to suggest that this novel fails to confront tragic issues: It begins with Will's decision to commit suicide, and, after repeated explorations of his memories of his father in imaginary dialogues with his ghost, in which he becomes aware that his whole life has been an attempt to escape his father and those aspects of the South which he represents, he is finally able to throw away the shotgun with which the father has killed himself and decide to live, love, and work against retirement. In the course of this process Will is explored at greater psychological depth than any previous Percy hero.

In general, this novel is less given to existential rhetoric than its predecessors, and even sharper in specificity of observed detail. The minor characters are memorable, drawn with marvelous economy and wit. In spite of the suggestions of the title, it is an unsentimental and unrhetorical affirmation of love against death.

The Hero of New Orleans

Noting that *A Confederacy of Dunces* (1980), by J. K. Toole, was resurrected long after the author's death and published by a university press, the reader may well approach it with a certain wariness. It does not look promising. Walker Percy, in his foreword, tells how reluctantly he was persuaded by the author's mother to read the smeared carbon, hoping only that it would be so bad he would not have to read much; and how soon he was convinced, against all odds, that it is a very good book. The reader may suspect that he means surprisingly good, considering all the circumstances, or worthy but dull. Fortunately, this is not the case; the book needs no concessions. It is consistently entertaining and irresistibly funny, a comic epic in the great tradition of Cervantes and Fielding, with a suspenseful and elaborate plot skillfully managed and the little world of New Orleans encompassing the whole modern world.

As Percy says, the central character, Ignatius Reilly, is "without progenitor in any literature"—though Percy indicates the necessary points of reference in the comic tradition by calling him a "mad Oliver Hardy, a fat Don Quixote, a perverse Thomas Aquinas rolled into one" and describing him as gargantuan and Falstaffian and the book as more a *commedia* or tragicomedy than a mere comedy. To these analogies I would add Nathanael West's *Day of the Locust* for similarly local and fantastic satire, Flannery O'Connor for the Southern Catholic grotesque-satiric-comic mode, and Percy himself for the New Orleans scene and the philosophical-theological preoccupation. But *A Confederacy of Dunces* is faster and lighter than anything of these three writers, much closer to farce.

Unlike most comic heroes, Ignatius is not attractive and he has little in the way of redeeming virtues: Not only is he a fat, lazy slob but he is not idealistic like Don Quixote, kind-hearted like Tom Jones, or witty like Falstaff; he is completely selfish, without charity or humor. The title comes from Swift: "When a true genius appears in the world, you may know him by this sign, that the dunces are all in confederacy against him." This is how Ignatius sees it. But Ignatius is, of course, not a true genius, and his troubles are not the result of any confederacy of dunces. His scorn of the modern world is (in terms of the novel) fully justified; but then his condemnation of it for lack of theology and geometry and the guides he proposes for it (Boethius and Hrotswitha) are equally ludicrous, and his gluttony, sloth, and lack of love for everything except his dead dog, Rex, as well as his spiritual pride, are very obvious.

His favorite occupation, aside from eating junk food, is watching television and movies while making a running commentary on their moral and aesthetic depravity; theoretically, he is writing a diatribe against the modern world, "the disaster course that history had been taking for the past four centuries"; but this proceeds on Big Chief tablets at the rate of six paragraphs a month. His pyloric valve closes in reaction against the modern world, and he constantly seeks sympathy on this ground; but his mother, after supporting him through eight years of college and several more of sponging, finally rebels and insists that he find a job. His unwilling efforts to do so are the mainspring of the plot, as he becomes first a clerk at Levy Pants and then a hot-dog vendor in a pirate costume.

At the end, the disasters Ignatius has created for himself are all averted through Fortuna's wheel (as he would say) and he is rescued and carried off to the Bronx by Myrna Minkoff, his opposite in every way, whom he detests both personally and on principle. In having to let Myrna adopt him as her latest cause and pretend eagerly to accept the modern world—including group therapy—Ignatius receives his appropriate punishment; but perhaps the gratitude he feels toward her at the end is genuine. Aside from Ignatius's equivocal fate, justice is meted out, in the classic tradition of comedy, at the end. Lana Lee, the one real villain, is in jail, and her cohort, George, the schoolboy pornographer, is on the run; the bully Mrs. Levy has lost her power; everyone else comes off better than he expected or hoped. Burma, the unmilitant black, has a job, an award, and the good graces of the police; Darlene, the kind-hearted stripper, has a job for herself and her cockatoo; Gus Levy has saved his fortune by picking up a suggestion from Ignatius and converting Levy Pants to Levy Shorts; Mancuso has fame and the respect of his fellow policemen; and Mrs. Reilly is marrying Mr. Robichaux.

One of the finest things about the book is the vividness with which the speech of each character is rendered so as to be at once individual and exactly representative of his class, race, and locality—and, most important of all, both expressive of his nature and funny. There are Ignatius's high-flown posturings and self-justifying pontifications, his mother's wispy murmurings from her alcoholic fog, vaguely complaining but full of endearments, her matchmaking friend, Santa Battaglia, and the gentle old man Mr. Robichaux, who is convinced that the police are all Communists, the incompetent policeman, Mr. Mancuso, the hard-boiled Lana and Darlene of the Night of Joy, and, best of all, Burma Jones, the black man who, to avoid being charged with vagrancy by the police, accepts a job as janitor of the Night of Joy and finally resolves the plot as a form of sabotage. His speech is both funny and moving:

> "Well, I gonna tell that po-lice I gainfully employ, keep him off my back, tell him I met up with a humanitaria payin me twenty dollar a week. . . . And he say, 'Now maybe you be becomin a member of the community.' And I say, 'Yeah, I got me a nigger job and nigger pay. Now I really a member of the community. Now I a real nigger. No vagran. Just nigger.'" (47)

Later, he says, "I turnin into a expert on flos. I think color cats got sweepin and moppin in they blood, it come natural. . . . I bet you give some little color baby one-year-old a broom in he han, he star sweepin his ass off. Whoa!" (144). At the end, though things are looking up, he is still far from the advertisement world he dreams of: "You got you . . . a son teachin school probly got him a bobby-cue set, Buick, air condition, TV. Whoa! I ain even got me a transmitter radio. Night of Joy salary keepin peoples below the air-condition level" (301).

Why this book should have been rejected by numerous publishers is a mystery. Perhaps they were offended by its lack of any positive satiric norm, by its impartial ridicule of both sides of most political, social, and religious issues. But its mode is quite different from the stark irony of Swift or Flannery O'Connor, the grim satire of Nathanael West, the existentialist quest of Walker Percy. It is less subtle and profound, often closer to farce than to their kind of religiously based comedy. Naturally, it is uneven; some jokes are repeated too often and some misfire. (Two that do not are the picture of Dorian Greene, clearly a fairy descendant of Wilde's Dorian Gray, and Ignatius's *Journal of a Working Boy, or, Up from Sloth*, his version of Horatio Alger.) But it is fully mature, individual, and completely finished, and it embodies a unique and powerful comic vision.

PART · 5 *Aspects of the Culture*

Southern Fictions in Visual Art

These paintings and sculptures are Southern fictions in the literal sense that they are works made in the South. The title of the exhibition suggests also, however, that there is a resemblance between these works and Southern prose fiction — the novels and stories of Faulkner, Welty, O'Connor, and later writers. The Southern quality that all these works share is, I believe, real and important, though to define it in a few pages is an assignment comparable in difficulty to inscribing the Gettysburg Address on the head of a pin. (W. J. Cash, in what is still the best book on the subject — *The Mind of the South* — required well over four hundred pages.)

If patriotism is the last refuge of a scoundrel, as Dr. Johnson said, then regionalism is surely the first refuge of the pretentious untalented, of those provincials who want to be big frogs in little puddles. Yet regionalism is inescapable: Like it or not, we must come from somewhere and exist in one place rather than another; and awareness of places is an essential part of self-knowledge. Place and time are the two coordinates that define our existence, so to speak, and to know who we are is to understand the point at which they intersect. Only through self-knowledge can the artist achieve authenticity and truth to personal experience. Bad art (unless technically incompetent) is usually an imitation of art of another time and place; bad American art has usually imitated European art of the recent past. Regionalism is obviously no virtue in itself; it is never an excuse or justification; but it is a necessary part of the artist's vision. As Max Apple said in the introduction to his anthology *Southwestern Fiction,* "there are no boundaries to regionalism; when you see the Southwest you are seeing everything. The local

Gallery talk and program essay for the exhibition Southern Fictions, Contemporary Arts Museum, Houston, September 1983.

language and customs, the small matters that separate us, these things, properly noticed, become the bond that unites us."[1]

Regional awareness may manifest itself as hate as well as love, and is usually ambivalent. The classic example is Faulkner's *Absalom, Absalom!*, in which Quentin, asked at the end why he hates the South, replies "quickly, at once, immediately; 'I dont hate it,' he said. *I dont hate it* he thought, panting in the cold air, the iron New England dark; *I dont. I dont! I dont hate it! I dont hate it!*"[2] An equally impressive and paradoxical example is James Joyce, who would have nothing to do with the Irish Renaissance, detested literary patriots and professional Gaels, exiled himself from Ireland, but then spent the rest of his life writing obsessively about Dublin.

Conceding, perhaps reluctantly, that regionalism is inescapable and important, we may yet wonder whether the South still exists as a meaningful region. Perhaps the South itself has now become a Southern Fiction, at least in Texas. In Houston, where the population is highly mobile, cosmopolitan, and often transient; and especially in speaking of visual artists, who, in order to obtain instruction and recognition, must be in touch with artists, teachers, critics, and dealers in the major art capitals of the world, it must be admitted that doubts do arise.

There are obviously many Souths, or many subregions of the South; cattle and cowboys and oil and chemicals have made Texas in some respects more Southwestern than the rest of the Confederacy. Houston, as megalopolis, in some respects has more in common with the nation's other very large cities than with the rest of the South. All superficial regional differences in speech, dress, customs, manners, and the like have been steadily eroding for a long time under the accelerating pressures of the mass media (television most of all) and of the advertisers and franchise chains who have made all America look the same. Yet I should venture to assert that the South does still exist, and that Texas, and even Houston, are still part of it.

There are, I believe, distinctively Southern qualities that are characteristic of most people throughout the region and that are clearly recognizable in the art they produce. (These are not, of course, absolute distinctions — Southerners are not completely different from everyone else — but matters of degree and emphasis.) Let me suggest two such qualities that seem relevant to this exhibition. In the first place, Southerners tend to be more humane than people in other regions. They are human — sometimes all too human. Traditionally, they give human relations priority over all other values: family most of all, extending to the farthest boundaries of kinship, but also hospitality to the stranger and an immense variety of relationships in between. This implicit value judgment is expressed in the warmth, ease, and courtesy of Southern manners at their best, and in the effort made to amuse and entertain. This quality of thoughtfulness, sympathy, and compassion derives not from aristocratic lineage (real or imaginary) but from a shared heritage of guilt, suffering, and tragedy in the Civil War and its long aftermath. Southerners are more aware of their ancestors, of tradition, of the burden of the past than are most other people. And what this makes them realize (except for the occasional ones who are imprisoned in the past, like Faulkner's Hightower) is their common humanity. Because they have known evil and defeat, Southerners do not expect innocence, automatic progress, or absolute righteousness, either for themselves or their country. Southerners still profess high ideals and a more demanding code of personal honor than others; but these high professions are balanced by a constant awareness that, as John Henry said to the Captain, "A man ain't nuthin but a man."

The second quality I would propose as distinctively Southern is a propensity for creating and believing fictions — anecdotes, stories, legends, myths — about themselves. These fictions are not lies in the sense of being deliberately contrary to fact; they contain at least a kernel of truth; but they are imaginative constructions ranging in motive from the teasing humor of the tall tale to the desire to escape unpleasant reality. For obvious examples, the myths that the Old South was populated exclusively by ladies and gentlemen descended from aristocratic Cavaliers, following as closely as possible the manners of medieval chivalry as depicted by Sir Walter Scott, and living on large plantations manned by slaves who loved their masters and were happy in their servitude. Many of these myths were nostalgic and defensive back-projections from the hard times of Reconstruction and after; but the basic ones were believed by many antebellum Southerners themselves, who often tried to embody them in real life. To distinguish myth from reality has been a central preoccupation of Southern artists since antebellum days. *The White Rose of Memphis,* by William Faulkner's great-grandfather, Colonel W. C. Falkner, is an early example: Throughout the book, the romantic and chivalric doings on board the steamboat are counterpointed by the realistic episodes on the river banks. Faulkner himself constantly explores the meaning of the myths and legends of the South and their relation to reality. In Robert Penn Warren's *All the King's Men* Jack Burden slowly and painfully discovers the truth about Willie Stark, about his own fathers, and about himself. Katherine Anne Porter's great story "Old Mortality" deals with the protagonist's long effort to find out the truth about the romantic legend of the Southern belle Amy and to apply the lessons learned to her own life. Southern historians, too, have found a rich field not in simply "debunking" the myths, but in studying the complex interactions of myth and reality in the South. In addition to Cash's *Mind of the South* and C. Vann Woodward's *Burden of Southern History*, a brilliant later book by Bertram Wyatt-Brown, *Southern Honor* (1982), provides an excellent example.

The South of Ransom's beautiful poem "Antique Harvesters"—"the Proud Lady, of the heart of fire, / The look of snow," who does not age, and who is served gladly, without hope of reward, by chivalric young men—is a central symbol of the imaginary land where all men are honorable and all ladies virtuous. The Southern woman, says Cash, "was the lily-pure maid of Astolat and the hunting goddess of the Boeotian hill. And—she was the pitiful Mother of God. Merely to mention her was to send strong men into tears—or shouts."[3] Such myths have been used to manipulate the South from very early times. I myself remember that great demagogue Cotton Ed Smith, who in my youth was rounding out a very long career in the U.S. Senate based on an unvarying platform of States' Rights, White Supremacy, and the Purity of Southern Womanhood. It would be hard to say now which part of this famous trinity is more completely obsolete—or which part the South was most relieved to get rid of. But it was not only Southerners who were victims of such stereotypes. When I left my native South Carolina for my first extended stay in the North, at Princeton, I made friends with a boy from Minneapolis who promptly assured me that Southerners knew how to manage horses and women, and therefore he was counting on me for guidance. No doubt he saw me as the archetypal slave owner, putting horses and women (black) through their paces and firmly in command. As a middle-class small-town Southerner, I had little experience and less assurance in dealing with either horses or women; but I let him keep his illusions.

If I am right in suggesting that a special susceptibility to illusion and myth about itself has always been characteristic of the South, and that its historians and literary artists have in recent years been preoccupied with the exposure of self-deception and the discrimination of myth from reality, the next question is whether or not the same preoccupation is apparent in the works of the visual artists in this exhibit. In the first place, about half of them are primarily workers in collage or related forms—assemblages, combines, installations—rather than in painting or sculpture in the traditional sense. Certainly one of the aims of collage is to break down the distinction between the world of illusion and the world of reality by bringing real objects into the art world. The viewer is to be prevented from making a safe and comfortable separation between art and reality, as the audiences of modern plays and novels are prevented from escaping into a more beautiful and comprehensible world of illusion. Even photography is used in ingenious ways by these artists to break down the barrier between art and reality. Fiction is thus revealed as fiction, while at the same time the aesthetic qualities of ordinary objects and materials are revealed in a new way.

(I am not saying that all collage has the intentions I have suggested; the subject is far too complex for such generalization. If all collage is in a sense abstract, it is also in a sense narrative both of the history of the materials and of the artist's process of working. Much of it is also funny through deliberate incongruity; much of it incorporates elements of folk-naïve and popular art. Perhaps it is worth noting that two of the leading recent collagists, Robert Rauschenberg and Jasper Johns, were born and raised in the South, though they are no longer Southerners in the same sense as those in this exhibit—that is, artists now working in and identified with the South.)

As to the other basic quality I have ascribed to the South, humaneness, this exhibition is part of a large movement in the visual arts that may be called Rehumanization. As Charmaine Locke said in the foreword to *Images of the House*, "We are seeing a return to humanistic issues, a reevaluation of the personal, the experiential, as sources for art."[4] The same trend is apparent in the current New Orleans Triennial, as it was in the two preceding ones. While this movement is certainly not peculiar to the South, it seems to be even stronger here than elsewhere, and it takes certain distinctive forms, which this exhibition undertakes to display. Rehumanization means a shift from the Minimalist and Conceptualist art that has dominated the recent past to the personal and the human. A revival of figuration is central to it; abstracts are not excluded (e.g., some swampy ones here by Melissa Miller), but it is no longer the dominant mode. Most of the artists have been called Neo-Expressionists or Figurative Expressionists. As far as formal media are concerned, the deliberate breakdown of distinctions continues: The viewer cannot tell painting from photography from sculpture (which may be hard as welded metal, as in James Drake's installations, or soft as old clothes in Donald Beason's) or any of these from the pieces of reality with which they are combined. (There are, of course, some thoroughly traditional paintings and sculptures.) But of formalism in the sense of impersonal detachment there is none: These works are highly expressive of emotion, and are in this sense expressionistic. Marc Brasz is a striking example. (Many of them also have a direct relation to the specific school of German Expressionism—e.g., those of Richard Stout.) Many of these works are very personal and openly autobiographical, drawn without disguise from the artist's own life. Even those works with an obvious mythological or archetypal motif are often described by the artist in personal terms. Many of the works deal with domestic scenes, with both the interior and the exterior of the house, and with the family, in which the artists do not hesitate to include themselves.

The Southern preoccupation with fiction is apparent in these works in a more obvious sense than that already discussed in relation to collage. Many of the works are anecdotal or narrative in that they tell or imply stories (e.g., Alexandra Kleinbard's large wall reliefs with their gestural figures). This is itself a humane quality, and no more exclusively Southern than love of family: As Sidney long ago observed, a good story can hold children from play and old men from the chimney corner. But Southerners traditionally like good stories even more than other people: They spend more time telling them and listening to them, and, as Southern orators have always known, they are more likely to be convinced by a story than by an abstract argument. The Old South was perhaps more influenced by art than any society in history, though unfortunately the art was not of very high quality and was confused with history. As we have seen, Southerners, when they were not pretending to be Periclean Greeks or Romans of the Republic, were attempting to imitate in real life the fake medieval world of Sir Walter Scott's novels, complete with names, manners, costumes, and tournaments. Their passion for Greek Revival architecture, for high-flown rhetoric, and for imaginary genealogy has not yet disappeared, though the "best people" are no longer referred to as "the chivalry" and there is some awareness that even the Old South was dominated by the frontier rather than by aristocratic planters. But Southerners, "the most sentimental people in history," have always been easily self-deceived; while not valuing art for its own sake, they have always been too ready to take fiction for fact. Hence they have needed help from their artists in distinguishing the two, and from Mark Twain, whose account in *Huckleberry Finn* of the funereal art of Miss Emmeline Grangerford and of the feud is a devastatingly comic picture of the real Old South, to Tennessee Williams with his pathetic and terrifying Southern ladies, they have received it. Because narrative has been out of fashion in painting since the sentimental "literary" painting of the Pre-Raphaelites, to reinject a narrative element into the art is to recover a lost domain.

Many of these works are funny—for example, Donald Beason's soft sculptures of horses made out of old shoes—but the humor is more often grotesque and grim, intended more to disturb than to amuse. For example, Julian Schnabel's collages made of broken plates, Melissa Miller's "dramas that play when our backs are turned," and most of Nic Nicosia's domestic dramas, staged and photographed.

There is a strong apocalyptic vein in many of these works, a sense of doom and foreboding, of waiting for something dreadful to happen. This theme contrasts with the images of domesticity, which are seen as imperiled or being destroyed—the house is often in flames (Art Rosenbaum, Melissa Miller). The human form is often shown as distorted, made into a mannequin or mummylike figure or modeling-armature—in short, dehumanized. Awareness and horror of this fearsome possibility of loss of humanity are, of course, far from peculiar to the South; but are perhaps stronger here than in other regions. Consider, for literary analogies, the novels of Walker Percy, especially *Love in the Ruins* and *The Second Coming;* or the poems of James Dickey, such as "May-Day Sermon," "The Fire-Bombing," or *The Zodiac.* No doubt this tendency is related to the fundamentalist and revivalist religion that is prevalent in the South, with its doomsday terrors and fire and brimstone rhetoric. But it is also true to say that because the South has been more aware of the importance of human values, of the relation of the individual to family, domestic life, and community rather than his problems in isolation, it is natural that the Southern artist should be even more sensitive than others to the threats to these values implicit in our contemporary world.

It is noteworthy that, though many of these works are by implication strongly critical of our civilization, none is in any sense propagandistic or programmatically political. One reason that the Old South lacked much interest in the arts is that its best intellectual energies went into politics and that its commitment to slavery imposed a political orthodoxy on artists that obviously was severely limiting to them. The artists here represented are plainly not limited by adherence to any political orthodoxy or unorthodoxy; they are aware socially, but not in terms of political abstractions. But their South is very different from the South of stereotype, myth, legend, and fictions in general. The world of minorities is well represented—blacks, Chicanos, Indians—but the dominant subject is what used to be called the poor white. The poor white is seen not as stereotype—neither the white trash caricatured by Erskine Caldwell nor the hillbilly nor the Klansman—but as ordinary middle-class American; and so, for the most part, are the minorities. We have had this kind of treatment in literature for some years: from good early treatment of blacks by such white writers as DuBose Heyward and Julia Peterkin we have moved to such fine black writers as Ralph Ellison, James Baldwin, Al Young, and Alice Walker.

Indian writers such as N. Scott Momaday, Leslie Silko, and William Least Heat Moon have dealt with their own race. In *Southern Fried and Ruby Red* William Price Fox deals with poor white South Carolinians and the country music scene, as does C. W. Smith in Texas, with his *Country Music,* and Beverly Lowry with *Daddy's Girl.* It is amusing to reflect that whereas Nashville was once the Athens of the South, noted mainly for its educational distinction, symbolized in its replica of the Parthenon, and its location as the headquarters of the Fugitive-Agrarians, with their defense of what they took to be the lasting values of the Old South, Nashville now is the home of the Nashville Sound, the capital of country music; and in strange conjunction one can still see *Hee-Haw* and the Lost Cause, the old classical-chivalric ideals and Opryland; though there is little doubt which side has the power and the future.

There is much fantasy in the collection and a strong surrealist element, though not the fantastic realism of Magritte, Delvaux, Dali, and the like. The technique is much closer to the folk and the comic, sometimes even the comics and pop. The folk-naïve and neoprimitive strains are also powerful. For example, David Bates with his *Grassy Lake* or Francie Rich with her portraits *Queen without a Crown, Squirmy Baby,* and *Old Woman with Dog.* Works such as Lee Smith's *Spirits at Dog Dump* are in this folk tradition, but highly emotional, directly related to personal experience, fantastic but also narrative and direct. Jimmy Jalapeeno and Susan Whyne combine the folk tradition with classical techniques and allusions in a fascinating manner, as in the former's *Aphrodite* or the latter's *Mars and Flamenco Dancer,* which is both fantastic and very emotional, somewhat in the manner of Chagall.

It is tempting to draw further parallels between these artists and other modern Southern writers, in addition to those already mentioned. Flannery O'Connor's grimly humorous satiric realism, which shades into the grotesque and fantastic, for example, is suggested by many of these works (perhaps especially those of Melissa Miller and Russ Warren), and so are Donald Barthelme, William Goyen, and that converted Southerner Max Apple, who are in their very different ways comic and fantastic writers. Larry McMurtry, who used to wear a T-shirt labeled "Minor Regional Novelist," is like them in his scrupulous recording of the regional scene as well as in his frequent use of the comic-grotesque tone. And that greatest of all regional artists, William Faulkner (though one must immediately say, greatest with the possible exception of Yeats; and must note that it might be better to call both the most regional of great artists rather than the other way around),

provides innumerable similarities in his rendering of life at once Southern and universal. No writer could be a better example of the humaneness and the special concern with distinguishing fiction from fact—or
better, with discerning the truth that lies in fiction, legend, myth, and
stories of all kinds—than Faulkner. How things and people look in one
place rather than another was as important to Faulkner as to any visual
artist; and yet he was very clear that this regional aspect was not as
important as the universal. The title of *Light in August,* he said, was
intended to suggest a special quality of the light in Mississippi when
about the middle of August "suddenly there's a foretaste of fall, it's
cool, there's a lambence, a luminous quality to the light." But that
luminosity, he continues, is "older than our Christian civilization"; it
seems to come from "back in the old classic times . . . from Greece,
from Olympus."[5] Although he does not say so, he is obviously thinking of Greek tragedy, in which the human condition was similarly portrayed in terms both local and universal. The Southern fictions of this
show, like Faulkner's, strive to become fictions that are true and universal as well as Southern.

Jewish Intellectuals of New York

An outsider (especially if a solitary WASP) tends to think of New York Jewish intellectuals as a nest of hornets, technically social but ferocious. What *Creators and Disturbers: Reminiscences by Jewish Intellectuals of New York,* by Bernard Rosenberg and Ernest Goldstein, and *A Margin of Hope: An Intellectual Autobiography,* by Irving Howe,[1] reveal is that New York really has been a nest for them, protective and nurturing. The native New Yorkers in both books not only had no sense of belonging to an ethnic minority—in many parts of the city, *goyim* were so rare as to be curiosities—but, in strong contrast to most intellectuals elsewhere in America, they were not isolated by their special gifts and interests. Their immigrant parents encouraged them, their schools put them in advanced classes, teachers and librarians helped them; by the time they reached their teens, they were part of like-minded peer groups, often deeply engaged in radical politics. Some New Yorkers, both native and immigrant, feel that the city is a truer Jewish homeland than Israel: "I'm an unhyphenated Jew, with my roots in my shoes, and I feel most comfortable in New York because there are more Jews here than in Israel"; "Israel's no homeland for me. I've got a homeland. The Jew is *not* somebody from Judea, not any more. Two thousand years have made the Jew an international being."[2]

The editors of *Creators and Disturbers* sidestep the qustions of defining "Jewish" and "Intellectuals"; as to "of New York," they divide their intellectuals into three categories: immigrants from Europe (seven), native New Yorkers (thirteen), and transplants from elsewhere in the United States (four). As to their choice of these particular intellectuals, they say only that the book is "not celebrity-centered" and that the omission of the great physicist I. Rabi, who was "unavailable," is "the kind of gap we hope to fill in subsequent volumes." This way of putting it seem disingenuous: The book contains few top-rank Jewish intellectuals, and it is hard to believe that they were excluded because some of them are celebrities. There are not only no scientists or mathematicians but also no poets and few of the fiction writers or critics who have dominated the literary scene.

According to the title page, the book consists of "reminiscences" "drawn from conversations with" the editors. The pieces are, however, presented as if they were essays written in the first person by the subjects. (They are clearly not literal transcripts, since they are said to be based on "interviews conducted in depth and over an extended period"; quotation marks are not used; only in one or two cases are the interviewer's questions indicated.) The pieces, then, appear as essays by the subjects, though they were actually written by the interviewers. This is the way ghost writers produce books by celebrities, though here even the obligatory "as told to" is omitted. This procedure blurs the distinction between talking and writing, off-the-cuff response to a question and considered written statement; it seems very unfair to those subjects who are professional writers. More important, it renders doubtful the value of the interviews as documents.

After voicing these complaints, I am glad to say that the book is nevertheless immensely readable and full of fascinating information. The subjects are all good talkers. Perhaps the best is I. B. Singer, the great Yiddish fiction writer and journalist, whose interview begins the book. It is a wonderfully provocative statement confounding all possible generalizations. Singer promptly separates himself from the tradition of Yiddish writing, which was, he says, sentimental and social: Yiddish writers "constantly fought for what they thought was a just world. They scolded the rich and praised the poor. I never felt that this was my function in literature. I was interested in specific stories and individual, exceptional people" (32). Singer is the only person interviewed who was neither surprised nor shocked by the Holocaust, because "the whole history of humanity is one big holocaust. . . . Even before the Hitler destruction I had the feeling that human life is one big slaughter. That was my feeling. Not just as a Jew. As a human being" (37). He believes in God, but not in his goodness or mercy; and he is conscious of the relation between his own pessimism and his humor: "The humorist sees mostly how easy it is to hypnotize people, to make fools of them, and how many fools God has created who don't even need to be hypnotized. They are born fools!" (41).

Starting with Singer makes everything else seem downhill, both because none of the other subjects is comparable in literary stature (Grace Paley is rather disappointing, and though Ted Solotaroff is good, Alfred Kazin and Irving Howe can only summarize what they say better in their own autobiographies) and because they naturally operate on the sociological-historical level that Singer has disdained. On that level, it is worth noting that Singer, then seventy-eight, was one of only two of the seven immigrant subjects still surviving, so that the first section already has a clear historical value. The interviews in the rest of the book cover everything from labor unions to psychoanalysis, from music (jazz, pop, and classical) to the various branches of Judaism, from architecture to education and the world of publishing. While it is obviously impossible here to summarize this wealth of material, a few recurrent themes may be mentioned. First is the basic difference between German Jews, who, both before and after the days of the famous refugees from Hitler, were mostly gifted, well educated, and successful in America as in Germany; from Brandeis to Kissinger and Weinberger, their primary goal was assimilation, and hence they were politically moderate or conservative and usually anti-Zionist or indifferent; and the Yiddish-speaking Jews from Eastern Europe and Russia. These were usually Orthodox and Zionist, anti-assimilationist, and politically radical — at least to start with. Thus the immigrant Henry Pachter says that in Germany he felt some hostility toward Eastern Jews because they refused to be acclimatized: "It was embarrassing to see them talk with their hands and to hear their pidgin German. Here, in the U.S., it's different. Yiddish is not a derivation of English; non-Jews don't understand what Yiddish speakers say. In Germany they talked a German dialect which was despised and ridiculed" (119). But in New York he "found all my old German Jewish prejudices against Eastern Jews confirmed. They are provincial, with few exceptions narrow and self-righteous, and have generally more chutzpah than most other tribes" (133). On the other hand, Gerson Cohen, whose parents were Russian immigrants, Zionists, Neo-Orthodox, and Hebrew-speaking, was shocked to discover that "there were *our* Jews and what the family referred to as 'Yehudim.' I learned that these were 'Deutsche Yiddin,' German Jews, 'Silk Stockings'" (220); they were rich and did not speak Hebrew or even Yiddish.

A second theme is why these Jewish intellectuals stay in New York, in spite of the physical and, many say, cultural deterioration of the city, its crime and unpleasantness. Perhaps the chief reason is that it is the world's largest Jewish city: "Here I have the Jews, so here I am at home, and I never was at home before." Schools and libraries are often mentioned, and other cultural advantages. The labor leader Victor Gotbaum cites the welfare tradition: "We have evidence in New York of social welfare and social conscience. It's no accident that our people are taxed 21 percent of their income. We do it because we believe in social services. . . . We may be vulgar, we may be dirty, but we have more sensitivity about those in need than any goddam city in the United States" (262). Relations between Jews and blacks (at their warmest in the world of jazz, on which there is a fine piece by Dan Morgenstern) are often mentioned. It was the teachers' strike of 1968 which revealed a basic divergence: "Jews had been partners in the civil rights movement so long as it appealed to universalism and to assimilationist ideals"; but when the black power movement resorted to violence in the pursuit of black self-interest, the Jews parted company. In education, black self-interest called for "reducing the importance of tests and pressing for racially-based hiring, while Jews had (and still have) a self-interest in preserving racially and religiously neutral policies" (396, 399). As always, the Jewish aim was to abolish quotas and to establish equal opportunity based on objective testing.

The Holocaust naturally bulks large in almost every interview. As the editors put it, the "liberalism or radicalism and humanitarianism of Jewish intellectuals, with their antecedents in the Enlightenment, barred them from anticipating Hitler's handiwork" (13). Pachter puts it more specifically: "As a Marxist of course I too had to believe that the banks were powerful enough to tell Hitler to let the Jews alone." And Alfred Kazin, a Socialist, found that "the Holocaust made me believe more and more in certain ideas of human nature which I had been loath to accept." Marxism "could never explain the Holocaust, or why the Nazis went out of their way, even to their military disadvantage, to capture and destroy Jews" (208–9). For religious Jews, however, the Holocaust "challenged the whole idea of God" and drove them into looking for new categories. Every person interviewed has strong opinions about Hannah Arendt, whose books on the origins of totalitarianism (1951) and the Eichmann trial (1963), as well as her own position as a superior representative of high German culture, provoked powerful reactions.

The establishment of Israel, similarly, is an inescapable topic. Hans Morgenthau was an anti-Zionist and thought of Israel as a "nation of schnorrers" until the 1967 war, when his pride in Israel's triumph led him gradually to redefine his Jewish identity. Many others went through a similar process. On the other hand, the architect Percival Goodman disapproves of the Israelis' martial virtues and argues that "the big Israeli export . . . should be peace," and Henry Pachter, considering Israel "the greatest misfortune that ever befell Jewry," nevertheless reluctantly accepts his identification with it: "I have to be responsible for Begin's mistakes."

Finally, all the interviews show the subjects, under the impact of the Holocaust and the emergence of Israel, forced to rethink their religion and politics in relation to their Jewishness. Alfred Kazin states the problem with particular frankness: Ultra-Orthodox Jews are anti-Israel and "embarrassing from the Western, hygienic, super-sophisticated point of view, which the Israelis have." Furthermore, he has a "very deep quarrel with Orthodox Jews" because they think of themselves as the "elect": "Whenever I see an Orthodox Jew I recognize the face that secretly burns up Christians" (206). Yet he is convinced of the reality and importance of religion, and his religion is meaningful to him only in relation to his Jewishness. The only professional sociologist in the book, Joseph Bensman, defines his Jewishness in a similarly complicated way. He can identify with Jews as "intellectual disturbers and creators" (thereby giving the book its title), which he calls a "kind of Jewish élitism." While he is committed to Israel, he is also committed to the United States ("at least in the sense that only its stupidities can make me really angry"), to his work, to his friends, and "to an intellectual tradition that I see being sold out every day by its practitioners." In all these ways, he is a "marginal man who accepts his position" (387), and this may be the decisive component of his Jewish identity.

Irving Howe's interview makes him appear almost paradigmatically typical of the New York Jewish intellectual. Child of immigrant Yiddish-speaking parents who were poor and got poorer, growing up in the Bronx where only the janitors were non-Jewish, he had excellent teachers and made the most of excellent libraries. At fourteen he joined the Young People's Socialist League and began the political activities that were central to his life thereafter; by sixteen or seventeen he thought of himself as a Marxist. At CCNY he was a leader of the anti-Stalinists, moving toward Trotskyism; *Partisan Review* impressed him deeply, and after the war "it became clear to me that I belonged to a generation called the New York intellectuals," centering on this magazine. First made aware of his Jewishness in the army, he returned to Yiddish literature after the war, editing, translating, and interpreting; he was instrumental in the "discovery" of I. B. Singer. Although not a Zionist, Howe took the Israeli side in the controversies over Arendt's *Eichmann,* which were "like a therapeutic session where you discover that, welling up within you, there is a great mass of feeling that . . . had been suppressed." His concern with Yiddishkeit culminated in his much-praised *World of Our Fathers* (1977). Describing his disenchantment with political ideology at the end, he hopes that he is "more humane, tolerant, and broad-minded" (287).

These bare bones are fleshed out in Howe's fine "intellectual autobiography," *A Margin of Hope,* which reveals him as an individual (and in his own language, without intermediaries). It is not that the book tells much about Howe's personal life; it is concerned with his ideas, and with his personal experiences only as they affect or are affected by those ideas. (There is, for example, hardly anything about his relations with women; even his parents are given minimal attention, and the archetypal rejection and eventual acceptance of the father that seems obligatory in all autobiographies is barely sketched in.) He attempts no novelistic characterizations or dramatized scenes, and I think he is wise not to. Howe's great gift as a critic is for lucid and readable exposition of ideas, enlivened by occasional flashes of wit or eloquence; and this gift is fully exploited here. He manages to write about himself at great length without sounding pretentious, defensive, or apologetic; his tone is thoughtful and candid, and his resources of self-knowledge are considerable. He does not seem concerned to make himself look good or to settle old scores; he is quite ready to say so when he thinks he was wrong, and he comes close to a recantation at the end, as we shall see.

Radical politics, the Young People's Socialist League and then the Trotskyist Socialist Workers Party, were Howe's Garden of Eden, his days of innocence and whole-hearted belief, with the kind of in-group bonding that other adolescents find in sports and social fraternities. "Never before, and surely never since, have I lived at so high, so intense a pitch, or been so absorbed in ideas beyond the smallness of self."[3] This Marxist orientation prevented him from grasping the full horror of the Holocaust: "Marxism, by remaining fixed upon class analysis and social categories appropriate only to the bourgeois-democratic epoch, kept us from seeing the radically novel particulars of the Nazi regime" (250). On the other hand, it facilitated his postwar entry into the circle of New York intellectuals centering around the quasi-Trotskyist *Partisan Review.* For Howe to call them *the* New York intellectuals seems unduly exclusive and proprietary; what are later ones to call themselves? And there had been other groups of intellectuals — even intelligentsia, perhaps — in other American cities. But Howe is probably right in calling these the first in New York, and his picture of their lives, aims, and activities is the best I have seen. His own aim was to be a social critic, with Edmund Wilson and George Orwell as models, and beyond this to be "one of those free-ranging speculative writers who grapple with the troubles of their time yet command some of the accumulated knowledge of the past" (195). Putting it in colloquial and ethnic terms in his interview, he says, "we had . . . a mania for range; that's why when I say literary intellectual I mean something other than a critic. . . . Behind this is a very profoundly Jewish impulse; namely, you've got to beat the goyim at their own game. So you have to dazzle them a little."[4] They cultivated a style some called New York Baroque, a mixture of mandarin elegance and street outcry; they were contentious, plebeian, rude, and Russian-flavored (with exceptions, of course, to each of these epithets).

One of Howe's best qualities is that he is not doctrinaire. In his early days he "fell crazily in love" with T. S. Eliot, "more with the rhythms and music of his verse than its meanings. I knew he was a reactionary but didn't really care."[5] Although utterly unlike them in background and basic assumptions, he likes and appreciates Tate, Ransom, and Blackmur (and it is worth mentioning that all three of them recognized his talent early). As he grows older he comes to appreciate the ideal of the gentleman, of being quiet and unassertive, modest and humane: "a life of the mind that can keep some distance from competitiveness and clamor" (324). He becomes enchanted by ballet. And he becomes deeply aware of the limits of politics: "The notion that as soon as 'we' take power, all will be well; the notion that democracy, even in its most debased forms, is anything but a precious human conquest; the notion that social change will occur through the automatic workings of the economy, just like the opposite notion that history can be forced through the will of a sacrifical band—none of these can be taken seriously by thoughtful people, none ever should have been" (345). It is almost a recantation or palinode. Yet at the end he is still trying to make a case for socialism on moral grounds, while conceding that "if at any point a socialist proposal were to conflict with the fundamental values of liberalism, I would unhesitatingly opt for the latter" (346). This nostalgic yearning for at least a vocabulary of his lost Eden is rather appealing, but it leads him into an unfortunately anticlimactic conclusion: an imaginary conversation that starts with the proposition "God died in the nineteenth century, utopia in the twentieth" (351) and finds nothing definite to affirm.

Black English

Does "Black English"—a dialect peculiar to American blacks—exist? The connotation of the term and the issue that it raises have a curious recent history.

In the old days, before, say, 1950, it is my impression that the casual observer, or man in the street, believed in the existence of a distinctive black dialect, though he would have been unlikely to call it Black English. The representation of the dialects of various ethnic minorities was a major form of American humor (from newspaper columnists and cartoonists to *Abie's Irish Rose*), and in the South black speech was accurately rendered from Mark Twain and Joel Chandler Harris to Ambrose Gonzales, Octavus Roy Cohen, Julia Peterkin, and DuBose Heyward. Not only authors but also most white Southerners prided themselves on the fluency with which they could reproduce typical black dialect. Peculiarities were, of course, exaggerated, for comic or other effects, most obviously in the language of "stage darkies" from minstrel shows to Rochester, Stepin Fetchit, Amos n' Andy, and innumerable later black comics in movies and television shows and situational comedies. The assumption that there is a distinctive black dialect, ethnically identifiable, is essential to this kind of humor; though with the more recent black comics, at least, awareness of their bidialectalism—their equal fluency in standard English, which allows them to shift dialects at will—is equally essential.

By the early 1950s, however, scholarly investigations of American regional dialects had begun to appear, all pointing to the same conclusion: that there was no significant difference between the speech of blacks and whites of the same geographical origin and economic and educational status. Analyzing the interviews that were their primary source of evidence, scholars found that differences between black and white speech, which seemed on the surface to be considerable, were essentially statistical: that is, every apparent characteristic of black speech was also to be found in white speech, but with greater frequency among the blacks.[1] (This conclusion had been anticipated by Cleanth Brooks's study of 1935, in which, comparing the language of the *Uncle Remus* stories with L. W. Payne's records of current Alabama-Georgia dialect, he found the difference to be merely one of degree: The distinguishing marks of the dialect—as of most Southern speech—are its archaism and its resemblance to the provincial dialects of southwestern England, both these features being preserved from the language of the original settlers in the seventeenth and eighteenth centuries; the blacks' dialect, being more isolated and less subject to educational and other influences, had simply changed less. Brooks's point was that Southerners, black or white, had no reason to consider their language inferior or incorrect; it was merely more conservative than, and somewhat different in origin from, the language of other regions.)[2] The skewed statistics, or greater linguistic conservatism, of blacks were obviously related to segregation, and the conclusions of linguists were in complete accord with, and gave support to, the movement toward integration in the 1950s and 1960s. The term *Black English* was rarely used because of possible racist implications; earlier racist explanations of black speech in terms of differences in anatomy (flat noses, thick lips, clumsy tongues, thick skulls, and small brains), temperament (careless, lazy, incapable of sustained attention, childlike, excitable), or climate (slow and lethargic because of the heat) were indignantly rejected. Dialectal differences between blacks and whites, it seemed clear, were culturally determined and transmitted; in the era of integration there also seemed to be no doubt that the pedagogical objective should be to eliminate these differences as rapidly as possible.

The next phase began about 1965. By this time enormous numbers of blacks had migrated to the cities and formed black ghettoes; rather than integration, Black Power was militantly asserted, and "Black Consciousness" and "Black Is Beautiful" became popular slogans. Sociolinguists in the inner cities were confronted by the urgent problem of formulating programs to deal with the linguistic and other educational difficulties—often desperate—of vast numbers of black children and adolescents. In their laudable concern to avoid suggesting that black speech was simply inferior or careless standard English, they refused to label it substandard or nonstandard or even dialectal, and hence arrived at the remarkably imprecise term *Black English*. Obviously the sociolinguists had powerful motives for arguing, and believing, that regional differences were unimportant, so that their government-sponsored programs would be applicable not just in Washington but also in New York, Philadelphia, Detroit, Chicago, Los Angeles, and so on. Reviewing the Urban Language Series published by the Center for Applied Linguistics in Washington from 1966 to 1974, Lee Pederson remarks that the "Great Black English Controversy" was "a pseudo-issue for linguistics, but a gut-issue for marketeering."[3]

To establish Black English as not only separate but equal and uniform throughout America, it was necessary first to ignore or discredit the work of the dialect geographers and then to provide an alternate genealogy for Black English. This genealogy was based on the rediscovery of Gullah, the strange, archaic dialect spoken on the Sea Islands and nearby coasts of South Carolina and Georgia. Gullah had not only been recognized by the dialect geographers as the single distinctive black dialect in this country[4] but was also admitted to be a genuine creole. (Creoles are pidgins that become the principal and native languages of speech communities—e.g., Haitian French, or Papiamento in Curaçao.) Furthermore, the definitive study of it, *Africanisms in the Gullah Dialect,* had been produced in 1949 by a great black linguist, Lorenzo Turner. Creolists and sociolinguists proceeded to construct an elaborate hypothesis assuming not only that Black English was a separate and distinct dialect but also that it always had been and that insofar as it resembled white English, it was because blacks had influenced whites, and not the other way around. According to this hypothesis, the creole that now survives only in Gullah was once spoken by slaves all over America (Plantation Creole), and by a process of decreolization became modern Black English.[5]

At this point I must make a brief personal digression. Although not a professional linguist, I have been more than casually interested in these questions. I grew up in South Carolina not far from the Gullah area; I spent a little time in Africa; and I am acquainted with the speech of a wide variety of American blacks. When J. L. Dillard's *Black English* appeared in 1972, therefore, I was interested enough to work up the background and write a substantial review.[6] I praised it as "the first book-length study by a qualified linguist of the speech of black Americans" and "a convincing demonstration that black English exists as a distinct and fascinating dialect and that its study and use in teaching black children is very important." As popularization I thought it somewhat unscrupulous in turning conjectures into assumptions,[7] and as polemic somewhat addicted to exaggeration and overkill. For example, Dillard sees the Academic Establishment—in a mythological drama pervading the whole book—as engaged in a conspiracy to suppress the true knowledge of Black English, denying that it is different from the white regional dialects whose origins it traces back to Britain. This ancient and evil conspiracy (which somehow takes on overtones of British snobbery as well as of power and privilege) is now being exposed and overthrown by creolists, sociolinguists, and other students of minority languages, especially the Black English of the urban ghettoes. Down with Anglo-Saxon attitudes; up with minorities!

To simplify, we may call the three principal theses of the book the ontological, the historical, and the educational. (1) Black English is different from (Southern and standard) white English not only in vocabulary but also in structure. It is not a corruption of white English but probably influenced white English more than it was influenced by it. At any rate, it is a separate, distinctive, and legitimate dialect. (2) Black English originated in a West African–English Pidgin that developed into a Plantation Creole once spoken by slaves all over the United States and still spoken by the Gullahs of Coastal South Carolina and Georgia; the characteristic structure of this creole is still preserved in modern Black English. (3) Bidialectalism (or biloquialism or bilingualism) should be the method and goal of language instruction. This means recognizing both the legitimacy of the black student's native speech and the special problems he has in learning standard English; in practice, it means teaching him standard English as if it were a foreign language. My own view was that Dillard was successful in establishing (1) and (3), but that (2), the historical thesis deriving Black English from a hypothetical creole perhaps like modern Gullah, while not inherently improbable, rested on a tendentious interpretation of insufficient evidence.[8]

Since that time, what new evidence I have seen and what new arguments on both sides I have read, together with my own further reflections, have inclined me to take a less positive position on (1) and (3) and to feel even greater skepticism abut (2). But let us look briefly at some of the specific issues.

1. Following William A. Stewart and others, Dillard argues that Black English differs not only in vocabulary but also in structure, and that its verb system "reveals the greatest difference from white American dialects—as from British dialects—and the closest resemblance to its pidgin and creole ancestors and relatives."[9] Aspect is more important than tense. Tense can be omitted in Black English, provided the necessary time cues are given elsewhere: *He go yesterday.* Distinctions of meaning are shown most clearly in the various negative forms. "When *he ain' go* is the negative of *he go,* the verb base marks a point-of-time category. This, again, is a creole language characteristic, and is very different from Standard English" (42). "*He ain' go* is the negative for a momentary action, whether or not in the past. *He ain' goin'* is the negative of a progressive action, whether or not in the past"

(43). Thus forms such as *He stood there and he thinkin'* are possible. Verbs in the Aspect category "are marked for the ongoing, continuous, or intermittent quality of action rather than for the time of its occurrence. . . . This is perhaps the most basic difference from Standard English, since a speaker of Standard English must mark tense but can choose to indicate or to ignore the ongoing or static quality of an action. Black English gives the speaker an option with regard to tense, but its rules demand that he commit himself as to whether the action was continuous or momentary" (43–44). These categories express important differences in meaning. "If one says of a workman, *He workin' when de boss come in* he is paying the worker no compliment; the work is coterminous with the presence of the boss. . . . On the other hand, *He be workin' when de boss come in* means that the work went on before and after the boss's entry. . . . One might also say to a scorned acquaintance's rare intelligent remark, *You makin' sense, but you don't be makin' sense,* meaning something like 'You've blundered into making an intelligent statement for once'" (45–46). *Been* marks an action that is decidedly in the past; it can be called Perfective Aspect; like West African languages, Black English has also a contrasting Immediate Perfective Aspect, for which the preverbal form is *done: I done go, I done sent, I done been gone.* The auxiliary *have* is replaced by *been, done,* and *is:* Thus for Standard English "Have you seen him?" there is Black *Is you see(n) him?* The contrast between *be* and zero as copula markers is significant: *My brother sick* means that the sickness is currently in effect, but of short-term duration; *My brother be sick* indicates a long-term illness (46–48, 52).

Dillard, by this kind of analysis, certainly makes the point very effectively that Black English is a legitimate dialect, not just an inferior or corrupt form of standard English. (No linguist would need to be convinced of this, but lay readers might.) On the other hand, the most authoritative scholars say that there is no feature of the verb system to be found among blacks that does not also occur among whites, though they are more common among blacks.[10] The examples given by Dillard of *be* as marker of habituative aspect have been shown to have parallels in Irish, Welsh, and Anglo-Irish;[11] it is not peculiar to Black English, and may well have arrived in it through the influence of Irish or Welsh settlers, of whom there were many in the South. The urban sociolinguists are ignorant of white Southern speech and especially of the speech of poor whites, say the linguistic geographers;[12] they do not compare the speech of their ghetto blacks to that of poor white migrants to the cities.

Analyzing numerous studies of the linguistic features of black speech, David Shores finds the most frequently mentioned of them to be: the uninflected plural (*five girl*), the uninflected possessive (*the boy hat*), the uninflected third person singular (*he think*), the uninflected past tense and participle (*he play, he has play*), the absence of the copula (*he here*), the uninflected *be* (*it be*), overinflection (*I knows*), final consonant reduction (*firs*), the existential *it* (*it is a man there*), and question inversion (*I want to know can he go*). But all these are also to be found in white Southern speech, and those who know most about regional dialects agree in finding the difference to be statistical only.[13] A particularly striking case is that of Beryl Bailey, a Jamaican creolist who, in a famous article of 1965, suggested "that the Southern Negro 'dialect' differs from other Southern speech because its deep structure is different, having its origins as it undoubtedly does in some proto-creole grammatical structure."[14] Using as her material the speech of the narrator in Warren Miller's *The Cool World,* she selected four structures as distinctively black: "the absence of the copula (zero copula), the marked forms which are 'past and future,' the negation markers *ain't* and *don't,* and the treatment of *there* and 'possessive *their.*'" In an equally famous article of 1970, Juanita Williamson, herself black and an experienced student of Southern dialects, analyzed numerous examples of Southern white speech in terms of these four "distinctively Negro" structures, and found the structures occurring frequently in them all. (The examples included an article by a white "redneck" klansman, the speech of white characters in a wide variety of recent Southern novels, and samples of Southern white speech quoted in various travel books, articles, and newspapers, with a final collection from Williamson's first-hand observation.)[15] In another brief but significant article, Williamson demolished the notion that "existential *it*" is peculiar to the black ghetto, tracing its honorable lineage not only to white Southerners but also to Shakespeare and *Cursor Mundi*.[16] And in another she proves that the sociolinguists are wrong in saying that whites always invert word order in questions, while blacks do not. "Descriptions of the black American's speech which indicate the omission of *be, do,* or *have* in the direct question is found in the speech of the black person but not in standard English do not take into consideration actual American usage."[17]

2. A few final words on the creolist hypothesis. Lorenzo Turner, in his great study, stressed the uniqueness of Gullah and the impossibility of extrapolating from it to other black dialects. Gullah was a very special case, a language spoken by slaves who lived for centuries in almost total isolation on the Sea Island rice plantations, developing their own combination of archaic English and African languages. Only a

few words of Gullah penetrated the surrounding region, and in my own experience black as well as white speakers in this region found Gullah fascinating but almost wholly unintelligible. To prove that Black English is a decreolization of Gullah would require far more evidence than has yet been forthcoming.[18]

Logically, there is no need to prove that Black English has a creole deep structure or substratum in order to establish its distinctiveness as a dialect. Whatever *dialect* means (and linguists do not agree), recognizability is a sufficient practical criterion; and this may be based on statistical incidence of vocabulary and pronunciation just as well as on grammatical structure. Why, then, so much emphasis on an argument so hypothetical and supported by so little evidence? Partly, I suspect, to justify a monolithic concept of Black English; partly to assert black identity and independence, turning the tables on the white man by proving that black influenced white linguistically; and perhaps most of all, to satisfy the yearning to find black roots in Africa. (The parallel with Alex Haley's *Roots* and the two enormously popular television series based on it is striking: The appeal is based on motives any decent person must find sympathetic, but in both cases, they lead to a highly simplistic version of history and a highly emotional concept of evidence.)

My own opinion is that history interpreted in terms of affirmative action or radical chic is not going to help blacks; there is no black history any more than there is black truth or black justice. For human beings, black or white, there is no escape from the constant struggle to keep in touch with reality; to abandon blacks to fantasies is to patronize and ultimately to betray them.

3. No genealogy or pedigree is required to demonstrate the legitimacy of black dialect. Everyone needs to respect and take pride in his native way of speaking, which should never be dismissed by teachers as merely careless or incorrect. Leonard Bloomfield stated the principle well in 1933: "For the native speaker of sub-standard or dialectal English the acquisition of standard English is a real problem, akin to that of speaking a foreign language. To be told that one's habits are due to 'ignorance' or 'carelessness' and are 'not English,' is by no means helpful. Our schools sin greatly in this regard."[19] But Bloomfield had no doubt that the objective should be the prescriptive teaching of standard English. Only Black Power militants, extreme linguistic relativists, and holders of other paradoxical positions would be likely to deny that bidialectalism is a useful pedagogical device in elementary school, though I gather there is some disenchantment with teaching English as a foreign language, the methods used for teaching foreign

languages not being notably successful for their original purposes either. Interestingly enough, those who are most suspicious of bidialectalism as an educational aim are black college educators. In an article based on evidence from hundreds of black educators from more than sixty traditionally black colleges, David Shores found that "they refuse to accept Black English as a separate dialect independent of American White English."[20] What bothers them most is "that people in the Black English business give the impression that these features are in the speech of all Blacks and that all Blacks, regardless of age, region, and social class, speak alike. Furthermore, they view with suspicion . . . the whole enterprising nature (and I use the word advisedly, for Blacks have recognized that Black English is a booming business) of the investigation of Black speech. They are especially put off by the linguists who say that it was they who studied, described, and have struggled to get Black English accepted as a legitimate language" (184). They "consider the best policy as that of trying to eliminate nonstandard features from the speaking and writing of their students, insofar as that is possible" (185), recognizing that the public does not judge speech with the same tolerance that linguists do.

Some may consider these black educators to be excessively concerned with getting ahead as a goal for their students; but they are shrewd, practical people, and their attitude is understandable. They are certainly right in objecting to the notion of Black English as a monolithic entity and in their feeling that anyone who encourages students to believe Black English is acceptable at the top levels of our society is perpetrating a cruel hoax. Whites, whatever their native dialect, have exactly the same educational problem, though often in lesser degree. Everyone has to learn the basic difference between spoken and written language, and then the kinds of language, oral or written, appropriate to many different situations and contexts. To purify the dialect of the tribe, as Eliot and Mallarmé put it unforgettably, is a task worthy of a lifetime for us as for our dead masters; trying to learn to use words requires all the knowledge, cultivation of taste, and subtlety of discrimination we can manage to acquire. The way a man speaks—his idiolect, in linguistic jargon—is one of his most individual and revealing characteristics, and different in each person; hence the study of language is infinitely complex. Dialect geography will remain perennially fascinating because the relation of people to places is important to their individual and collective histories, and language is a cherished part of their heritage. In this light, the simplistic concept of Black English is not helpful; and Dillard's later vision of All-American English, consisting of Network Standard (pure, non-regional offspring of Colonial Koiné, itself descendant of Plantation Creole), surrounded from sea to shining sea by International English, is not an inspiring one. Let us hope instead for the continued flourishing of many black dialects—some, of course, indistinguishable from white—and rejoice that they have been accurately respresented by novelists of both races (Ellison, Wright, Baldwin; Faulkner, O'Connor, Welty) and that some of their special flavor and rhythm, with their exceptional vitality and flair for imaginative metaphor, may be seen in the poetry of Gwendolyn Brooks, Ishmael Reed, Philip Levine, and many others.

Notes

Cotton Mather

1. Kenneth Silverman, *The Life and Times of Cotton Mather* (New York, 1984).
2. Quoted in ibid., 277.
3. David Levin, ed., *Bonifacius: An Essay upon the Good* (Cambridge, Mass., 1966), iv.
4. Silverman, *Cotton Mather*, 171.

William James as Culture Hero

1. Elizabeth Hardwick, ed., *The Selected Letters of William James* (New York, 1961), xiv.
2. Quoted in Jacques Barzun, *A Stroll with William James* (New York, 1983), 81.
3. The first quotation is in ibid., 170, the second in Bertrand Russell, *A History of Western Philosophy* (New York, 1945), 811.
4. Further testimony is provided by the elaborate new edition of his works being published over many years by the Harvard University Press and the continued republication of his books among the most advanced offerings in phenomenology, poststructuralism, deconstruction, and other fields of current interest: for example, in 1984 the State University of New York Press reprinted Bruce W. Wilshire's very fine selection of James's *Essential Writings*. James is widely perceived as not merely a historical monument or national symbol, but a thinker still alive and relevant.
5. Howard M. Feinstein, *Becoming William James* (Ithaca, N.Y., 1984), 329.
6. Wilshire, *Essential Writings*, 23–24.
7. Russell, *History of Western Philosophy*, 812.
8. W. J. Bate, *Samuel Johnson* (New York and London, 1979), 297. B. H. Bronson's essay is in his *Johnson Agonistes and Other Essays* (Cambridge, 1946).
9. Bate, *Samuel Johnson*, 300.
10. William James, *The Varieties of Religious Experience* (New York, 1902), 157.
11. Hardwick, *Selected Letters of William James*, xviii.

12. Boswell, *Life of Johnson* (New York, 1933), 2:496.
13. Hardwick, *Selected Letters of William James*, 250.
14. Boswell, *Life of Johnson* 1:303.
15. Boswell, *Life of Johnson* 2:221.
16. Wilshire, *Essential Writings*, xxvii.
17. Barzun, *Stroll with William James*, 167.
18. Hardwick, *Selected Letters of William James*, 187.
19. James, *Varieties*, 318.
20. Hardwick, *Selected Letters of William James*, 248.
21. His writings on these and related matters were collected and edited by Gardner Murphy, *William James in Psychical Research* (New York, 1960).
22. Boswell, *Life of Johnson* 2:225, 176.
23. Barzun, *Stroll with William James*, 251.
24. Murphy, *William James on Psychical Research*, 67.
25. Boswell, *Life of Johnson* 1:421.
26. Wilshire, *Essential Writings*, 307.
27. James, *Varieties*, 46–47.
28. Boswell, *Life of Johnson* 2:274.
29. Bate, *Samuel Johnson*, 457.
30. Quoted in ibid.
31. Wilshire, *Essential Writings*, 311–12.
32. Quoted in Barzun, *Stroll with William James*, 260.
33. James, *Varieties*, 511.
34. Murphy, *William James on Psychical Research*, 270–71.
35. James, *Varieties*, 370.
36. Boswell, *Life of Johnson* 2:258.
37. James, *Varieties*, 374.
38. Wilshire, *Essential Writings*, 271, 275, 276.
39. Murphy, *William James on Psychical Research*, 215.
40. Johnson, *Vanity of Human Wishes*, lines 157–58, in *The Poems of Samuel Johnson*, ed. D. N. Smith and E. L. McAdam (Oxford, 1941), 38.
41. Wallace Stevens, "Disillusionment of Ten O'Clock" (1915), in *Collected Poems* (New York, 1955), 66.
42. Louis MacNiece, "Snow" (1935), in *Collected Poems*, ed. E. R. Dodds (New York, 1967), 30.
43. Wilshire, *Essential Writings*, vii, xxxvi, and 7.
44. Quoted in Barzun, *Stroll with William James*, 127.
45. Murphy, *William James on Psychical Research*, 224.
46. Quoted in Barzun, *Stroll with William James*, 107.

Revolution in American Poetry

1. Robert Frost, *Complete Poems* (1942; New York, 1964), 467.
2. Robert Penn Warren, *Selected Poems, 1923–1975* (New York, 1977), 241 (from *Promises, 1954–56*).

3. Walt Whitman, *The Complete Poems,* ed. Francis Murphy (Harmondsworth, 1975), 37.

4. Thomas H. Johnson, ed., *The Poems of Emily Dickinson* (Cambridge, Mass., 1955), 314.

5. See also Johnson's *Emily Dickinson: An Interpretive Biography* (Cambridge, Mass., 1955): Like Jonathan Edwards, "she saw that the pursuit of liberty, gained only by agony and travail, is the purpose of existence. . . . The seasons that create and destroy, the nations that must maintain eternal vigilance to stay free, are likewise part of the revolt which alone can assure survival" (19).

6. Gerard Manley Hopkins, *Letters to Robert Bridges,* ed. C. C. Abbott (London, 1955), 155.

7. D. H. Lawrence, *Studies in Classic American Literature* (New York, 1953), 183.

8. D. H. Lawrence, *Complete Poems* (New York, 1971), 260.

9. Quoted in *T. S. Eliot: The Man and His Work,* ed. Allen Tate (New York, 1966), 15.

10. Ezra Pound, *Personae* (1926), 89 (first published in *Lustra,* 1916).

Life and Art in Robert Lowell

1. Robert Lowell, *Selected Poems,* rev. ed. (New York, 1981), 246.

2. Ian Hamilton, *Robert Lowell: A Biography* (New York, 1984).

3. Thomas Daniel Young, *Gentleman in a Dustcoat: A Biography of John Crowe Ransom* (Baton Rouge, La., 1976).

4. Hamilton, *Robert Lowell,* 44.

5. From Lowell's essay in the 1959 special issue of the *Sewanee Review* honoring Tate on his sixtieth birthday.

6. Hamilton, *Robert Lowell,* 167.

7. Lowell, *Day by Day* (New York, 1977), 79.

8. Hamilton, *Robert Lowell,* 130.

9. Lowell, *History* (New York, 1973), 140.

10. Lowell, *Selected Poems,* 183.

11. Alan Williamson, *Pity the Monsters: The Political Vision of Robert Lowell* (New Haven, 1974); Vereen Bell, *Robert Lowell: Nihilist as Hero* (Cambridge, Mass., 1983); Helen Vendler, *Part of Nature, Part of Us: Modern American Poets* (Cambridge, Mass., 1980). Vendler is discussed below, in "Two Women Critics: Helen Vendler and Ursula Le Guin."

12. Lowell, *Day by Day,* 122.

13. Edmund Wilson, *The Wound and the Bow* (New York, 1947), 294–95.

Daniel Hoffman and the American Epic

1. Daniel Hoffman, *The Center of Attention* (New York, 1974), 13–14.

2. In *Corgi Modern Poets in Focus: 4,* ed. Jeremy Robson (London, 1971), 142–43.

3. Hoffman, *Center of Attention,* 53–54.

James Dickey: Southern Visionary as Celestial Navigator

1. Richard J. Calhoun, ed., *The Expansive Imagination: A Collection of Critical Essays* (Deland, Fla., 1973), 17.
2. R. V. Cassill, "The Most Dangerous Game of the Poet James Dickey," *Southern Carolina Review* 10 (1978): 7.
3. Both quoted by Robert W. Hill, "Editorial," in *South Carolina Review* 10 (1978): 3.
4. Robert Penn Warren, "A Poem about the Ambition of Poetry: *The Zodiac,*" *New York Times Book Review,* 14 November 1976.
5. Hendrik Marsman, "The Zodiac," from *Tempel en Kruis.* Translated from the Dutch by A. J. Barnouw. In *Sewanee Review* 55 (1947): 238–51.
6. Dickey, *Self-Interviews* (New York, 1970), 78.
7. But some references, like that to the present Astronomer-Royal ("Fred Hoyle and the steady-state," 28), are emphatically postwar.
8. Dickey, *The Zodiac* (Garden City, N.Y., 1976), 12.
9. W. H. Auden, *Collected Poems,* ed. Edward Mendelson (New York, 1976), 445 (from "The More Loving One," 1957); Robert Penn Warren, *Selected Poems, 1923–75* (New York, 1977), 17 (from "The Nature of a Mirror," in *Or Else—Poem/Poems, 1968–1974*).
10. Dickey, *Puella* (Garden City, N.Y., 1982), 23.

Robert Penn Warren as Hardy American

1. Warren, *Selected Poems, 1923–1975* (New York, 1977).
2. Warren's latest selection—*Selected Poems 1923–1985* (New York, 1986)—follows the same pattern that seems to me so successful in the earlier ones. But, presumably because of constraints of space, radical surgery has been performed on the earlier work—*disembowelment* is hardly too strong a term—in order to include the poems of the latest decade. Surely his publishers will soon produce either a two-volume *Selected Poems* or a complete *Collected Poems.*
3. This poem, together with much of *Or Else,* and many others discussed in this essay, is omitted from the 1986 *Selected Poems.*
4. Warren, *Selected Poems, 1923–1975,* 6.
5. Warren, *Being Here: Poetry 1977–1980* (New York, 1980).
6. Warren, *Rumor Verified: Poems 1979–1980* (New York, 1981).
7. Warren, *Chief Joseph of the Nez Perce, Who Called Themselves the Nimipu—"The Real People"* (New York, 1983).
8. Warren, *Rumor Verified,* 33.
9. Warren, *Chief Joseph,* 62.
10. Floyd C. Watkins, *Then and Now: The Personal Past in the Poetry of Robert Penn Warren* (Lexington, Ky., 1982).

11. Neil Nakadate, ed., *Robert Penn Warren: Critical Perspectives* (Lexington, Ky., 1981).
12. James A. Grimshaw, Jr., ed., *Robert Penn Warren's "Brother to Dragons": A Discussion* (Baton Rouge, La., 1983).
13. Charles H. Bohner, *Robert Penn Warren,* rev. ed. (New York, 1981).
14. James H. Justus, *The Achievement of Robert Penn Warren* (Baton Rouge, La., 1981), 302.

The Function of Literary Quarterlies

1. Randall Jarrell, *Poetry and the Age* (New York, 1955), 63–64.
2. Stanley Hyman, *The Armed Vision: A Study in the Methods of Modern Literary Criticism* (New York, 1955), 8.
3. Malcolm Cowley, *The Literary Situation* (New York, 1954).
4. R. P. Blackmur, *The Lion and the Honeycomb* (New York, 1955).

The Criticism of Allen Tate

1. Tate, *On the Limits of Poetry. Selected Essays: 1928–1948* (New York, 1948).
2. Tate, *Reactionary Essays on Poetry and Ideas* (New York, 1936), 139.
3. Tate, *Limits,* 288, 306.
4. Tate, *Reason in Madness: Critical Essays* (New York, 1941), 212.
5. Tate, *Limits,* 11.
6. Tate, "Poetry and the Absolute," *Sewanee Review* 35 (1927): 41–52.
7. Tate, *Limits,* 138.

A Little Man Who Was a Writer: R. P. Blackmur

1. Russell Fraser, *A Mingled Yarn: The Life of R. P. Blackmur* (New York, 1982).

Cleanth Brooks and the Responsibilities of Criticism

1. Cleanth Brooks, *A Shaping Joy: Studies in the Writer's Craft* (New York, 1971), xi.
2. The phrase is W. J. Ong's; I have discussed it in *Dionysus and the City* (New York, 1970), 197.
3. Brooks, *Shaping Joy,* 6.
4. Quoted by Henrich Böll in *Intellectual Digest,* May 1973, 65.
5. Brooks's latest publication, *The Language of the American South* (Athens, Ga., 1985), provides fresh and abundant evidence for this statement.
6. Brooks, *Shaping Joy,* 16, 50.

7. Brooks, "Telling It Like It Is in the Tower of Babel," *Sewanee Review* 76 (1971): 136–55.
8. Brooks, *Shaping Joy,* 144.
9. Brooks, *The Hidden God: Studies in Hemingway, Faulkner, Yeats, Eliot, and Warren* (New York, 1963), 22–23.
10. Brooks, *William Faulkner: The Yoknapatawpha Country* (New Haven, 1963), 338.

Robert Penn Warren as Critic

1. Brooks and Warren's first textbook, *An Approach to Literature,* which they edited with J. T. Purser in 1936, was more elementary than *Understanding Poetry* and covered all the literary genres. As their prefaces and postscripts to the first two editions of *Understanding Poetry* (1938, 1950) show, Brooks and Warren were concerned not to promulgate any specific critical doctrine, but criticism of any sort as opposed to history or biography or inspiration or philosophy or whatever might be loosely called scholarship. Their approach was New Criticism only in that the whole idea of stressing criticism was relatively new, and this approach paralleled Brooks's attempt to synthesize and reconcile the chief recent critics in his *Modern Poetry and the Tradition* (1939).

   By the time of the 1960 edition, however, Brooks and Warren had decided that *Understanding Poetry* did make certain assumptions, which they state explicitly: "Poetry gives us knowledge. It is a knowledge of ourselves in relation to the world of experience, and to that world considered, not statistically, but in terms of human purposes and values. Experience considered in terms of human purpose and values is dramatic—dramatic in that it is concrete, in that it involves a process, and in that it embodies the human effort to arrive—through conflict—at meaning." They continue: "Because poetry—like all the arts—involves this kind of experiential knowledge, we miss the value of poetry if we think of its characteristic knowledge as consisting of 'messages,' statements, snippets of doctrine. The knowledge that poetry yields is available to us only if we submit ourselves to the massive, and subtle, impact of the poem as a whole. We have access to this special kind of knowledge only by participating in the drama of the poem, apprehending the form of the poem. What in this context do we mean by form? To create a form is to find a way to contemplate, and perhaps to comprehend, our human urgencies. Form is the recognition of fate made joyful, because made comprehensible."

   In the fourth edition (1976), they drop this statement and revise the whole book drastically, calling the first section simply "Poetry as a Way of Saying" and emphasizing—as in the earlier editions—the teachability and flexibility of the book rather than any assumptions.
2. The most obvious foreign examples are French *explication de texte* and British public school teaching—less formal and systematic, and more per-

sonal than the French—of the Greek and Roman classics, with the discipline of translation both ways.

3. In a recent interview (*Possibilities of Order: Cleanth Brooks and His Work,* ed. Lewis P. Simpson [Baton Rouge, La., 1976], 3–4) in which they describe their conversions to literature, both Brooks and Warren attribute the experience to two things: first, having an instructor who could show them how a poem worked from the inside by taking it apart and demonstrating how the parts worked; second, realizing that this instructor wrote poetry himself and wrote it about a region (a landscape and a people) they were familiar with. All these things made them realize that poetry was alive and present, not something from the dead past. Warren discovered this in Ransom's classroom; Brooks, being (he says) too timid to take Ransom's course, discovered it from Davidson. The mind reels at the thought of Davidson's rage if anyone had ever dared to call him a New Critic!

4. There is clearly some relation to the change in Warren's own poetry in the period (mostly 1942–47, though the Wolfe is 1935 and the Conrad is 1951) represented by these essays. From 1943 to 1954 he wrote no poetry he has published except *Brother to Dragons,* and the movement was to poetry much more closely and obviously involved in history. In *All the King's Men* (1946), the historical pole of Huey Long and Louisiana in the 1930s is very obvious, but, as Warren has often pointed out, the other pole is the novel's origin in Spenser, Dante, Machiavelli, and Shakespeare.

5. Although this essay was not published until 1979, it may well have been written much earlier, since Warren, as we have seen, vowed in 1977 to write no more criticism. In any case, since it derives largely from a much earlier piece ("Uncorrupted Consciousness," in the *Yale Review,* 1966), it seems appropriate to discuss it before *Democracy and Poetry* (1975).

Two Doctors for Critics: René Wellek and Randall Jarrell

1. René Wellek, *Concepts of Criticism,* edited and with an introduction by Stephen G. Nichols, Jr. (New Haven, 1963).

2. "Literary Criticism and Philosophy," *Scrutiny* 5 (1937): 375–83; 6 (1937): 59–70; 6 (1937): 195.

3. Mary Jarrell, ed., *Randall Jarrell's Letters: An Autobiographical and Literary Selection* (Boston, 1985).

Two Women Critics: Helen Vendler and Ursula Le Guin

1. Helen Vendler, *Part of Nature, Part of Us: Modern American Poets* (Cambridge, Mass., 1980).

2. Ursula K. Le Guin, *The Language of the Night: Essays on Fantasy and Science Fiction,* ed. Susan Wood (New York, 1979), 11.

George Garrett and the Historical Novel

1. Floyd C. Watkins and John T. Hiers, eds., *Robert Penn Warren Talking: Interviews, 1950–1978* (New York, 1980), 71, 128–29.
2. *Death of the Fox* (Garden City, N.Y., 1971), 527.
3. *Do, Lord, Remember Me* (Garden City, N.Y., 1965), 253.
4. *The Succession: A Novel of Elizabeth and James* (Garden City, N.Y., 1983), 538.

A New Classic: Madison Jones, A Cry of Absence

1. Madison Jones, *A Cry of Absence* (New York, 1971), 260.

Two Southern Gentlemen as Heroes

1. Walker Percy, *The Second Coming* (New York, 1980), 360.

Southern Fictions in Visual Art

1. Max Apple, ed., *Southwest Fiction* (New York, 1981), xix.
2. William Faulkner, *Absalom, Absalom!* (New York, 1951), 378.
3. W. J. Cash, *The Mind of the South* (Garden City, N.Y., 1954), 97.
4. Charmaine Locke, *Images of the House* (program essay), Contemporary Arts Museum, New Orleans, 1981.
5. Fred Gwynn and Joseph L. Blotner, eds., *Faulkner in the University* (Charlottesville, Va., 1959), 199.

Jewish Intellectuals of New York

1. Bernard Rosenberg and Ernest Goldstein, *Creators and Disturbers: Reminiscences by Jewish Intellectuals of New York* (New York, 1982); Irving Howe, *A Margin of Hope: An Intellectual Biography* (New York, 1982).
2. Rosenberg and Goldstein, *Creators,* 91, 323.
3. Howe, *A Margin of Hope,* 42.
4. Rosenberg and Goldstein, *Creators,* 284.
5. Howe, *A Margin of Hope,* 57.

Black English

1. Raven I. McDavid, Jr., and Lawrence M. Davis, "The Dialects of Negro Americans," in *Studies in Linguistics in Honor of George L. Trager,* ed. M. Estellie Smith (The Hague, 1972), 303–12; David L. Shores, "Black

English and Black Attitudes," in *Papers in Language Variation,* ed. David
L. Shores and Carole P. Hines (University, Ala., 1977), 177–87.

2. Cleanth Brooks, *The Relation of the Alabama-Georgia Dialect to the
Provincial Dialects of Great Britain* (Baton Rouge, La., 1935) and "The
English Language of the South" (1937), in *A Various Language: Perspec-
tives on American Dialects,* ed. Juanita Williamson and Virginia Burke
(New York, 1971), 136–42. In his recent *The Language of the American
South* (Athens, Ga., 1985), Brooks restates, with additional evidence, his
thesis about the origins of the Southern language and gives some extremely
perceptive discriptions of its nature and its literary uses.

3. Lee Pederson, "The Urban Language Series," *American Speech* 50 (1975):
106.

4. Riley B. Smith, "Research Perspectives on American Black English: A Brief
Historical Sketch," *American Speech* 49 (1974): 24–39; Thomas Pyles,
"Early American Speech Adoptions from Foreign Tongues," in Williamson
and Burke, *A Various Language,* 77.

5. Although suggested as early as 1941 by Melville J. Herskovits, the "Creolist
Hypothesis" was first proposed in 1965 by Beryl Bailey, "Towards a New
Perspective in Negro English Dialectology," reprinted in *Readings in
American Dialectology,* ed. Harold Allen and Gary Underwood (New
York, 1971), 421–27. It was then developed by William A. Stewart in 1968,
"Continuity and Change in American Negro Dialects," reprinted in *Per-
spectives on Black English,* ed. J. L. Dillard (The Hague, 1975), 233–47,
and elsewhere; and most extensively expounded by J. L. Dillard in his
Black English (New York, 1972) and *All-American English* (New York,
1975).

6. "You Makin' Sense," *New York Review of Books,* 16 November 1972.

7. Stewart, for example, calls for further work on the two questions, the relationship between Gullah and other black dialects, and the relationship between black dialects other than Gullah and white dialects. Dillard seems
to feel no need of confirmation. William Labov, in his *Social Stratification
of English in New York City* (Washington, D.C., 1966) and *Language in the
Inner City* (Philadelphia, 1972), is careful to specify the exact nature and
applicability of his evidence; the latter book, for example, deals with the
speech (which he prefers to call Black English Vernacular) of "black youth
from 8 to 19 years old who participate fully in the street culture of the inner
cities." Dillard tends to ignore such specifications.

8. I am here quoting my review, "American, Black, Creole, Pidgin, and
Spanglish English," of Dillard's later book, *All-American English,* which
appeared in the *New York Review of Books,* 17 July 1975.

9. Dillard, *Black English,* 40.

10. McDavid and Davis, "The Dialects of Negro Americans," 306–7.

11. William A. Stewart was apparently the first to note this usage, in his 1967
article "Sociolinguistic Factors in the History of American Negro Dialects," reprinted in Dillard, *Perspectives on Black English,* 231: "On var-

ious occasions, I have pointed out that many speakers of non-standard American Negro dialects make a grammatical and semantic distinction by means of *be*, illustrated by such constructions as *he busy* 'He is busy (momentarily)' or *he workin'* 'he is working (right now)' as opposed to *he be busy* 'he is (habitually) busy' or *he be workin'* 'he is working (steadily),' which the grammar of standard English is unable to make." William Labov noted that this "provides no strong argument for a Creole origin; the closest analogy is with the Anglo-Irish *be*, stemming from the Celtic 'consuetudinal' or habitual copula" (*Language in the Inner City*, 51). The Anglo-Irish, Irish, and Welsh forms are cited in *American Speech* 48 (1973): 144–46 and *American Speech* 50 (1975): 323–25.

12. See McDavid and Davis, "Dialects of Negro Americans"; Raven I. McDavid, Jr., and G. J. Forgue, *La Langue des Americains* (Paris, 1972), 242–50.

13. See Shores in Shores and Hines, *Papers in Language Variation,* and McDavid and Davis, "Dialects of Negro Americans."

14. Bailey, "Towards a New Perspective, 422.

15. Juanita Williamson, "Selected Features of Speech: Black and White," in *A Various Language,* ed. Williamson and Burke, 496–507.

16. Williamson and Burke, *A Various Language,* 434–36.

17. Juanita Williamson, "A Look at the Direct Question," in *Studies in Linguistics in Honor of Raven I. McDavid, Jr.,* ed. Lawrence M. Davis (University, Ala., 1972), 207–14.

18. The movie *Conrack* gives an accurate impression of the Gullah region, though with the commercialization of Hilton Head and St. Simon's Island, acculturation may take place with terrifying speed. Whatever one's doubts about decreolization, McDavid has well said that a process of neocreolization seems to be taking place in the urban ghettoes.

19. Leonard Bloomfield, *Language* (New York, 1933), 499.

20. Shores, in *Papers in Language Variation,* ed. Shores and Hines, 183. Naturally enough, a great many blacks (and whites, too) have rushed to enlist under the banner of Black English. For example, Deborah Harrison and Tom Trabasso, eds., *Black English: A Seminar* (Hillsdale, N.J., 1976), based on a seminar given at Princeton in 1973; Thomas Kochman, ed., *Rappin' and Stylin' Out* (Urbana, Ill., 1972); and Geneva Smitherman, *Talkin and Testifyin* (Boston, 1977).

Index

MONROE K. SPEARS
recently retired as Moody Professor of English at
Rice University. He is a former editor of the *Sewanee Review,* co-editor (with H. B. Wright) of *The
Literary Works of Matthew Prior,* and the author of
several books, including *The Poetry of W. H. Auden:
The Disenchanted Island* and *Dionysus and the City.*
His poetry has appeared in numerous periodicals
and in his book *The Levitator and Other Poems.*

American Ambitions: Selected Essays on Literary and Cultural Themes

Designed by Martha Farlow.

Composed by A. W. Bennett, Inc., in Sabon.

Printed by The Maple Press Company on 50-lb. S. D. Warren's Sebago Eggshell Cream offset and bound in Joanna Arrestox A and Kennett cloths with Simpson Kilmory endsheets.